EUROPEAN LEGAL DEVELOPMENT

What shapes the development of a legal system? The economy? Legal ideas? Social and political movements? Drawing on the other eight volumes in the series, *European Legal Development: The Case of Tort* aims to challenge conventional comparative law explanations of the factors that shape the law. It goes further into ideas that law could be conceived as either driven by external factors or is primarily the product of deliberations among lawyers. Choosing the examples of product and medical liabilities, the book considers the convergence of developments across legal systems. By contrast, examining road accidents and relations between neighbours, it notes areas in which the development of tort law has diverged. Tort law emerges as only part of the legal response and its place depends on the activity of the legislator, as much as on judicial and scholarly ideas about the place of fault liability within the schemes of compensation.

JOHN BELL is Professor of Law at the University of Cambridge.

DAVID IBBETSON is Regius Professor of Civil Law at the University of Cambridge.

[redacted]

EUROPEAN LEGAL DEVELOPMENT

THE CASE OF TORT

This volume brings together many of the themes in the series, *Comparative Developments in the Law of Torts in Europe*. It presents a way of looking at legal development that goes beyond that found in the existing literature. It looks in greater depth at ideas such as legal transplants, the path dependence of particular legal traditions, the connection between law and particular social cultures. It argues that legal development can be studied fruitfully by examining changes in the law in the books and the legal outcomes which the law generates within its social, political and economic environment. Path dependence is a crucial feature in explaining why similar societies do not operate with the same legal rules and may not even produce the same outcomes. These ideas are examined in relation to liability for fault. Having reviewed the law around 1850, two broad themes are pursued in relation to the period 1850 to 2000. The first is the homogeneity of legal outcomes in relation to liability for products and the liability of doctors and hospitals. The second is the divergence of legal outcomes in relation to liability for road accidents and industrial nuisances. The book concludes with an analysis of the factors shaping legal development in Europe.

PROFESSOR JOHN BELL is Professor of Law (1973) at the University of Cambridge.

PROFESSOR DAVID IBBETSON is Regius Professor of Civil Law at the same university.

COMPARATIVE STUDIES IN THE DEVELOPMENT

[redacted]RTS IN EUROPE

[redacted]itors

[redacted]vid Ibbetson

EUROPEAN LEGAL DEVELOPMENT

The Case of Tort

Volume 9

JOHN BELL

and

DAVID IBBETSON

CAMBRIDGE
UNIVERSITY PRESS

CAMBRIDGE
UNIVERSITY PRESS

University Printing House, Cambridge CB2 8BS, United Kingdom

Cambridge University Press is part of the University of Cambridge.

It furthers the University's mission by disseminating knowledge in the pursuit of education, learning and research at the highest international levels of excellence.

www.cambridge.org
Information on this title: www.cambridge.org/9781107023116

First published 2012
First paperback edition 2014

A catalogue record for this publication is available from the British Library

Library of Congress Cataloguing in Publication data
European legal development: the case of tort.
p. cm. – (Comparative studies in the development of the law of torts in Europe; v. 9)
Editors: David Ibbetson and John Bell.
Includes bibliographical references and index.
ISBN 978-1-107-02177-8 (hardback)
1. Torts – Europe – History. 2. Liability (Law) – Europe – History.
I. Ibbetson, D. J. (David J.) II. Bell, John, 1953–
KJC1663.E97 2012
346.403–dc23 2012019849

ISBN 978-1-107-02177-8 Hardback
ISBN 978-1-107-47562-5 Paperback

Hardback only available as
ISBN 978-1-107-02311-6 3-volume set

CONTENTS

FIGURES

PREFACE

The European Legal Development series arose from a project funded by the AHRC from January 2005 until February 2008.

The aim of the project as a whole was to examine the nature of legal development in Western Europe since 1850, focusing sharply on liability for fault. Behind this there is a more abstract purpose, to attempt to cast some light on the factors which have influenced the way in which the law has changed over this period. Legal historians have looked at the general question, usually focusing on the rather facile distinction between the English common law and continental European legal systems. Though rooted in the sources, these works have been marred by a somewhat unsophisticated methodology and an inevitably selective use of evidence. Comparative lawyers have developed far more sophisticated methodologies, but their theoretical perspectives have too often borne little relation to empirical data. Over the last 25 years, tort lawyers have looked at the same types of question; but their analysis has invariably been at a high level of generality and has rarely looked at the historical component. By bringing together experts with different disciplinary backgrounds – comparative lawyers and legal historians, all with an understanding of modern tort law in their own systems – and getting them to work collaboratively, we have aimed to produce a more nuanced comparative legal history, and one which is theoretically better informed.

The topic of legal development is broad and, to make it manageable, with colleagues we undertook a programme of work built up from a number of case studies. The first six books in the series, covered Product Liability, Relations between Neighbours, Medical Liability, Technological Change, Traffic and Railways, and Legal Doctrine. They examined the development of tort law in relation to those topics in a number of Western European countries. The next two books examined the influences on legal development, the Impact of Ideas and the Impact of Legal Institutions and Professions. To make the study manageable, these works concentrated on the liability for fault between 1850 and 2000 as our major area of study.

Around 1850, there were many similarities in approaches to liability for fault across the legal systems of Western Europe. But since then, there has been significant divergence. Our method has been first to chart the changes and then to seek the explanations for what happened.

This volume aims to bring together many of the themes in the series, and to develop and apply a method of analysis appropriate to comparative legal history. It therefore aims to present a way of looking at legal development that goes beyond that found in the existing literature. It looks in greater depth at ideas such as borrowings between systems, the path dependence of particular legal traditions and the connection between law and particular social cultures. It argues that legal development can be studied fruitfully by examining changes in the law in the books and the legal outcomes which the law generates within its social, political and economic environment. The methodology of the book is set out in Chapter 1, but briefly, it involves looking at the law in the books, legal outcomes and the legal environment through both general surveys and detailed case studies. Although we have based ourselves very significantly on the research undertaken by our colleagues in the project, we have also undertaken our own detailed research on specific areas of the law. We have also developed a theoretical framework for studying legal development which was not contained in the other books in the series. That theoretical framework is set out in both Chapter 1 and in the concluding Chapter 5. Chapter 2 seeks to set the scene for the development of tort law between 1850 and 2000 by setting out the background to liability for fault as conceived in Western Europe around 1850. Chapter 3 examines examples of the homogeneity of legal outcomes with a focus on liability for products and the liability of doctors and hospitals. Chapter 4 offers a contrast by examining examples of the divergence of legal outcomes in relation to liability for road accidents and industrial nuisances. Through these examples, studied with both surveys and detailed case studies, we demonstrate the way a more sophisticated understanding of legal development can be justified, built around the importance of path dependence in explaining the distinctive features of the legal development of the different jurisdictions in Europe, despite the similarity of the modern social problems which they faced and, very often, the similarity of their values.

The research for the European Legal Development project as a whole involved scholars from a range of countries, in particular, England and Scotland, Spain, the Netherlands, Germany, France, Sweden, Austria and Italy. Each working group drew on the expertise of both senior and more junior scholars familiar with different European legal systems, and contained a mixture of comparative lawyers and legal historians. We are grateful for their energy and enthusiasm, as well as for the many insights they have brought to the project. As well, in producing this volume we have taken advantage of the kindness of many other friends and colleagues in helping us to understand aspects of their legal systems which were otherwise opaque to us. We thank them, and hope that we have not unwittingly misrepresented them. In particular, we are grateful to Matthew Dyson and Colm McGrath, who began as PhD students on this AHRC project, and who made a significant contribution to the formulation, discussion and execution of its many strands.

John Bell
David Ibbetson

ABBREVIATIONS

ABGB	Allgemeines bürgerliches Gesetzbuch (Austrian Civil Code) 1811
AC	Law Reports, Appeal Cases
AJDA	Actualité Juridique – Droit Administratif
All ER	All England Law Reports
ALR	Allgemeines Landrecht (Prussian Civil Code 1794)
BGB	Bürgerliches Gesetzbuch (German Civil Code 1900)
BGHZ	Entscheidungen des Bundesgerichtshofs in Zivilsachen
Burr.	Burrow's King's Bench Reports *tempore* Mansfield
BW	Burgerlijk Wetboek (Dutch Civil Code 1838)
C.	Codex of Justinian
CA	Court of Appeal
Cass. ch. réunies	Cour de cassation, chambres réunies
Cass. civ.	Cour de cassation, chambre civile
CE	Conseil d'Etat
CE Ass.	Conseil d'Etat, Assemblée Plénière
CE Sect.	Conseil d'Etat, Section du Contentieux
chr.	Chronique
CJ	Chief Justice
col.	column
Comparative Studies	Department of Transportation, *Comparative Studies in Automobile Accident Compensation* (Washington: Dept of Transportation, 1970)
concl.	Conclusions
Crim.	Cour de cassation, chambre criminelle
D.	Receuil Dalloz; Digest of Justinian
DC	Receuil Dalloz, Dalloz
	Receuil Dalloz, Hébdomadaire
Doctrine	N. Jansen, *The Development and Making of Legal Doctrine* (Cambridge University Press, 2010)
DP	Receuil Dalloz, Périodique
ER	English Reports
Exch.	Exchequer Reports

F. & F.	Foster and Finlayson's Nisi Prius Reports
G.	Gaius, Institutes
Gaz. Pal.	Gazette du Palais
gl	Glossa
	Hansard, House of Commons Debates
HL	House of Lords
HLC	House of Lords Cases Reports
HR	Hoge Raad
Ideas	M. Lobban and J. Moses, *The Impact of Ideas* (Cambridge University Press, 2012)
Inst.	Institutes of Justinian
JCP	Semaine Juridique – Juris-Classeur Périodique
KB	King's Bench
KFG	German Road Traffic Law of 3 May 1909
Lebon	Recueil Lebon (Conseil d'Etat)
LJ	Law Journal; Lord Justice
MDU	Medical Defence Union
Medical	E. Hondius (ed.), *The Development of Medical Liability* (Cambridge University Press, 2010)
MR	Master of the Rolls
Neighbours	J. Gordley (ed.), *The Development of Liability between Neighbours* (Cambridge University Press, 2010)
NJ	Nederlandse Jurisprudentie
obs.	Observations
OJ	Official Journal of the European Union/European Communities
P.	Partida
Products	S. Whittaker (ed.), *The Development of Product Liability* (Cambridge University Press, 2010)
Professions	P. Mitchell (ed.), *The Impact of Institutions and Professions* (Cambridge University Press, 2012)
Req.	Cour de cassation, chambre des requêtes
RG	Reichsgericht
RGZ	Entscheidungen des Reichsgerichts in Zivilsachen
RJ	Repertorio de Jurisprudencia
RTR	Road Traffic Reports
S.	Recueil Sirey
SC	Session Cases
STS	Sentencias del Tribunal Supremo
StVG	Straßenverkehrsgesetz (Road Traffic Act) 1952
S-VC	Recueil Sirey
TC	Tribunal des Conflits

Technology	M. Martín-Casals, *The Development of Liability in Relation to Technological Change* (Cambridge University Press, 2010)
TR	Durnford and East's Term Reports
Traffic	W. Ernst, *The Development of Traffic Liability* (Cambridge University Press, 2010)
Wils.	Wilson's Kings Bench and Common Pleas Reports
WLR	Weekly Law Reports

1

Introduction

This book analyses the nature and causes of the development of fault liability in tort in the period 1850–2000. The concept of 'legal development' is used frequently in historical and comparative law literature, but it requires further elucidation because of the central place that it plays in this work. To begin with, it is necessary to explain the understanding of 'law' that is appropriate in this context, and then to proceed to explain the idea of development. While it is important to understand law as a set of normative standards that govern conduct, law needs to be understood in a number of other ways as well.

I The distinctiveness of law

Law should be seen as a problem-solving enterprise. The problems are seen as (first order) resolving disputes, maintaining order and achieving fairness; (second order) ensuring confidence in the institutions of justice, ensuring effectiveness of the system and ensuring solutions can be replicated; and (third order) reinforcing social values through words and symbols.

The distinctive contribution of law is solving problems through rules and through institutions. Law is thus a distinctive way of dealing with social problems. It reduces complexity by offering an ordered system of rules, principles and procedures within which problems can be resolved. Lawyers value not only doing the right thing, but doing it repeatedly. So the key to a legal solution is to develop routines and rules that will deliver the right solution repeatedly. Such routines are embedded in agreed procedures and institutions. At the same time, there needs to be flexibility to adjust to the unforeseen and unfair.

Any solution to a new problem has two institutional settings. The first is the organisational institution: the bodies that make rules, the people who have to administer the rules, and the procedures they have to follow. The second is the conceptual institution of the law: its framework of concepts through which it routinely delivers justice to particular cases, not only in this new problem, but in the myriad other contexts within which it operates. Lawyers are concerned about the consequences of individual decisions in order to ensure that the solution to a new problem does not disrupt the ability of established institutions and concepts to deliver routine justice. An account of legal development, therefore, has to involve not just the changes in rules, but also changes in the institutional setting of the law and its environment.

To understand the capacity of the law as a set of rules to be open to development, it is necessary to appreciate that rules are inherently incomplete, in need of interpretation, and therefore contestable. Rodolfo Sacco usefully developed the concept of 'legal formants' to describe the conception of this legal system with which lawyers work:

> even the jurist who seeks a single legal rule, indeed who proceeds from the axiom that there is only one rule in force, recognizes implicitly that living law contains many different elements such as statutory rules, the formulations of scholars, and the decisions of judges – elements that he keeps separate in his own thinking. In this essay, we will call them, borrowing from phonetics, the 'legal formants'. The jurist concerned with the law within a single country examines all of these elements and then eliminates the complications that arise from their multiplicity to arrive at one rule. He does so by a process of interpretation. Yet this process does not guarantee that there is, in his system, only a single rule.[1]

It would be clearer to say that national legal scholars writing books and articles and judges making decisions on the basis of the law operate with the regulative ideal that the law should be coherent and consistent, even if it may not be fully so in actual reality. In other words, they seek to interpret the law *as if* it were completely coherent and consistent, even though they know that, as a matter of fact, it is not. This produces the notion that there is a single formulation of the law valid at a particular moment of decision. As Sacco says, this regulative ideal is implemented by an act of interpretation which has authority because of the position occupied by the scholar or judge. So it would not be typically right to say that the legal community has a single view of what the law is.

[1] R. Sacco, 'Legal Formants: A Dynamic Approach to Comparative Law' (1991) 39 *American Journal of Comparative Law* 1, 22. See also S. Mancuso, 'Legal Transplants and Economic Development: Civil Law vs. Common Law?' in J.C. Oliveira and P. Cardinal (eds.), *One Country, Two Systems, Three Legal Orders – Perspectives of Evolution* (Heidelberg: Springer, 2009), 75.

It is better to characterise the law as a conversation within the legal community in which certain participants carry particular authority. The idea of 'formants' suggests that there are competing, always incomplete, versions of what the law is on a particular matter. These are contributed by different participants in the legal discussion – legislators, judges, scholars and advocates. They may agree on the basic sources and principles of the system, but come to different formulations of the rules. There are debates about what the law requires and certain discussants in many legal systems have strong authority, such as higher courts or legislators or some leading scholars. Others will contribute their ideas without particular authority, e.g. lower courts and many other legal scholars. Looking back in time we have at best a partial reconstruction of the elements of that conversation between members of the legal community. The state of the law at any one time comes from a snapshot of the conversation and where it has reached, focusing on the contribution of certain authoritative participants, but also cognisant of the way those authoritative statements are being received. These snapshots are published as doctrinal articles, textbooks, lawyers' opinions and advice, or as judicial decisions on particular cases.

The combination of the ideas of formants and the legal conversation produces a sense that statements of what the law is are provisional and incomplete. Although the regulative ideal may lead any one discussant to make claims that a particular view is the 'right' statement of the law, the picture which an observer of the legal system acquires is of a diversity of opinions.[2] For our purposes, it is sufficient to identify 'dominant opinion(s)' within the legal conversation and the different views that are sufficiently respectable to be available as potential grounds for decision. So it is necessary to reflect the diversity of currents of opinion, as well as areas of agreement. It is this messy picture that enables the law to be revised or developed over time, often without a formal change in the wording of a rule.

II The concept of 'legal development'

If there are always diverging and incomplete statements of the law in the 'formants' of legal argumentation, then how do we define 'development'? Development is a change either in the way in which the law is understood by the legal community as a standard of conduct or in the way it is applied in practice.[3] The law operates as a normative standard of conduct.

[2] Sacco, 'Legal Formants', pp. 25–26.

[3] It follows that there is no significant difference between the concept of legal 'development' and the notion of legal 'change'. The former term is intended to convey a more organic

It provides individuals with distinctive reasons for action from the legal point of view. Legal actors and legal subjects understand the normative requirements of the law starting from its verbal formulation and its conceptual structure. Legal development will be most obvious when the verbal formulation of a legal text alters.

In addition, within this normative meaning, we need to distinguish between what is required by the law and the strength of that requirement (its *force*). A legal provision may be clearly formulated, but its authority may be weak, e.g. because the formulation of the rule only emerges from the case-law of lower courts and is contested in scholarly literature. For the most part, the normative meaning is controlled by the legal community. By contrast the application, especially the practical application, is governed by factors not fully under the control of lawyers.

So when we talk of 'development' we are essentially looking at the differences in formulation and meaning of statements about what the law is, as well as how it is applied. In particular, there are the following areas of difference which affect the meaning of a rule:

1. Formulation
2. Interpretation
3. Context and relevance
4. Operation.

A Formulation

If we adopt Sacco's analysis that there is no formulation of a legal rule that is both canonical and comprehensive, then we are faced with constantly varying statements of what the law is: from legislators, judges, advocates, parties and textbook writers. As codifiers like Portalis recognised long ago, it is impossible to be comprehensive, however detailed the legislative text.[4]

But even though there may be a canonical formulation of a rule, it will typically be at a very general level, such as article 1382 of the French Civil Code: 'Any human act whatever which causes damage to another obliges him by whose fault it occurred to make reparation.' Typically, it will need

difference from one period to another, rather than minor differences in content. It is not intended to suggest that there is always a movement towards something that is 'better' in any sense.

[4] J.-E.-M. Portalis, 'Discours préliminaire sur le projet de Code civil' in F. Ewald (ed.), *Naissance du Code civil* (Paris: Flammarion, 1989), 39–42.

a lot of interpretation to turn it into prescriptions for action in particular cases. It serves more as a reference point for legal debate, rather than the source of a precise prescription of what citizens must do. That is to say, it provides the focus of argument, rather than the content of the argument. So, for example, there will be a debate about the meaning of 'fault' within article 1382. That debate may have different content at different periods. At one time, there may be a dominance of a subjective idea of fault, but a more objective idea at another.[5] Different ideas may be applied in different contexts at the same time. Formulations may remain static, even if interpretations change. But a change in the formulation would be a significant indicator of change in understanding.

A formulation of a rule will often take a lot for granted. In particular, it presupposes a lot of knowledge about legal concepts. Legal words are not just part of ordinary language, but take their colour from the broader framework of legal concepts and their interrelationships that have developed over time. The concept of a 'mental map' developed by Geoffrey Samuel is illuminating here.[6] He suggests that lawyers locate problems within a matrix of interconnected concepts. The solution to a new problem, such as the liability of hospitals or for industrial nuisances, is located on the map of existing legal concepts, e.g. tort, contract, property. So a rule formulated to stress the importance of the 'fault' of the person causing damage will depend on the relationship of that idea to other notions in the relevant body of tort, contract or property. Indeed, each of these concepts themselves is what MacCormick would term an 'institution' – a bundle of interconnected rights, duties, values and norms.[7] This embedding of ideas is an important feature of the law as a system of norms. To understand particular legal rules, you need to understand the concepts used in the formulation of the rule, and you need to understand the connection between concepts. For the study of legal development, it is necessary to look not only at the formulation of the rules, but the way legal concepts may change over time.

[5] J.-L. Halpérin, 'French Doctrinal Writing' in N. Jansen, *The Development and Making of Legal Doctrine* (Cambridge University Press, 2010) (hereafter '*Doctrine*'), 73 at pp. 81–86; G. Viney and A. Guégan-Lécuyer, 'The Development of Traffic Liability in France' in W. Ernst (ed.), *The Development of Traffic Liability* (Cambridge University Press, 2010) (hereafter '*Traffic*'), 50 at pp. 60–62.

[6] *Epistemology and Method in Law* (Aldershot: Ashgate, 2003), 222.

[7] Neil MacCormick and Ota Weinberger, *An Institutional Theory of Law* (Dordrecht: Kluwer, 1986), 9–13, 49–74.

Of course, the formulation may remain very static over time. Indeed, that is the argument about English law in many areas: the formal test of negligence does not appear to change in time. This does not mean that the law has not changed, but merely that changes can be accommodated without reformulation of the rule. Indeed, there may be reasons related to the hierarchy of norms why the formulation of the rule may remain static. On the whole, the legislative formulation is likely to remain more fixed than the formulation of the textbook writers. The former have a canonical status by virtue of the high authority afforded to them, the latter have a relatively low authoritative status and can hence be departed from by later writers with considerable ease.

So the predominant test for whether there has been a change in formulation is whether the wording used in the dominant formants of the system remains the same or not. The change in formulation is typically the act of the legislator or of the law-making judge, though even in a common law system doctrinal writers can play a significant part.

B Interpretation

Even if the formulation remains the same, the interpretation may well change. For example in relation to the sale of products, article 1648 of the *Code Civil* was originally understood as entitling the disappointed buyer of defective goods compensation for out-of-pocket expenses incurred in the transaction when the transaction was annulled. The French courts and doctrinal writing subsequently re-interpreted 'costs consequent on the sale' in article 1648 of the *Code Civil* to cover damages paid by the buyer for personal injury caused by the defective product and other damage consequent on using the product.[8] In that example, the scope of the article changed radically, whilst the formulation of the text and its underpinning conceptual structure remained the same.

It is here that interventions by judges and doctrinal writers become significant parts of the legal conversation. Under Sacco's analysis, every application potentially involves an act of interpretation: the formulation of a new 'formant'. But the concept of 'interpretation' involved in legal development focuses on much more general features of the way in which a particular text is applied. An interpretation in this sense involves an orientation in the way a text will be used to govern a plurality of cases.

[8] S. Whittaker (ed.), *The Development of Product Liability* (Cambridge University Press, 2010) (hereafter '*Products*'), 15 and 95.

Interpretations in this sense are not so much the act of an individual interpreter, but they are collective understandings of how a text is to be used to solve problems and disputes. Over time, those common reference points may change. Such changes indicate differences in perception of the law among the legal community, or a section of it.

Interpretations can focus around different aspects of a rule. There can be substantive changes in interpretation, e.g. what kinds of loss are covered by a particular article of the Code, and we have procedural interpretations, e.g. reversals of the burden of proof, which challenge the rule less directly, but do change its effect. Indeed, the change in the burden of proof can be seen as one of the most common interpretative devices in legal development. For example, this was the route used in the 1960s and 1970s in Italy, Germany and the Netherlands to create a form of strict liability of manufacturers for injuries caused by products, without altering the existing legal texts themselves.[9] A similar approach was adopted in Spain and the Netherlands with regard to the liability for traffic accidents.[10]

It would be right to include reconceptualisation within substantive interpretation. By this is meant the creation of a different way of categorising a problem legally. Many of the areas covered in the European Legal Development project fall into this kind of interpretation. Whereas the code provisions remained at a very high level of abstraction, dealing with fault in general, the courts and academics were able to introduce distinctive interpretations of the code that formed a coherent body of law governing specifically 'road accidents', 'medical liability' or 'product liability'. Clearly, there are significant limits to the extent to which new categories can be introduced without reformulation of the core text.

So legal change in interpretations can be identified from changes in collective understandings of how a text is used to solve problems and disputes, whether this is in the form of attributing to it a new (substantive) meaning, a change in ideas about the burden of proof, or even the development of a distinctive body of law around a specific problem area.

C *Context and relevance*

The context of a legal rule can be examined in two ways. First, a legal rule forms part of a block of legal provisions that regulate a particular situation. For example, in the area of product liability, the law of contract and

[9] *Ibid.*, pp. 16–20, 123–128, 160–161, 208–209.
[10] *Traffic*, pp. 136 and 175.

the law of tort interacted to provide solutions for injured consumers in different ways in different legal systems. In some systems, such as France, a great deal of protection was provided to consumers through contract. On the other hand, contractual solutions were rejected, at least against manufacturers, in countries such as Italy and Germany.[11] In medical law, the interaction between criminal law and civil law was important in some countries, or at the same country at different times.[12] It is here that an understanding of the 'mental map' of the different legal systems becomes essential. Where would the local lawyer locate the analysis and the solution to the problems which are being studied? When one studies the place of 'fault' in tort, one is looking at how one part of the legal system relates to other parts. In the various volumes in the European Legal Development project, authors have focused on showing the importance of fault liability in tort within their own legal system and they compare this across the various systems. At the same time, they have been sensitive to the functional equivalence of other legal mechanisms in their own system, which substantially match the use of fault liability in some other systems.

Secondly, there is also the external context of legal norms. In the area of accidents at work (e.g. exploding boilers or liability for products used by employees), the existence of workmen's compensation provides an alternative which diminishes the importance of tort law.[13] The victim does not need to make use of tort law in order to find compensation. Here one needs to relate legal solutions to those that can be achieved through other means, e.g. insurance, social security or regulatory frameworks. This context could also render the existing tort law significant, for example when the legislator is unable to enact legislation to require motorists to insure against accidents to third parties.[14]

An account of legal development has to have regard not only to the formulation of rules and their interpretation, but also to the context of the block of legal provisions governing a particular kind of situation, e.g. the liability of doctors, and other legal and non-legal mechanisms that

[11] *Products*, pp. 123–128, 208–212.

[12] E. Hondius (ed.), *The Development of Medical Liability* (Cambridge University Press, 2010) (hereafter '*Medical*'), 79 and 161–165.

[13] M. Martín-Casals, 'Technological Change and the Development of Liability for Fault: A General Introduction' in M. Martín-Casals (ed.), *The Development of Liability in Relation to Technological Change* (Cambridge University Press, 2010) (hereafter '*Technology*'), 1, 15–18.

[14] G. Viney and A. Guégan-Lécuyer, 'The Development of Traffic Liability in France', *Traffic*, 50 at pp. 61–63.

may also provide compensation to victims, e.g. insurance and statutory compensation schemes.

D Operation

The way in which rules of law operate is dictated not only by their formulation or interpretation, but also by the way in which they are used and enforced. Even where a legal framework or remedy is available, citizens or their lawyers may not make use of it. In this area, it is important to distinguish between pre-litigation phases and litigation procedure. One of the major topics that recurs in this project is the extent to which legal rules are actually used. For example, in the area of exploding boilers, we discover that the typical victim (the employee) never seems to have brought an action against the person responsible for the explosion (the employer).[15] In relation to medical liability, the major use of litigation seems to have been in relation to serious personal injury,[16] and at least at some times and places the principal claimants may in reality have been insurance companies exercising their rights of subrogation. The extent to which the tort provisions are not used to start litigation suggests that there may be other mechanisms in use to deal with problems, and that will lead to an enquiry into context and relevance. But the use of law and litigation for particular kinds of problem may also colour the way the law is interpreted. If the law is invoked only for serious personal injuries, then this may well affect the kinds of result that the courts try to achieve. On the other hand, procedural changes may lead to different changes in the way in which the law operates. For example, the decline of the English jury led to greater precision in the formulation of rules in the judgments of the judges on facts rather than through directions to juries, and the consequential increase in the power of judges meant that in the short term there appears to have been a shift in the working of the rule towards the interests of the defendants rather than of the plaintiffs.[17]

The operation of the legal system can be studied predominantly from the evidence of the kinds of case that come before the courts and the rules of procedure in force in them. Statistics of litigation rates are difficult to find, and statistics about choices not to litigate are next to impossible. Firstly, there are not always reliable statistics on the amount of litigation.

[15] *Technology*, pp. 12–13.
[16] Hondius, *Medical*, pp. 8–10.
[17] See D. Ibbetson, 'The Tort of Negligence in England' in *Doctrine*, 46 at p. 60.

Secondly, and more importantly, they are not sufficiently fine-grained to reveal much about litigation on the sorts of issue that are studied in this book. In part, this is because the information may be categorised at a higher level of generality (e.g. 'obligations') and partly because the kinds of category with which the project was dealing are modern constructions that are being applied retrospectively. Within the various chapters in the first six volumes, there is some statistical information, but it is largely indicative and needs to be correlated with other information before its significance is obvious.

E Agents of change

Most of the theories of legal change focus on deliberate change, but this is not the only focus of this work. Development may be desired deliberately, e.g. when the formulation of the rule is changed by legislation or judicial overruling, or when a route around a particular legal obstacle is found in non-legal means, such as social insurance. But legal change may also be the by-product of other changes. For example, changes in procedure may be introduced for reasons unconnected with the state of tort law. The abolition of the civil jury in England would be an example. Social changes, such as the development of a universal healthcare system, would be largely independent of tort law, since most health problems do not arise from wrongdoing. But such changes may have an impact on tort law. For example, in England the existence of insurance and healthcare reduced the pressure for change away from fault liability for road accidents, unlike in most of the other European countries studied in the project.[18]

Some theories of legal development focus heavily on the invisible hand of market or social processes as an explanation of why the law develops. The model that has been retained for the project is open to the possibility that this is an adequate explanation, but pays most attention to deliberate change in the law and its operation. The economy and society are important environmental conditions within which the law operates. But those environmental conditions operate across a number of legal systems, especially in the areas that were chosen for the European Legal Development project – road accidents, medical injuries, illness caused by asbestos occurred in all countries. The legal rules were not always the same and changes in the law as a result of the growth of these problems were not

[18] See P. Bartrip, 'No-Fault Compensation on the Roads in Twentieth Century Britain' (2010) 69 *Cambridge Law Journal* 263, and below p. 123.

always the same. Lawyers were typically aware of the legal developments in other countries, but in many cases chose distinctive paths to providing solutions to the problems that had occurred.

As agents of change, lawyers can be seen in two ways. They can be seen as essentially reacting to demands on the legal system, providing a public service to enable the resolution of problems that are presented from the outside. Lawyers can also be seen as generating legal problems, as part of a business strategy. They are in need of business and so look out for opportunities to divert issues into the 'legal' framework. In nineteenth-century England, solicitors gained much from the private bill procedure authorising railways etc. Pure litigation might have been less important, were it not part of the overall strategy of the repeat clients. Solicitors would have been company secretaries, involved in the management of businesses and business decisions. In the late twentieth century, the solicitors are business advisers, offering a range of services, only some of which are law. Other lawyers are keen to develop reputations that will play with repeat players such as insurance companies representing the victims of road traffic accidents.

Summary

Each of these different features contributes to the meaning of the law. Even when the formulation of the rule has not changed, the meaning of the law may no longer be the same – if the interpretation has changed, if the operation of the law has changed, or if the context within which the law is used and applied changes.

The research in this project has demonstrated that all these different features of development happen. There is not a single feature which can be labelled 'development'. As a result, it is necessary to assess which changes have happened in a particular topic area and what these contribute to an understanding of the bigger picture of legal development.

So, in terms of an analysis of legal change, the questions to ask are

- Has there been a change in the formulation of the legal rules?
- Has there been a significant change in the leading interpretations of the relevant legal rules either by higher courts or by doctrinal writing?
- Has there been a significant change in the use of the legal rules as the basis for transactions or litigation either by citizens or by lawyers?
- Has there been a change either in the place of these rules within the overall scheme of the law or in relation to non-legal sources that govern the activities and redress in the area of law under scrutiny?

III Theories of legal development: getting beyond the metaphor

Jurisprudential and comparative law scholarly literatures include a number of important models for understanding and explaining the reasons for legal development. This section analyses a number of the leading theories and suggests an appropriate approach for the purposes of the study undertaken for the European Legal Development project, which can be replicated in other studies. Two major questions arise for the analysis of legal development. The first question is how far the law should be viewed as a self-contained social sub-system, independent of its economic or social environment. The second question is whether law should be viewed internally as a single coherent system or as a set of distinct systems (or even as not very systematic at all).

However 'law' may be analysed in jurisprudence, for the purposes of comparative law and legal history, as the previous section suggested, it makes sense to study law as a system in the full sense, rather than just as a system of norms. A system in the full sense is described by Gerber, who argues that we do not look at law simply as sets of rules. Authoritative texts, institutions, decision-making communities and patterns and modes of thought are the elements of legal systems that are the proper object of study.[19]

A Law as self-contained

A number of important theories focus on the distinctiveness of law as a social sub-system. These try to explain the distinctive character of law and why it may not simply reflect economic circumstances or social ideas. Although some of the theories are couched in metaphorical language which is ultimately distracting, their core is an importantly distinctive analysis of the character of law and its place within society. Any theory of legal change needs to take on board these insights in order to target appropriately the issues.

B Law as a distinct social system

At its core, Luhmann and Teubner argue that one of the distinctive contributions of law is to manage complexity.[20] Law provides an element of

[19] D.J. Gerber, 'System Dynamics: Toward a Language of Comparative Law?' (1998) 46 *American Journal of Comparative Law* 719.

[20] G. Teubner, *Law as an Autopoietic System* (Oxford: Blackwell, 1993), ch. 2; N. Luhmann, *Law as a Social System*, trans. Klaus A. Ziegert, ed. Fatima Kastner, Richard Nobles, David Schiff and Rosamund Ziegert (Oxford University Press, 2004), 219–220.

stability in a complex world by being a system through which the complexity is reduced and stability of expectations is offered.[21] Reality is messy and complex; law sets out to impose order on it. So, in tort, the law sets out circumstances where one person has to pay compensation to others, including for which other people's harmful actions you have to pay. We know that such rules can be simplistic and even unfair in particular instances. But we accept the order resulting from the rules even with their imperfections, rather than the greater disorder resulting from the absence of rules. Luhmann says that law deals with complexity by establishing conditional programmes containing the conditions of their solution (*constraints*) – a simplification of the decision-making process: the decision-maker need only know the programme and the material relevant to it.[22] So in tort, the lawyer only has to focus on a small number of factors to determine whether someone is legally obliged to pay compensation to another. There be many other moral or social factors that would lead us to say that the person causing the harm ought to pay, but they are irrelevant to the *legal* issue of compensation. This core insight of systems theories into the social contribution of law is sound and provides a focus for the distinctiveness of legal development.

Of course, such stability comes at a price – the legal world's perspective on what is right does not always conform to that accepted in the wider world. Stability of expectations also cannot be guaranteed absolutely, since the law, however self-referential, has to interact and communicate with other social systems. All that can be guaranteed is that legal change is not an *automatic* consequence of social change and that the law adapts at its own pace and in its own terms to changes in its environment. This vision of the law as a social *system* is important for understanding how law works – both in its contribution to society and, even more clearly, in its internal processes. Systems theory assumes that law's unity can only be programmed or reproduced by the system itself, not by factors in the external environment.[23] In this sense, the system is (operatively) closed. Such a conception tells us nothing directly about the connection between law and its environment; it merely asserts that change in one does not necessarily lead to change in the other. For example, although tort law might seem to involve moral standards, as Lord Atkin pointed out, it is more restricted – not every morally blameworthy person is obliged by

[21] Luhmann, *ibid.*

[22] N. Luhmann, *A Sociological Theory of Law*, trans. Elizabeth King and Martin Albow (London: Routledge & Kegan Paul, 1985), 174–177.

[23] Luhmann, *Law as a Social System*, p. 73.

the law to pay compensation to his or her victim.[24] The plausibility of this analysis of law depends on how law is assumed to function. The stabilising of expectations through a series of distinct social systems makes social life manageable. But the legal system in its own terms cannot ensure social stability nor can it control the pace of social development.[25]

C Law and other systems

A systems theory of law needs to explain not only the distinctiveness of law and legal argumentation, but also connections with other social systems. Whilst Luhmann argues that the legal system is best analysed as self-referential (autopoietic), he acknowledges that there are connections with other systems. Likewise Teubner rightly points to the fact that law often responds to the evolution of the external environment in its own particular way: by adaptation in symbiosis, rather than by direct incorporation of the external ideas.[26] Teubner draws the analogy from biology. Cells have a life of their own, but react to an environment. The cell undergoes internal change in response to changed conditions, but it remains somewhat self-contained and reproduces itself as it grows.[27] Teubner accepts that the system evolves, but in a hypercycle by which the law has its own pace of development. It is self-reproducing, but it is not causally independent, i.e. free from the indirect effect of events occurring outside it.[28]

Luhmann and Teubner stress the 'operative closure' of a legal system, but 'cognitive openness',[29] i.e. the law is self-referential in its normal operation, but it scans the environment to see where it should adapt. But they recognise that legal systems are more open than this picture suggests. For example, there are 'open concepts' which refer out to other social subsystems – some legal standards, such as 'reasonable care' or 'the bon père de famille', deliberately refer out to the standards of other social systems. This arises because law is purposive. Law has its own programmes, but justice serves as the overall programme of programmes. As Teubner comments:

[24] *Ibid.*, pp. 121–123; *Donoghue v. Stevenson* [1932] AC 562, 580.
[25] Luhmann, *Law as a Social System*, p. 161.
[26] Teubner, *Law as an Autopoietic System*, pp. 61 and 95.
[27] *Ibid.*, especially ch. 3. [28] *Ibid.*, pp. 35 and 49.
[29] N. Luhmann, 'The Self-Reproduction of Law and its Limits' in G. Teubner, *The Dilemma of Law in Welfare States* (Berlin: de Gruyter, 1986), 229.

> Justice as law's contingency formula explicitly goes beyond internal consistency. It is located at the boundary between law and its external environment and means both the historical variability of justice and its dependency on this environment. Invoking justice – and this is the core of the contingency formula – makes explicit law's dependency on it social, human and natural environment.[30]

Juridical (legal) justice does not respond by maximising doctrinal consistency, but by responding sensitively to external demands and at the same time striving for high level of consistency: 'Internal consistency plus responsiveness to ecological demands – this is the double requirement of juridical justice.' [31] In this way, the self-referentiality of the law is maintained: law looks at itself and decides whether it complies with justice. But law is creating its own picture of the external world.[32] In this picture, law is always going to find it hard to relate to the outside world. There are three limitations: law has to come to decisions and cannot wait to research thoroughly, it has limited means at its disposal actually to discover what justice in the outside world really requires, and it has limited instruments (binary solutions of 'lawful' and 'unlawful'). Law will adapt imperfectly.

D Lessons

The lesson of this analysis is that we should not expect any direct connection between the legal system and other social systems. At the same time, the law is not unaffected by its environment. The weakness of both Luhmann's and Teubner's theories is the explanation of why the law needs to change. The missing element is the essentially instrumental function of law. Teubner's analysis suggests significant self-contained activity. But law is intended to achieve social purposes which are set by political and social institutions. Lawyers play their part in formulating these social objectives and determining how they will be realised. The model of the biological cell lacks this intentional, purposive direction. Law is a system for social governance. Unlike the biological metaphor used by Teubner, law is not self-contained and existing for its own purposes. It exists to achieve appropriate governance of certain social relationships for a clientele made up of legislators, clients and citizens. The instrumental character of law is more explicit in Luhmann. The idea of a 'programme' requires a programmer who has ideas of what the law is to achieve. The key social

[30] G. Teubner, 'Self-subversive Justice: Contingency or Transcendence Formula of Law?' (2009) 72 *Modern Law Review* 1, 9.

[31] *Ibid.*, at 10. [32] *Ibid.*, pp. 10 and 17.

institutions involved in law-making are bridges to the non-legal world. The legislator is linked to the political process and has an agenda largely determined by it. The lawyers are paid by clients and are trying to achieve outcomes in the non-legal world, as well as in the legal world. Luhmann does devote some space to discussing these. But, the law is not a single programme, rather a collection of programmes developed at different times. The current lawyer has essentially to integrate the programmes from past and present and to make them serviceable and compatible. The regulative ideals of coherence and consistency, a certain kind of order, are inherent in the nature of law as a social sub-system. That provides a much more active role for those who run the legal system at any one time.

E Watson and the culture of lawyers

In a sense, Watson's model of legal development also focuses on the central role of those who run the legal system and their ways of making the legal system evolve. He argues:

> Law, then, despite its practical impact, is very noticeably the culture of lawyers, and especially of the lawmakers – that is, of those lawyers who, whether as legislators, jurists or judges, have the control of the accepted mechanisms of legal change. Legal development is determined by their culture; and social, economic, and political factors impinge on legal development only through their consciousness. This consciousness results from the lawmakers being members of the society and sharing its values and experiences, though they are members with a particular standing. Sometimes this consciousness is heightened by extreme pressures from other members of the society, but always the lawmakers' response is conditioned by the legal tradition, by their learning, expertise, and knowledge of law, domestic and foreign ... law is largely autonomous and not shaped by societal needs.[33]

For Watson, the legal community should be the focus of attention when considering legal change, especially those that control law-making in the legislature and in the courts. They are the key actors in legal change and the intermediaries through which social and economic influences are mediated. His thesis suggests that law can be both ahead of social and economic change, as well as lagging behind it. This would be the case particularly in relation to the concepts and institutions through which the

[33] A. Watson, *The Evolution of Western Private Law* (Baltimore: Johns Hopkins University Press, 2001), 263–264.

law is organised. His illustrations show a movement of concepts and ideas from one system to another.

Watson's thesis has been subjected to refinements. Ewald rightly suspects that Watson's claim is really that law is sometimes insulated from social and economic change, rather than that law does not reflect some of the forces external to the law.[34] Certainly, it would seem to be extreme to separate law from economic forces.

Watson's argument is evidenced by the importance of legal transplants. There are a number of rules imported successfully from one system to another. But Dupré argues that one has to be more sophisticated about 'importing'. Creation of new law on the basis of foreign legal materials can neither be simply reception, nor the adoption of foreign law without reasons, but rather part of a deliberate choice to follow another system as part of a strategy for legal development.[35] For her, the key determinants of such a process of positive adoption are both internal to a particular society – social context, the need for radical change, and institutional optimism – and external – the reputation of the imported legal system.

With these refinements, we are nevertheless left with Watson's focus on the legal community (particularly those involved in influencing and enacting legislation) as the gateway of legal change. Teubner may be right that 'justice' is one of the ideas around which the interaction between legal and other sub-systems is organised. But Watson is equally right that the legal community has a major role not only as intermediary, but also as guardian of the system. Any account of legal change must therefore reflect both the ideas and the social institutions and people through which change happens.

F Renner

Although his discussion relates essentially to problems within Marxist theory of law, Karl Renner's insight should not be lost. He argued that legal rules might well continue for some time, perhaps even for centuries, not to reflect the economic system that was currently in operation.[36] In that sense, legal rules and concepts might be seen as having a life of their own. The legal tradition develops around concepts and ideas and these

[34] W. Ewald, 'Comparative Jurisprudence (II): The Logic of Legal Transplants' (1995) 43 *American Journal of Comparative Law* 489, 496.

[35] C. Dupré, *Importing the Law in Post-Communist Transitions* (Oxford: Hart, 2003).

[36] K. Renner, *Institutions of Private Law and their Social Functions*, trans. A. Schwarzschild, ed. O. Kahn-Freund (London: Routledge & Kegan Paul, 1949), ch. 2.

may continue to influence the structure (form) of the legal rules, even if the content and application are appropriate for a changed economic and social situation. All the same, the key changes were for him in the social context. For him, legal change is likely to come in 'jumps', rather than smoothly following economic change, but the changes in the economy change the function and purpose of the law, even if the concepts and rules of law do not change.[37] This applies in property (Renner's concern), but it also applies in other areas such as tort. As a result, the observer should not be surprised if the concepts and even rules of the law do not change, even when the economic and social environment does change.

Summary

From the various theories examined, we see that legal development does not follow automatically from social, political and economic change. There will be a period of adaptation, and there will be some deliberate decisions about the direction the law should take. Whereas Renner, like Luhmann and Teubner, leaves us the idea of the relative autonomy of law in relation to the economic system, Watson leaves us with the idea of the relative autonomy of lawyers. Any explanations of legal development that we propose in this book take account of this potential divergence between the changes going on within the legal system and those in the surrounding environment. At the same time, the role of law in serving the purposes of society requires it not to fall too far out of step with its environment. Indeed, the issues brought to the attention of legislators, judges and scholars will arise largely because of developments in that environment of the legal system.

IV Is law systematic?

A major objection to the approach adopted by all the authors discussed so far would be that they assume that law should be systematic. From a common law perspective, Atiyah has contended that lawyers are more comfortable in describing their solutions to legal problems as 'pragmatic' and are impatient with attempts to produce more holistic systematic solutions. Both from Civilian and common law perspectives, van de Kerchove and Ost[38] and Sampford[39] would go further and argue that law is not actually

[37] *Ibid.*, p. 253.

[38] M. van de Kerchove and F. Ost, *The Legal System between Order and Disorder*, trans. I. Stewart (Oxford: Clarendon Press, 1994), 171–176.

[39] C. Sampford, *The Disorder of Law* (Oxford: Blackwell, 1989), ch. 8.

systematic. So, rather than see the systematicity of law as an explanation of what happens, it may be better to see it as a regulative ideal.

A Pragmatism and law

How far does systematicity matter? Atiyah identified two distinctions in the way that lawyers talk about law: reason is contrasted with practicability, theory with pragmatism.[40] The first distinction suggests that common lawyers reject 'strict logic' as the basis for decision, but this really means that they are rejecting a simplistic picture of law as applying principles that contain all the answers in favour of a more complex picture in which rules contain exceptions based on justifications not limited to those that underlie the rule in question. The job of the lawyer is to come to a 'common sense' application of the starkly formulated legal rules and principles. The second distinction in the common law, reflecting the lower status of theory, is also connected with the lower status of academic debate among practitioners, especially in the common law where judges are typically the opinion-formers.[41] (This, of course, contrasts with the higher status of doctrinal writers in Civilian systems. In the following chapter, we will see that the common opinion of legal scholars had a high status in the Civilian systems in 1850 and a much lower status within the English common law.)[42] On the one hand pragmatism enables decisions which are sensibly departures from established rules, but without having to renegotiate the whole legal framework. But the weakness can be a lack of coherence and an unwillingness to engage fully in justification.

Atiyah argues that the preference of lawyers (particularly practising lawyers) for pragmatism understates one of the significant characteristics of law to which the lawyers would adhere:

> Law is a *purposeful* enterprise. We live by law in modern societies for *reasons*, we have intelligible and discoverable goals. The whole concept of the rule of law requires not just that we have rules, and that government is bound by rules, but also that those rules should be based on purposes and reasons which are open to public debate.[43]

Pragmatism might be taken to be the assertion that something is right because the judge or legislator says so, an assertion of authority. But

[40] P.S. Atiyah, *Pragmatism and Theory in English Law* (London: Stevens, 1987), 6–7.
[41] *Ibid.*, pp. 34–39.
[42] Below, pp. 70–71.
[43] Atiyah, *Pragmatism*, p. 144.

actually we do expect reasons to be given, even if the reasons do not persuade everyone and even if the reasons sometimes do little more than parrot assumptions that are largely untested. Indeed, Atiyah identifies in the common law tradition the prevalence of *implicit theory*.[44] Shorthand expressions such as 'fairness', 'reasonableness' and 'common sense' are used instead of an elaborated expression of the justification. Judges' own approaches to their jobs are often implicit, because there is an inadequate theory of when they can be innovative and when not.[45] The focus of attention is typically on solving the particular problem at hand, rather than a general solution.[46]

Detailed legislation encourages this in relation to the interpretation of statutes. His argument is that pragmatists actually work with an implicit theory and if they do not try to explain it, then they are really asking the wider community to trust them.[47] On this analysis, appeals to pragmatism do not really mean that the value of law as a system is being denied, but the effort of making explicit how a solution fits within the legal system as a whole is seen as unnecessary in a particular context. We can take from Atiyah the lesson that the justifications that lawyers give may well be incomplete. Not merely may they be under-theorised, but they may take for granted a series of ideas as unnecessary to be made explicit. Such implicit arguments have to be made explicit in any analysis of legal development.

The lawyer's conception of systematicity needs also to be made explicit. Even if there are general values for which the law as a whole strives, there may well be local solutions which run counter to what these higher-level principles require. Canaris helpfully suggests that the existence of programmes (road traffic law, medical law, etc.) means that legal system has defined values. Legal reasoning shows the internal logic (*Folgerichtigkeit*) of such programmes as applied to a decision, not necessarily the inherent justice of the outcome.[48] He identifies various levels of system within the law. General principles hold things together at a lower level than values, and detailed rules hold specific programmes within the law together.[49] As a result, although any system or sub-system within the law is purposive and aims at values such as justice, a system-correct solution may go against justice in particular respects. So there is a potential conflict at

[44] *Ibid.*, p. 151. [45] *Ibid.*, pp. 155–159.
[46] *Ibid.*, p. 28. [47] *Ibid.*, pp. 143–144.
[48] C.-W. Canaris, *Systemdenken und Systembegriff in der Jurisprudenz* (Berlin: Dunker & Humblot, 1969), 45
[49] *Ibid.*, pp. 53–55.

times between higher-level legal principles and the operation of specific legal programmes.[50] In reality, the systematic coherence of the legal system will always be work in progress. It is a regulative ideal, rather than a fully achieved reality.

B Law as chaos

The paradigm of law as system is challenged by those who see the value of order as grossly overstated in the ambitions of law. Of course law does introduce an element of order and does thereby reduce complexity in an artificial way. But some would argue that, in an imperfect world, an element of disorder is a natural condition for a legal system.

In brief, the legal system consists of legislation, judicial decisions and doctrinal writings produced at different times, typically for very specific purposes. Those who made legislative and judicial decisions did not have the time (or often the inclination) to conduct an exhaustive review of the existing law and relate any new provision systematically to it. Modern British statutes attempt to do this but this is not undertaken in France, where there is typically no schedule of repeals or amendments. Detailed British judicial decisions do not cover all the areas of previous law, nor do the more exhaustive surveys of the advocate general in French and Dutch legal systems, for example. The result is that the interpreter has to make the necessary alignment of the different provisions.

Contemporary interpreters of law can adopt one of two attitudes. On the one hand, they can try to carry out faithfully the instructions provided in the authoritative sources within the specific branch of law at hand, but not worry about whether this fits well with what the law demands in other branches. On the other hand, they can see their mission as being to integrate the whole legal system, as far as this is possible. This means that incompatibilities have to be reduced.

The regulative ideal of systematic coherence of the legal system means that the rule-maker or interpreter attempts, as far as possible, to make sense of one rule of the law in relation to other parts of the system. One assumes that the law speaks today to the citizen and is consistent in its demands. The ideal of coherence is seen by the use of systematic, rather than literal interpretation of statutes, the need to integrate constitutional and other branches of law, and the ambition of legislation to integrate

[50] *Ibid.*, p. 110.

with existing rules of law. Having a regulative ideal provides an ambition for legislation, case-law and doctrinal writing.

Sampford[51] and van der Kerchove and Ost [52] argue that it is not a necessary or even desirable regulative ideal. Clearly, coherence of some kind is important in law but perhaps not as an ideal that prevails over other ideals such as justice. Indeed, experimentation may be a way of trying to achieve justice. For instance, systematic interpretation is a central feature of the approach to interpreting statutes in most legal systems. At any one time, the law will never be fully systematically coherent. Courts will disagree with one another, or even internally with themselves. Legislation is often enacted with inadequate regard to rules already in force, so there are incoherences in what is required in different statutes. Doctrinal writers will also disagree among themselves. The result of disagreement and debate is progress. It is important to recognise that the law does exist at any one time in a state of some chaos. But it is important not to exaggerate this. As van der Kerchove and Ost remark, the legal system is 'partially disordered'.[53] In that way, it adapts to the objectives set for it. But there is a constant attempt to give it order, because one of the distinctive contributions of law is to reduce complexity by instituting order, albeit an artificial order.

In such a situation, when they describe a legal system, lawyers will typically be reporting what is the regulative ideal of the aspiration of the law, rather than what is the reality of what is achieved at any one time. One view to be explored would suggest that the law is not best viewed as a single coherent system, but as a collection of more or less tightly connected systems. Thus, there might be a close connection between crime and tort in relation to fault, but not between fault and various regulatory laws on planning or health and safety. The fact that a particular approach is adopted in one part of the law does not mean that it is universally applied within the law as a whole.

C Law and its relationship to economic change

In terms of the European Legal Development project and its concern about the relationship of legal and economic or social development, Teubner would argue that it is futile to search for a clear causal relationship

[51] C. Sampford, *The Disorder of Law*, ch. 8.

[52] M. van der Kerchove and F. Ost, *The Legal System between Order and Disorder*, ch. 4.

[53] *Ibid.*, p. 173.

between economic change and legal change. For him, there is no direct relationship, but a 'co-evolution' between law as one social system and other social systems, such as the economy:

> Autopoietic closure does not mean that the [legal] system is independent of its environment. Evolution's relation to the environment is not brought about, however, by direct, causal, external influence on legal developments. Rather, it evolves through processes of co-evolution in which the co-evolving systems exert an indirect influence on each other.[54]

A more traditional instrumental or intentionalist narrative would set a different line of enquiry and try to show the way in which the law is deliberately used to handle economic or social change. It is unlikely that the picture will be clear cut. Rather, it is a question of choosing a narrative that is more persuasive. The best way of assessing whether a causal or a non-causal analysis makes sense is to examine whether the narrative of one or other of these approaches is well suited to presenting a story that adequately accounts for the known data. A comparison of causal and non-causal narratives would seem appropriate.[55]

Luhmann and Teubner argue that legal change happens primarily through processes within the system, either a change in the conditional programme (Luhmann) or a mutation within the cell (Teubner) through which the law accommodates a new social phenomenon. This one can typify as *internal legal change in the content or operation of the law.* Changes in the outside environment *may* be a trigger, but will not always be so. One could characterise Watson as having much the same focus. On the other hand, Teubner suggests that society has a number of social sub-systems, of which law is only one. If a new problem arises, it may not be the law that adapts most, but another sub-system and the place of the law is squeezed.[56] This one can typify as *external change to the place of the law.* A holistic view of legal development has to take account of the second, external change. As a result, an enquiry on legal change has to look not only at changes within the law, but also at the place of law within social sub-systems. Renner's approach is to see the only real change as *external change to the place of law.* The economy or society change and so the significance of the legal rules, how they are used and what they

[54] Teubner, *Law as an Autopoietic System*, p. 61.

[55] Teubner's critique of the introduction of 'good faith' by means of a directive on consumer protection: G. Teubner, 'Legal Irritants: Good faith in British Law' (1998) 61 *Modern Law Review* 1.

[56] Teubner, *Law as an Autopoietic System*, pp. 109ff.

signify change, even if the inner content does not (or does not change at the same pace).

V Path dependence and national difference

When considering legal change, the question arises why different systems take different paths faced with very similar social problems. When problems are new in a number of socially similar legal systems, why do not the same novel solutions become adopted? One explanation often offered is that each system is locked into a set of concepts, procedures and ideas from the past which are carried forward to resolve new problems. This explanation is often called 'path dependence'. The term, borrowed from economics, implies that systems do not progress necessarily towards the same end, but find different points of equilibrium, depending on the path along which they have travelled.[57] Zweigert and Kötz argue that, if we want to find explanations for differences between legal systems, we should look to history, inherited traditions and legal concepts.[58] This fits very much the idea that previous solutions create a path dependence which shapes the future development of the law.

Three features combine to make a path dependence analysis plausible. First, path dependence suggests that legal development will almost unconsciously work within the framework of previous solutions. Lawyers take for granted certain assumptions about how to deal with legal problems and work within those parameters, often without consciously reconsidering their appropriateness. Secondly, law develops incrementally, especially when being driven through case-law or doctrinal commentary.[59] The law develops deliberately by small steps, often because it is dealing with one problem at a time. Certainly case-law develops by handling specific situations as they arise. This feature of *incrementalism* is a limited form of legal development and works by keeping most of the law the same. Thirdly, lawyers typically reason by analogy. Thus, explicit justifications for legal decisions will be drawn from established principles.[60] Analogy

[57] John Black, Nigar Hashimzade and Gareth Myles, *A Dictionary of Economics* (Oxford University Press, 2009).

[58] K. Zweigert and H. Kötz, *An Introduction to Comparative Law*, 3rd edn, trans. Tony Weir (Oxford University Press, 1998), 68–72.

[59] J. Bell, *Policy Arguments in Judicial Decisions* (Oxford University Press, 1983), 226–234; R. Goff, 'The Search for Principle' (1983) *Proceedings of the British Academy* 169, 182–186.

[60] Z. Bankowski in P. Nerhot (ed.), *Legal Knowledge and Analogy: Fragments of Legal Epistemology, Hermeneutics, and Linguistics* (Dordrecht: Kluwer, 1991), 198.

is a method of reasoning by which new fact situations are brought within the ambit of established legal rules and so a decision can be presented as made according to law.[61] This method is seen most by the citation of previous decisions either in judgments or in the other documents in a case, e.g. the arguments of the advocate general. This is supported by notions of equal treatment and also by the idea that the decision on new facts is still taken according to law. The importance of analogy in legal reasoning is perhaps the most significant feature, since it forces lawyers deliberately to link new decisions with those in the past.

A *Theories of path dependence*

'Path dependence' is used to explain why change in the actions of individuals and of institutions tends in a particular direction, especially over time. The basic idea is that individuals are faced with complex situations. They often do not know what is the best thing to do, or what will be the consequences of their actions. To cope, they basically play safe – they act in ways that are similar to what they have done before and that they know work. Stinchcombe argued that doing something new can be expensive and unpredictable: 'The most important [costs of new activities] are the risk and cost of thinking. The poorer the capacity of people to predict the consequences of an innovation, the more likely they are to (rationally) prefer what they already have, whose consequences they can predict from their experience.'[62] The literature in economics and management identifies a number of features that explain why we as individuals continue to do the same thing, even if this is not the most efficient outcome. As has just been noted, Stinchcombe identifies the cost of innovation. We may continue to do the same thing, because it is simply not worth the cost of change. In law, change in one area often has implications and therefore costs of change for other branches of the law, as well as for other social activities.

But we may continue to do things because they are appropriate or at least no more inefficient than other courses of action. The external environment may provide positive signals that particular conduct is correct. We learn from our experiences. Crouch[63] offers a simplified analogy of

[61] L.L. Weinreb, *Legal Reason. The Use of Analogy in Legal Argument* (New York: Cambridge University Press, 2005), 98.

[62] A.L. Stinchcombe, *Constructing Social Theories* (New York: Brace and World, 1968), 123.

[63] Colin Crouch, *Capitalist Diversity and Change. Recombinant Governance and Institutional Entrepreneurs* (Oxford University Press, 2005), 78.

the new student learning to cook bacon. Sometimes he fries it, sometimes he boils it, but he will gradually get to know the method he likes best and becomes adept at it. There is a learning curve. Once we have learnt from experience, then the future becomes easier and we can move on to more problems. If decisions are taken in law, then there will be a reaction from the legal community. If that is positive, then legislators or judges are given incentives to continue to do the same in future.

Applied to institutions, like the law, path dependence would seek to explain why, having set down one path and created over time a set of legal frameworks, procedures and rules, a legal system may adopt a particular approach to new problems (and, some would say, not adopt the most efficient approach to solving a particular problem). John Armour and colleagues[64] have examined path dependence as the underlying idea of the 'legal origins' theory of LaPorta and others, and have suggested ways in which such a theory needs to become more sophisticated, notably in explaining the mechanisms by which the internal momentum of a legal system and its approach to a problem are reinforced. It would appear to us that the place of analogy in legal justifications and the feedback received from such decisions does provide some explanation for the internal momentum that a legal system acquires.

What features of a legal system would path dependence involve? Zweigert and Kötz differentiate legal systems according to *style*, which involves the interaction of a number of features which, operating together, make a system distinctive.[65] For them, historical development, characteristic mode of legal thinking, distinctive concepts, the identity and use of legal sources and its overall ideology will work together to define a particular system's approach.[66] They are well aware that these features change over time, and this is why they are more sceptical of concepts like 'legal culture' as a way of describing differences. Samuel points out the way in which structural schemes serve to make the legal system intelligible in certain ways, making certain analogies seem appropriate.[67] These ideas would both suggest that, within a particular legal tradition or family, there are characteristic frameworks within which problems are approached and solutions are justified. The claim is that being tied to working within

[64] J. Armour, S. Deakin, V. Mollica and M. Siems, 'Law and Financial Development: What We are Learning from Time-Series Evidence' (2009) *Brigham Young University Law Review* 1435.

[65] Zweigert and Kötz, *An Introduction to Comparative Law*, p. 67.

[66] *Ibid.*, pp. 68–72. [67] Samuel, *Epistemology*, pp. 306–308.

these frameworks creates an often unconscious approach that drives one system to operate differently from another system.

If this notion is expanded, it seems that path dependence would involve a number of features. First, the lawyer approaching a new problem has to take certain premises, rules, concept maps and forms of justification as starting points for his or her activity. Deciding according to law within a particular legal system requires these starting points to be taken for granted and used as the framework within which solutions according to law are found. This approach offers a heuristic for searching out and debating an appropriate solution.

Secondly, any justification of a solution needs to demonstrate itself faithful both to the content of the legal tradition of that jurisdiction and to its traditions of reasoning. As has been said, the tradition will make certain analogies appropriate and others implausible.

Thirdly, there are certain rules and outcomes that cannot be altered easily, however inconvenient or objectionable they may be. The incremental character of legal development prevents a wholesale revision of an area of law. This has two consequences. First, legal argument in court or legislative reform will tend to work within established frameworks of legal rules and concepts. The lawyers involved will be dealing with specific problems that have arisen in a case or a set of cases or that have given rise to a demand for law reform. There is neither the time nor the appetite to call into question the whole body of law within which the problem is conventionally approached. So solutions are sought within the established rules and concepts, suitably adapted to deal with the problem in hand. This is achieved either by interpretation, by extension of a concept into a new area, or, very occasionally, by a legal fiction. Analogy is a very common form of legal reasoning. In an analogy, a similarity is found between the problem at hand and a problem that has already been settled. The solution for the new problem is found through applying a previous solution that dealt with a similar situation. Secondly, the limitations of partial remedies may make it more acceptable to do nothing than to make a small change to resolve one particular problem, which may render the law less coherent in a number of other respects.

The first two features, using existing legal materials as starting points and justifying decisions in relation to the existing law, essentially set out an ideal for deciding according to law. To do so, the lawyer must justify his or her solution to a new problem by showing how it fits within existing legal authorities or is a legitimate extension of them. This is the model of 'rational reconstruction', of inventive fidelity to the system as a whole.

Existing theories of 'path dependence' seem more focused on the first of these ideals of decision-making according to law. Our own work here will look at all three features.

Such a model of rational reconstruction may be contrasted with a 'pragmatist' account according to which the decision-maker has to provide the best solution he can to the new problem within the constraints offered by the features of the law he is not permitted to change. On this account, the legal decision-maker is guided principally by ideologies and policies that he wishes to achieve. The legal materials exist as constraints, both substantive and procedural, which force him to relate his proposed solutions to what may be a prevailing consensus within the legal or social community that he is serving. It is a model of constrained responsibility. Rather than an unconscious path dependence, this account would focus on deliberate actions designed to fit within or push the boundaries of the established framework.

B Path dependence theories and moments of change

The economics literature on path dependence focuses especially on the persistence of inefficient outcomes and their effect on future decisions.[68] Even though new issues and changes in the environment may cause some disturbance, there are a number of stable alternative states into which a person or an institution may settle, depending on where they started.[69] Path dependence serves to explain the particular response to change of that person or institution. The emphasis on the effect of the market may appear to stress a kind of 'invisible hand' explanation of economic and legal stasis or change. But the politics variant of path dependence pays attention to the human agency reasons why decisions are not responsive to the signals from the market.[70] Although we have seen that Stinchcombe raises the issue of the costs of change, there is also the self-interest of those in power which makes them wary of change:

> Inefficient outcomes have long lives. But inefficiencies do have welfare costs for actors, and the fact that these may persist or even accumulate as countries travel further down a particular policy path can serve to magnify their impact. At some point – a *tipping point* – the returns to be

[68] S.J. Liebowitz and S. Margolis, *The Economics of QWERTY* (New York University Press, 2002), ch. 7.

[69] *Ibid.*, p. 157.

[70] M.J. Roe, 'Chaos and Evolution in Law and Economics' (1996) 109 *Harvard Law Review* 641, 665–666.

> gained from network externalities of convergence on common practices may well become outweighed by the utility loss of living with 'bad' policies. Once this tipping point is reached, we should expect actors to seek policy change to correct the inefficiency. However, note that rectifying inefficiencies need not necessarily imply wholesale overthrow of a policy or complex of policies. If the benefits of long-standing coordination among actors are significant, and inefficiencies can be corrected through modifications to existing practice, we should expect to see strategies of adjustment that fall in between continuation of the status quo and complete policy reversals.[71]

So the model of path dependence makes us look for established practice, feedback from the environment, but also factors for resistance to change that are institutional, as well as those based on conscious individual decisions. The result of this perspective is not to assume that change will be smooth and incremental. It may well come at specific points of pressure or crisis, when tipping points of conflicting pressures for and against change are upset.[72] Although the economics literature talks a lot about the persistence of 'inefficient outcomes', path dependence analysis need not be limited to inefficiency. It seems perfectly proper to talk about different kinds of legal system as efficient in their own way, but all the same creating a path dependence towards particular ways of dealing with new problems.[73]

C *The limitations of path dependence*

Despite its correct identification of many of the constraints within which the law operates, two areas have been identified in which theories of path dependence have to become more sophisticated in order to provide an explanation of legal development or the lack of it. First, some versions of it are over simplistic – they exaggerate the importance of inertia and underplay the potential for change.[74] For simplicity of modelling, the economics literature's account of path dependence focuses on a single, monotonous task that is repeated. If we get used to doing a thing, like driving a car on the left-hand side of the road, then it becomes natural and we resist changing it. All our real world decisions are more complex, especially in

[71] P. Pierson (ed.), *The New Politics of the Welfare State* (Oxford University Press, 2001), 373.
[72] Roe, 'Chaos and Evolution', p. 663.
[73] Such an analysis fits with the approach of Liebowitz and Margolis, *The Economics of QWERTY*, p. 165.
[74] Crouch, *Capitalist Diversity and Change*, p. 78.

law. Secondly, the versions focus on institutions and not enough on the individual actors who make decisions at key moments. There is too much emphasis on a kind of 'invisible hand', rather than conscious decisions.

1 The potential for change

Even though law creates routines, within what might be seen as a settled area of law, there is the uncertainty of whether this new situation is going to produce as good a solution as the previous ones. Road accident victims are varied – pedestrians, cyclists, drivers, passengers, bystanders. Road conditions are varied; drivers have varied experience and have varied types of insurance cover. It is not straightforward to come up with solutions appropriate to each circumstance. We often provide different solutions to different situations. So the position of the friend or family member carried in the car for free was treated differently from other victims in English and French laws for a long time. There continue to be points for decision, even once the initial decision has been made. These will often be issues of how the law is interpreted or applied, but they have an importance to the issue of what the law is actually doing in particular countries.

Crouch suggests that the context within which people work is heterogeneous. There are multiple environments. Decision-makers are faced with situations within which they have not previously used their knowledge and they are forced to extend their repertoire in ways that have not been anticipated. Scientific innovation occurs by putting several teams of researchers together who are not doing collaborative work. Stretching one group to start thinking about the problems of the other stretches their potential. Lawyers faced with road accidents were not just tort lawyers, but were criminal lawyers, contract lawyers, litigators, judges, parliamentarians and road-users. The way problems were presented was not confined to tort, but involved sometimes criminal law, sometimes contract, sometimes social insurance. As a result, lawyers had complex approaches to the problem which gave them different insights when deciding tort cases. Fault fitted criminal liability, but did not fit contracts for the carriage of passengers. Social insurance was more victim-orientated than tort law. Whilst unconscious processes may account for some of the 'naturalness' of some analogies, there are a number of other parts of the picture that ensure the individual decision-maker could make alternative decisions.

In particular, the law is not isolated from other social processes. Crouch[75] makes the point that the potential for change may sometimes

[75] *Ibid.*, p. 87.

come from within (endogenous) an institution and sometime from without (exogenous). The research scientist example shows the way in which one group may draw on material that they treat as redundant and for which they have no use in order to help the other group solve its problems. Crouch argues that given access to endogenous new ways of behaving, actors can change their minds. He takes the idea of Lévi-Strauss about *bricolage* (rummaging around) in primitive societies, and applies it to modern sophisticated societies:

> these arguments highlight a relatively underappreciated implication of path dependence theory: that more than one path of institutional development is possible, even if only one becomes established. Alternatives exist somewhere within agents' repertoires, but have become forgotten or hidden through disuse or failure to appreciate their possible relevance. Something like this is embodied in Douglas's adaptation of Lévi-Strauss's idea of *bricolage*, a rummaging around in disused but available practices for ways of solving new problems.[76]

The national law contains a repertoire of solutions, which the national lawyer may choose. As we will see,[77] English law and French lawyers in the period 1900 to 1920 did a lot of *bricolage* in relation to road accidents, trying out different legal solutions until one became imposed by the Court of Appeal or the Cour de cassation. Conscious choices were made that were disputed at the time.

2 Individual actors

If lawyers in new situations have genuine choices to make, then there is a clear place for individual actors. If lawyers not only participate in their own legal community, but are operating also in relation to other legal communities and to non-legal communities, their individual ways of thinking can be distinctive. In the course of this book, we will draw attention to the place of a number of key individuals who have made significant contributions to particular legal developments – as legislators, judges, policy-makers and scholarly writers. At the same time, we have already noted that the law is a collective enterprise, and so we must give an account of the development of the legal systems as a whole and how fault liability was used to deal with new problems, not just an account of great individuals.

[76] *Ibid.* [77] Below, pp. 122–123, 125.

Summary

So the more sophisticated version of path dependence leaves the comparative lawyer with a number of questions:

- When a question first occurred, what were the obvious analogies or similar situations on which the national lawyer could draw? Why was a particular path attractive?
- What were the experiences which reinforced the chosen path? What were the advantages to those in power, e.g. to legislators or judges and to those influencing them?
- Given that circumstances are varied and change, why didn't some rules change?
- What is the tipping point for change: where is the pressure building up and why?

VI Legal change in the European Legal Development project

This section locates the types of legal development identified in the first six books of the project, which will be the constant reference point for the discussion in the rest of this book.

Liability for Products identifies a new social phenomenon that emerged essentially in the late nineteenth century and accelerated from 1950. The problem was the greater role of the manufacturer in controlling the design, distribution and marketing of products. The retailer became less the person on whose skill, judgment and reputation the purchaser relied, and more the distributor of the pre-packaged item that the manufacturer had prepared for the consumer. The key relationship was not so much that in contract between the retailer and the purchaser and moved to be more that between the manufacturer and the consumer. Because of a weaker contractual nexus, tort law was expected in most countries (but less so in France) to play the role of creating a remedy. A series of crises affected some countries, e.g. Thalidomide (1960) in Germany and England, or Colza Oil in Spain (1982), and created a climate that favoured treating this as a distinctive problem requiring easier compensation than was currently available.

Until the European Directive of 1985,[78] there was little change in the formulation of the substantive rules of law applicable.[79] Instead, the legal

[78] Council Directive 1985/374/EEC of 25 July 1985 on the approximation of laws, regulations and administrative provisions of the Member States concerning liability for defective products, OJ L 210, 7 August 1985, 29 ('The Product Liability Directive').

[79] The Spanish law of 1984 following the Colza Oil scandal was quickly superseded by the Directive.

systems saw a re-interpretation of the general provisions on tort, particularly those relating to fault. First, following American developments in the 1940s and 1950s, culminating in the *Restatement on Torts (2d)* in 1965, European systems typically conceptualised 'product liability' as a distinctive legal problem, even though this was not recognised in their codes. Secondly, the difficulties for the consumer to prove fault and the privileged position of the manufacturer to identify the causes of defects led to procedural interpretations, notably the reversal of the burden of proof.[80] There were also re-interpretations of fault to include conduct such as putting items into circulation without instructions on use, or not withdrawing them from circulation when an unexpected defect appeared.

In terms of context, it is the change in social practices that triggered the identification of liability for products as a distinct area. In terms of the importance of the law, the business imperative of customer satisfaction led to voluntary schemes of redress where there were simple defects.[81] So, again, this confined the law to more serious harms where manufacturers (or their insurers) would insist on a more clearly defined legal obligation before settling a claim for compensation from a consumer. A further feature of the context would be the long-standing role of legislation in regulating the quality of products

In terms of the operation of the law, it is difficult to identify change, since this was a new category of problem. The creation of small claims jurisdictions[82] provided remedies for many cases of defects in products, but these would not lead to reported cases. So the few reported cases tend to deal with the more serious personal injuries, and this provided a context for the development of 'product liability' as a distinct field within basic tort principles. The other phenomenon in the United States was the class action, which enabled large numbers of consumers to bring actions relating to the same product. Whilst there was some co-ordination between litigants, e.g. in relation to Thalidomide, there was no systematic introduction of this procedure so as to encourage the development of this area of law.[83]

[80] *Saiwa* in Italy (1964), *Hühnerpest* in Germany (1968), *Leaking Water Bottle* in the Netherlands (1973). The French had established an almost irrebuttable presumption in relation to sellers as early as 1925: see *Products*, pp. 208–209, 123–124, 160–161 and 95–96.

[81] G. Borrie and A. Diamond, *The Consumer, Society and the Law*, 3rd edn (London: Penguin, 1973), 33–34.

[82] See generally C. Whelan (ed.), *Small Claims Courts: An International and Comparative Appraisal* (Oxford University Press, 1991).

[83] See J.A. Jolowicz, *On Civil Procedure* (Cambridge University Press, 2000), 111–118.

Liability for Traffic Accidents covered two distinctive causes of personal injury, the train and the car. As is made clear in the relevant volume, there had been litigation in relation to accidents on the highway for many years, particularly accidents involving stagecoaches. The distinctiveness of the social problem in relation to both trains and cars was the difficulty for the owners to identify potential problems in complex machines and for the victim to demonstrate fault occurring in events at high speed and involving complex mechanical parts. It is clear that the scale of the problem of accidents, though dramatic, was not a radical change from the problems associated with horses and bad roads. But the character of the injuries became more significant, particularly after 1950 when medicine enabled more of the victims to survive.

This is a topic on which many systems formulated new rules. Prussia (1838), the Netherlands (1859) and then Germany (1871) enacted specific legislation to deal with railway accidents. Sweden (1906), Germany (1909) and the Netherlands (1924) introduced specific laws on road accidents, which were reformulated later. For the most part, these laws covered two issues. The first was whether the victim had to prove fault or would be compensated without proof of fault. The second problem was the extent to which the custodian of a vehicle would be responsible for the acts of the driver. Other systems were later in producing new rules: Spain in 1962, France in 1985. England never did produce a new law on road traffic liability, though it did produce some legislation in relation to railways. Many of the newly formulated rules took liability away from general fault liability and created a distinct regime of no-fault liability.

In many legal systems, the main approach for many years was interpretation of existing texts. In France, the radical re-interpretation of article 1384 of the Civil Code created first a presumption of fault and, after 1930, a presumption of liability, which was in effect strict liability with limited exceptions. In English law, after some attempts to use stricter liability through public nuisance and *Rylands v. Fletcher* or breach of a statutory duty, the law settled on the interpretation of fault liability with some alleviation of problems through the burden of proof.[84] In Spain, there was some early attempt to use stricter liability, but the law quickly focused on fault.[85] A presumption of liability was created by the courts in 1943, well ahead of legislation in 1962.

To understand the importance of the law it is necessary to examine the context of different categories of victim. In relation to railways, the

[84] See below, pp. 122–123. [85] *Traffic*, pp. 174–175.

restrictions on employees suing led to few tort actions, but compensation was often provided through the insurance which employers took out.[86] The passenger victims were typically protected through contract and their numbers were quite small. In many ways, the special legislation passed was overly concerned about this group, which was relatively rich and had political influence. Social changes caused by rapid increases in car ownership after 1920 and the very high incidence of death and injury on the roads provided not only a spur to legislation, but provided a context for judicial and academic debate. A major contextual feature is the development of compulsory insurance. Not merely did this bring about subrogation actions which transform the function of the courts. It also provided the resources from which relatively poor tortfeasors could pay compensation. These contextual features increase the relative visibility of this area within tort law. A major contextual change over the period involved the regulation of driving, the design of vehicles for greater safety, and the layout and surfacing of roads. These had very significant effects on the level of road accidents and the standards of driving and vehicle repair that would be treated as faulty. Similarly, the improvement to working hours and practices had a significant effect on the level of accidents.

In terms of the operation of the law, the most important feature is the difficulty for employees to gain compensation. As will also be seen in relation to technological change, the largest number of railway victims were employees, but they were excluded from compensation either because of the rules about accepting the risk of harm caused by your fellow employees or because of the limitations on vicarious liability, or because of the rules on contributory negligence. In addition, the cost of litigation for this group of victims made recovery problematic. In relation to cars, there were issues about whether passengers could recover if they were not carried for reward. For a long time, such gratuitous passengers were not able to recover in some systems, like France and England. Of course, the principal group of people involved were other members of the family. The importance of subrogation and similar rules led to many cases before courts actually being between insurers whose objective was to have a ruling that they could then use for the settlement of a range of other cases. Again, small claims procedures reduce the number of cases brought before the courts.

Medical Liability was not a new problem. There were actions against doctors in the fourteenth century and some of the major rules were laid

[86] *Ibid.*, pp. 12–13, 32–33 and 84–85.

down a long time ago. Three features changed in the period under review. First, doctors and other medical actors became more professionalised in their training, discipline and organisation. It is only in the nineteenth century that the profession of doctor was differentiated from other kinds of healer. The rules developed in France in 1810 for the training and registration of medical professionals, as well as for the restriction on the use of titles, were a starting point. With an identifiable group, it was easier to develop standards. Secondly, social expectations of doctors and other medical professionals increased over the period. Thirdly, particularly after 1950, medicine became increasingly technological and hospitals became major providers of medical services in increasingly complex ways. So whilst the problem of harm caused by doctors was not new, the level of expectation and sophistication in relation to medical services became significantly different. For that reason, the topic of medical liability only became differentiated in the 1970s.

The national chapters on the subject make it clear that the formulation of the rules really does not change much over the period, until the twenty-first century, when no-fault compensation schemes are introduced in countries such as Austria and France.

Interpretations of the rules change radically over the period. Three specific areas illustrate this. First is the notion of fault. All the chapters explain the extreme reluctance to find doctors to be at fault in the nineteenth century. The interpretation given to fault in the applicable rules was really a standard of 'gross fault'. Equally important is the interpretation of the notion of 'consent' to treatment, which now carries with it the idea that the patient should give an informed consent. Secondly, there was reluctance to find that the hospital was vicariously liable for the work of the doctor or nurses. In particular, liability for the system of activities within a hospital has only recently been acknowledged. Thirdly, concepts of 'causation' have been interpreted less restrictively in order to deal with the difficulties of proving the connection between a wrong and the kind of loss that has been suffered. For example in the Netherlands, there has been a reversal of the burden of proof from 1953.[87]

In terms of context, the liability of the medical professions has changed out of all recognition. There has been a move from hospitals as places where the elderly and infirm were sent effectively to die to becoming major centres of complex and technologically sophisticated treatment with a high chance of cure and rehabilitation. Medical training, understanding

[87] *Medical*, p. 145.

and professionalism have changed completely. It is the change in context that has led to changes in social expectations and so standards of fault. As Hondius points out, the patients' rights movement has led to a major change in the way issues such as the right to be informed are viewed.

Since this was not a recognised area until recent years, few operational arrangements have been put in place to deal with this kind of litigation. Doctors did take out insurance at an early stage and public authorities stood behind many hospitals. That ensured that the defendants in actions were well organised and solvent. In terms of procedure, the proof of fault and causation relies heavily either on expert reports or on expert evidence, according to the system. Since the experts themselves would have to come from the medical community, there were concerns whether they would be sufficiently critical and whether the judges would be willing to challenge their findings. Over most of the period, it would seem that expert opinion remained unchallenged.

Liability between Neighbours is a much more established field. Gordley states that the problem encountered in modern times is fundamentally the same as in Roman law.[88] Urbanisation and industrialisation put strains on the conceptual framework of tort. Gordley argues that this did not lead to radical change in the formulation of tort law. Others would argue that the social problems of industrialisation made very significant changes to the social problems with which the law operates.

In terms of formulation, all the national reports suggest that the general rules of tort law and property law found in the codes were used to deal with the problems of industrialisation and urbanisation in the nineteenth century. Indeed many of these were very old. New rules were introduced to deal with the planning of noxious activities, but these did not affect tort liability.

On the other hand, interpretations changed quite significantly. The increased importance of comfort and enjoyment in the use of one's property led to a more sophisticated notion of the interests protected by nuisance or equivalent remedies in other systems. Greater attention was paid to excessive user and the idea of abuse of rights as a theme that connected the different situations of liability. But these notions led inevitably to a more 'factual turn', rather than general rules (e.g. Dutch 1956). Fault was used as a justification for expanding the range of liabilities, e.g. for personal injury. The move away from seeing liability as protecting property

[88] J. Gordley, *The Development of Liability between Neighbours* (Cambridge University Press, 2010) (hereafter '*Neighbours*'), 1–3.

rights and covering more extensive interests in the enjoyment of property was significant.

In terms of context, clearly the social context within which the law operated changed significantly. But it was not simply a change in the social environment (smoke and pollution from factories; more densely populated towns). There were changes in social values with a greater importance given to enjoyment of property, even from the eighteenth century.[89] The other major context for the operation of the law was the increase in planning law. In many countries, there had been restrictions on land use in urban areas from medieval times. But these became systematised in the early nineteenth century in France and elsewhere later. This caused a significant change in the importance of tort law as a vehicle for disputing the use of land. As a result, the issues of compensation became relatively more significant.

There are no significant operational issues relating to tort law, but of course the presence of the whole system of planning law made significant changes to the way in which the conduct of neighbours was halted.

Liability in Relation to Technological Changes necessarily involves new social issues. Sparks from railways and exploding boilers were new technology. Asbestos was not a new product and its problems had been known as early as the sixteenth century. But the public health knowledge really came only in the twentieth century.[90] The harmful nature of sparks and boilers was immediately apparent, but the harm from asbestos was appreciated only after some time. In each topic, there are two classes of victims: employees and neighbours (within which one can include the families of asbestos workers who were contaminated by fibres on the workers' clothes and users of asbestos products). Harm caused at work and harm caused by industrial processes to neighbours were not new. It was the character of the harm and the scale that produced a new legal situation. The length of railway tracks could make a single engine cause a multiplicity of harms on a single journey. Steam boiler explosions caused harm on a scale that was not seen before. Asbestos created a latent potential for harm, which then affected a very large number of people over many years. All of these problems raised issues for regulation, as well as for compensation.

In terms of formulation, the relevant volume does not provide many examples of changes in the formulation of tort rules, except in Germany. New rules were formulated to provide compensation outside tort, and some rules on investigation of accidents were produced, which provided

89 *Ibid.*, p. 135. 90 *Technology*, pp. 19–21.

improved evidence. But, essentially, the existing rules of tort and property were left to provide the remedies for the harms caused.

Interpretations have been quite significant. In terms of sparks from railway engines, interpretations provided the appropriate scope for property rules (which would favour the landowner suffering the harm) and tort rules. England, Spain and Italy based liability mainly on tort and fault, introducing a stringent requirement to obtain compensation. Germany moved in a similar direction where railway activities were specifically authorised.[91] Indeed, most countries, except France, were reluctant to find liability where there had been public authorisation of the activity. In the area of asbestos, there have been major interpretative issues on fault, causation, damage and limitation periods.[92] A particularly difficult topic in recent years has been causation.[93] Since many diseases are latent for a long time and can perhaps be caused by a single fibre, a worker who is employed by a number of firms during a working life will find it difficult to attribute his illness to any particular employer's working environment. So the question of potential multiple causes has to be resolved and this has been undertaken by interpretation. Clearly, the interpretations involved affect the law beyond asbestos, so there are limits to the way in which the law can be manipulated.

The social context of technological change created the legal issue. The legal context of employment and the expectation that employees were deemed to accept the risks of their employment situation and fellow employees limited many of the earlier actions. The effect of contributory fault was also important. The move over the period to the apportionment of loss according to contributory fault favoured the employee, who might otherwise be barred. The removal of such limitations allowed the basic principles of tort to operate more directly, and so this made it more possible. The broader social context changed the importance of liability in these areas. The largest element in the context was the importance of regulation. Regulation was undertaken both by state authorities and by private bodies. The private bodies included not only insurers, but sometimes associations of owners, such as boiler owners.[94] Owners did not want the accidents and so self-regulation became an important part of business safety, e.g. in relation to steam boilers in a number of countries. But technological change also altered the importance of the area of tort law. Steam power for trains and boilers was gradually phased out as new

[91] *Ibid.*, pp. 138–140. [92] *Ibid.*, pp. 29–39.
[93] *Ibid.*, pp. 31–33. [94] *Ibid.*, pp. 13–15, 23–25.

power technologies came in to existence. Asbestos had a peak and then reduced in importance. The development of regulation and technology had relatively little to do with tort law, but affected its importance. Even more so, the existence of workmen's compensation systems reduced the number of accidents that were compensated through tort.

The operation of the law has been changed in a number of ways. The removal of many defences such as common employment (e.g. for workers injured by exploding boilers) made it possible for actions to be brought. Rules about the investigation of events, such as boiler explosions in England and France, provided indirect ways in which the victim was able to obtain the necessary information to form the basis of a claim against the owner of a boiler or factory. The technical sophistication of the trains and boilers made it difficult for a lay person to know what was the cause of an event that resulted in harm. If it was necessary to prove fault or causation, then expert views would be necessary. But expert evidence would be difficult unless the expert came on the scene of the accident soon after and was able to formulate a hypothesis about the links between the train or boiler and the harm to the victim. It is even clearer in the cases of asbestos that developments in the understanding of medicine and public health were needed to provide any plausible cause of action.[95] The existence of workmen's compensation made a big change to the extent to which tort was needed to provide compensation. In all of the areas studied, the law of tort can be seen to have a background, subsidiary role when we look through the lens of the technological developments themselves and the responses to them.

Doctrinal Legal Writing might be thought to be timeless. But it is important to remember that doctrinal writing is a social product. One of the important aspects of doctrinal writing is that it became much more focused on individual legal systems during the later nineteenth century, reflecting the way in which English lawyers had approached the common law since the thirteenth century. Countries like Germany and Italy came into being. National codes of private law were developed and enacted, so that academic attention was focused on articulating the principles underlying those documents. The professionalisation of legal practice and the growth of university courses created a market for works that focused on the law of a particular system in which these people would practise. While these features created an impetus to academic work and to writing

[95] *Ibid.*, pp. 20–21.

on the legal system, they also channelled energies towards distinctive approaches.

The formulation of the rules on which commentaries were written changed with the codes. No longer were the principles of the Digest or of natural law the focus of comment, it was the national code.[96] If comparison was made, it would be with the codes of other systems, rather than with what had been common sources in Roman law. Indeed, in many countries, the Roman law became less studied as part of the formation of lawyers and thus constituted a smaller part of the common heritage. In this aspect, it is the legislator who plays the leading role in enacting codes that formulate fault liability, but also in enacting provisions that restrict its scope by providing for stricter liability.[97]

In terms of interpretation, we see the growing importance of national courts as authoritative expositors of the meaning of codes, not only in the common law but also in Civilian systems, though the pace of change in the latter varied. Many of the books note the way courts made key decisions that changed the way in which the code or legal principles on fault were interpreted. This changed the relative importance of academic writers in some countries. Jansen comments that, particularly in France and Germany, doctrine became detached from legal practice and less influential in its development during the twentieth century.[98] In England and Scotland, there is a rise of the academic profession and thus a change in the authors of key works, some of which were designed for a mixed academic and professional audience, e.g. Clerk and Lindsell's treatise on the law of tort.[99] But in that community, there was nonetheless a significant deference to the judge.

As Jansen points out in relation to procedure, doctrinal changes are often influenced by changes in the institutional framework and procedure. He points to issues about the delineation of law and fact, and thus the extent to which concepts such as 'fault' or 'causation' became the subject of analysis.[100] The reporting of decisions is also important. Changes in the process of reporting generate new inputs. The French systems of reporting for most of the period involved the creation of the 'note d'arrêt' in the middle of the nineteenth century as a major vehicle of academic commentary. Often with some additional information from the Cour de cassation, scholarly writers developed theory on the back of particular

96 Jansen, *Doctrine*, pp. 5–6, 9–11, 41–42.

97 *Ibid.*, pp. 18–20, 40.

98 *Ibid.*, pp. 34, 35 and 41, but not Italy or the Netherlands: *ibid.*, pp. 36 and 37.

99 J.F. Clerk and W.H.B. Lindsell, *The Law of Torts* (London: Sweet and Maxwell, 1889).

100 Jansen, *Doctrine*, p. 40.

cases. As a result, cases became a major de facto focus of attention in doctrinal writing. The *conclusions* of the advocate general in France and the Netherlands provided an alternative genre of focused doctrinal writing in which individuals could develop a doctrinal position over a number of decisions. But the limited publicity given to such sources limited their impact until the advent of the internet. The longer judgments in England, Scotland and Germany provided more scope for the judges themselves to be shapers of doctrinal positions.

The social context of doctrinal writing focuses on the importance of law. Access to law does improve over the twentieth century, especially where this is supported by legal aid or funded by insurance. Litigation on motor accidents and on medical liability has a certain distorting effect on the kinds of question that come to court and on which academic commentators write. Jansen points to the move from the focus on wrongdoers to victims.[101] Others would point to the increasing importance of values such as social solidarity in areas such as workmen's compensation as opposed to leaving losses where they are found, unless someone has been morally at fault. The seriousness of the harms suffered and their increasing prevalence did much to stimulate debate about issues such as no-fault compensation schemes from the 1920s. The importance of the United States as a beacon of 'progress', especially after the Second World War, provided an alternative reference point to the debates on liability that had originated from Roman law, canon law and natural law. The American doctrine had a much more functional and instrumental approach.[102] It developed new categories around the solutions to problems. Thus were born topics such as 'liability for products' 'medical liability' 'traffic liability'. Each area had its own policy dynamic and doctrinal solutions. It is clear that these American influences, reinforced by personal visits to the United States, led to significant changes in the conceptual structure and the instruments of analysis (such as law and economics) that came to dominate doctrinal analysis.[103]

The Impact of Ideas examines the environment of social and political ideas in which tort law was operating in the period 1850–2000. Whilst *internal* doctrinal developments were a vital motor of legal change and even if judges and jurists in many jurisdictions seemed to speak only the

[101] *Ibid.*, pp. 21–22.

[102] P.S. Atiyah and R.S. Summers, *Form and Substance in Anglo-American Law* (Oxford University Press, 1987).

[103] Jansen, *Doctrine*, pp. 23–27, 36.

language of doctrine, they were often strongly influenced by influences *external* to the law. Through a number of national case studies, the volume charts these influences. As Lobban and Moses remark:

> The prevailing ideological mood of the mid-nineteenth century, which was so closely associated with leaving social interaction to be regulated primarily by private law – individualism and *laissez-faire* – came under increasing attack in the later nineteenth century from a variety of forces, including the growth of new collectivist ideas and pressure from organised working-class movements. In this context, politicians on both the left and the right turned to greater state intervention. The state now began to pass legislation to promote social welfare, creating special regimes of regulations and rules which would operate outside the sphere of traditional tort law. The growth of the state also saw the growth of experts, within and without government, who could identify or define new social problems, and suggest solutions. These new forms of regulation operated alongside, and, at times, in conjunction with, tort law.[104]

Their volume examines the way in which lawyers perceived private law, of which tort law is part, as distinct from the broad range of social legislation that arose from collectivist ideas and values such as social solidarity. During the nineteenth century, codification in many countries encouraged a distinct lawyerly methodology, and the same was seen in a different way in the common law. These lawyerly techniques did not look directly at social values and consequences, but sought coherence in doctrinal legal principle. Whilst this lawyerly methodology did not disappear, the twentieth century saw more explicit references to the underlying social values and purposes of the law in doctrinal writing and in some of the documents associated with judicial deliberations (even if not in the judgments themselves). Certainly legislation in a number of areas had direct and indirect impacts on tort law. Most notably, workmen's compensation laws provided an alternative source of compensation and fostered values such as social solidarity, which were picked up in judicial decisions in some countries, such as France. At the same time, *laissez-faire* ideas remained relevant to many branches of law, especially in supporting nascent industries.

Social ideas such as welfarism and social solidarity had different impacts on private law in different countries. In part, the shape of social theory in France, Germany and Britain was different, reflecting the distinct political and social culture of those countries as much as it influenced the

[104] M. Lobban and J. Moses (eds.), *The Impact of Ideas* (Cambridge University Press, 2012) (hereafter '*Ideas*'), 4.

development of the law. Indeed, there have been shifts in ideas in different countries at different times, moving from individualism to welfarism to consumerism and ideas of individual rights. So the law has, to some extent, reflected these different national cultures at their time. The complexity of the relationship between legal development and social ideas is shown by the role of non-legal experts in legal change. As objective scientific knowledge changes, then this also gives rise to demands for the law to adapt and change. For example, medical experts and those inspecting factories were important in recognising the causes of harms and promoting regulatory legislation. But this did not eliminate the need for tort law.

The social changes and the demands for legal action encouraged changes in legal methodology and in the books written by scholars about the law. Writing became less formalist and focused on the arguments in favour of substantive legal change, but more traditional doctrinal legal works continued to be produced. There were equally changes in the formulation of legal rules and principles. These movements were not necessarily confined to one country, so the interaction between the ideas in different legal systems reflects a similar interaction in philosophical and political ideas.

The Impact of Legal Institutions and Professions on legal development is also significant. The volume edited by Paul Mitchell,[105] examines in particular the role of legislators, judges and academics in the development of tort law. Although legislators may have very wide discretion, constitutionally, they operate in practice within a significant number of constraints. Changes in tort law often require significant work, which is a low political priority. Decisions are often made in response to crisis or the surfacing of a sensitive issue, and early action is needed. The processes of legislative change often involve drawing on the work of committees, which have had the time to deliberate and consult on issues before they produce proposals. Legislative reform will also be the result of comparison with other cognate countries. Judicial law-making is often contested and this may encourage self-censorship, even when there are problems that need resolving. This also creates a problem in identifying the influence of particular judges on legal development within continental systems that adopt the style of single, often terse judgments for multi-member courts. But there is some evidence to show that individual judges have an influence on legal development, even in these countries. In many cases, the

[105] P. Mitchell (ed.), *The Impact of Legal Institutions and Professions* (Cambridge University Press, 2012) (hereafter '*Professions*').

individuals in question have been academics and so there is external evidence of their personal opinions. Academics may contribute to doctrinal writing through their textbooks and articles. But it is in their legislative committee work and in their roles within the judiciary that less publicised routes of significant influence can be identified in a range of different legal systems.

Looking at these different professional inputs into legal development, it is possible to see connections between legal systems that go beyond the divisions between cognate legal families. Echoing the view of Lobban and Moses, Mitchell notes the way in which the division between Civil and common law systems is not the most useful tool of analysis in understanding the interaction between legal systems in Western Europe.[106]

VII A note on methodology

In examining the development of fault liability we need to take into account four distinct elements:

- The law in the books, i.e. the legal rules and principles that are capable of being formulated in words, whether they are found in legislative enactments, authoritative decisions of courts, or doctrinal writings. We need to recognise always that at any given time there may exist competing formulations.
- Legal outcomes, i.e. the results reached in actual cases determined by judges or other state officials. Parties will often negotiate in the light of expected legal outcomes, and so they have a significance for the operation of the legal system as a whole.
- Legal institutions, i.e. the framework within which the law operates, including the following: the formal canons of reasoning used by judges and officials to translate linguistic formulations into actual decisions on particular sets of facts; 'legal style', which we might define in terms of the judges' and officials' perceptions of their own roles within the system; legal practices, ways of doing things (especially lawyers' craft skills) which are often inherited and are based on just how it has happened to be convenient to do things; and the legal process. Related to these are what might be described as 'legal culture', a set of beliefs and attitudes (implicit and explicit) which give meaning to and condition

[106] *Ibid.*, p. 13.

activity.[107] Many of these are inherited from tradition and are consciously transmitted, e.g. by legal education, but they can be forcibly changed, as occurred in continental Europe with the advent of codification or in England with the enactment of the Human Rights Act in 1988.

- The legal and extra-legal environment, including the societal and economic context within which the rules operate and the existence of different mechanisms for dealing with similar fact situations, both within the law and outside it.

Each of these can be analysed in its own terms. We may examine the development of legal doctrine with a view either to comparing the different experiences of different systems or to studying the shaping of the rules independently of the system(s) in which they are located.[108] Alternatively we may look at the ways in which particular types of cases are decided without concerning ourselves too much with the precise doctrinal frameworks which are used.[109] Some comparatists, most notably Pierre Legrand, have argued that the legal culture and institutional frameworks are so different from system to system that the comparison of legal doctrine is futile; we are better advised to compare their cultures.[110] Finally we might give up entirely on formal legal structures and look instead at the way in which individuals or organisations adjusted their behaviour so as to avoid disputes or to resolve them.[111]

In the present work we adopt a different approach, aiming to integrate all four elements. This necessitates a structure for analysis.[112]

At its most basic level, the model of law which we adopt can be expressed diagrammatically (Figure 1):

107 The term is used in a variety of different ways: see J. Bell, *French Legal Cultures* (London: Butterworths, 2001), ch. 1.

108 For the former, see for example *Doctrine* in the present series. For the latter, J. Gordley, 'Comparative Law and Legal History' in M. Reimann and R. Zimmermann (eds.), *Oxford Handbook of Comparative Law* (Oxford University Press, 2006), 753–773.

109 See the volumes on *Products*, *Traffic*, *Neighbours*, *Medical*, and *Technology* in the present series.

110 P. Legrand, 'European Legal Systems are not Converging' (1996) 45 *International and Comparative Law Quarterly* 52; W. Ewald, 'The Jurisprudential Approach to Comparative Law: A Field Guide to "Rats"' (1998) 46 *American Journal of Comparative Law* 701.

111 The classic example of this is J.W. Hurst, *Law and Economic Growth: the Legal History of the Lumber Industry in Wisconsin* (Cambridge, Mass.: Belknap Press, 1964).

112 A version of what follows has appeared in D. Ibbetson, 'Comparative Legal History: A Methodology' in A. Musson and C. Stebbings (eds.), *Making Legal History* (Cambridge University Press, 2011), 131.

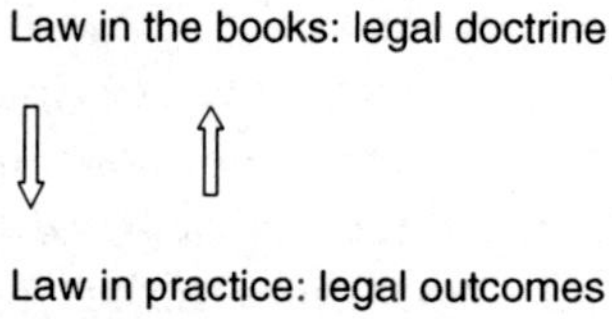

Figure 1. Legal doctrine and legal practice

At the top level is legal doctrine, the law in the books; at the bottom there are legal outcomes, typically the results of court decisions. While we cannot just assume that there is a relationship between legal doctrine and legal outcomes, there is no a priori reason to suppose that judges or other legal actors must always take notice of the law in the books when reaching decisions or performing other legal functions, nor any a priori reason to suppose that legal doctrine is responsive to changes in legal outcomes. As a working hypothesis, we may suppose, however, that in fact the two levels of law do influence each other to a greater or lesser extent, though the degree of influence is a matter for investigation. The law in the books will commonly reflect – and frequently reinforce – some widely held system of values underlying the decisions of judges and officials. Secondly, judges and other legal officials commonly justify their behaviour by reference to legal doctrine. This is not to say that any specific behaviour is *necessitated* by the legal doctrine, since this will commonly be sufficiently open-textured that officials have a considerable degree of discretion in its application, and it may be open to manipulation in order to justify doing something that is at first sight contrary to its meaning. It is perhaps better to put it negatively and say that legal doctrine should *not necessitate* behaviour that is *undesired*, recognising that exactly what is or is not desired may well itself be contentious. Thirdly, to the extent that judges and others can be relied upon to act in accordance with the 'law in the books', facilitative socio-legal institutions may be created. It would be impossible to have reliable mechanisms for the passing of property on death, for example, were it not for the existence of a law of succession which was by and large applied, or to have modern limited liability companies without a highly tuned set of legal mechanisms lying behind them. Finally, especially when formulated at a high level of abstraction, legal doctrine will commonly carry moral weight, providing an acceptable ethical basis for actual and hypothetical decisions. It simultaneously *describes* the basis of decisions and *justifies* them.

It is, therefore, a plausible hypothesis that there is a feedback loop between the law in the books and the legal outcomes in any system. Legal decisions are made by reference to the law in the books, always recognising that competing formulations of the latter might carry different weights. In their turn the legal outcomes reflect back into the law in the books: sometimes by giving more precise definition to it; sometimes by favouring one formulation of a rule over others; and sometimes by replacing one version of a rule by another. Legal institutions create the parameters within which this feedback loop operates. It determines, for example, the weight to be given to academic opinion as against judicial decisions, the degree of freedom available to reformulate existing rules and principles or to create new ones, the extent to which judges are required to give reasons for their decisions, which questions (if any) can be defined as questions of 'fact' that can be determined by a jury or trial judge and not be susceptible to further consideration by appellate tribunals, and how far foreign material can be brought into account.

If this feedback loop were a closed system, we would expect legal development to follow an evolutionary model, mimicking the development of biological systems. At any point there are a number of possible ways forward; there is a mechanism to select among them; and there is a mechanism whereby some choices become stabilised within the system while others do not.[113] However, we do not believe that the relationship between the two levels can be treated so mechanistically. There is a substantial degree of inertia within a legal system. Judges and other officials will be inclined to justify their decisions by reference to the existing dominant formulation of any rule rather than openly changing the rule; even where there is some dissatisfaction with a rule as formulated, there might not be sufficient strength of feeling that a tipping point is reached. For the purposes of comparative legal history, the methodology adopted must be one which allows us to understand non-change as well as change. Nor do we believe that law simply evolves as a closed system. In particular, deliberate legal change can be, and frequently is, introduced by legislation. The pressure for such change can have different aims; it might, for example, be seen as a way to reach different results in practice, or to give voice to a different perception as to the moral basis of liability. Equally, it may come from different sources, both individuals and pressure groups. Whatever the aim and whatever the source, however, the pressure must

[113] Luhmann, *Sociological Theory of Law*, p. 109.

be sufficiently strong that a tipping point is reached and the inertia of the earlier rule is overcome.

Behind all this we may hypothesise that there is a substantial element of path dependence. Legal decisions in any system are made within the framework of the existing law, a framework which might have deep historical roots. Legislative change can be shaped by existing models in related fields. The legal institutions embody ideas, modes of thinking and practices which have become solidly embedded, perhaps over many centuries. For this reason we examine the historical background to the different systems that we discuss before going on to analyse the post-1850 developments of the law.

The final element that has to be brought into account is the legal and extra-legal environment. Any area of law exists in relation to other areas of law, so that the same practical problem may be dealt with in different ways in different places at different times. The fact that such alternatives are available has its effect on the development of each area of law. If, say, medical incompetence is dealt with in one legal system primarily by the law of tort and in another primarily by criminal law or disciplinary regulations, we would expect the law of tort to develop differently in the two systems. At the very least, if there is pressure to change the tortious rules it is likely that the tipping point will be reached earlier in the former system than in the latter. Similarly, if there are alternative mechanisms for redress outside the law the pressure to change the legal rules will be that much the less, and hence the tipping point might be reached that much later; the availability of insurance, both generally and for specific things (e.g. for steam boilers in the nineteenth century), can be expected to have that effect on the subject matter of the present book. In the same way, changes in the legal environment may alter the way in which the feedback loop between the law in the books and the legal outcomes operates; if the cost of litigation were to rise, for example, we would expect the rate of legal change to drop, while if the cost of litigation were to fall we would expect it to increase.

Above all, the extra-legal environment affects the development of the law: social and economic changes create pressure to alter the law in the books, and influence the ways in which judges and other officials apply the law. So too do changes in social morality, for example a shift from a dominant mode of thought encouraging entrepreneurship to one in which those injured by others should be entitled to some form of compensation. The extent to which these external factors, as opposed to internal

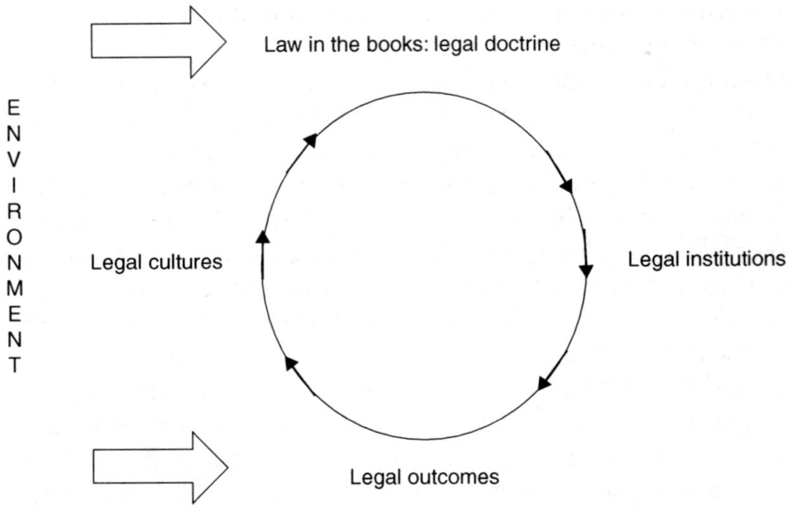

Figure 2. Legal development

ones, influence changes in the law is perhaps the most important question for comparative legal history.

We may indicate the relationship between the different elements by means of a diagram (Figure 2).

2

The place of fault in 1850

Although by the middle of the nineteenth century Western European legal systems generally accepted a principle of liability for fault, each system had reached this position along its own route and each system retained its individual substantive, procedural and cultural characteristics. Before the post-1850 developments can be analysed in comparative terms, it is necessary to map out the relevant characteristics of each system and, so far as possible, to see the trajectory of their development at that time. This can be only a sketch, but it is essential if we are to understand the extent to which the development of substantive rules is path dependent,[1] i.e. how far changes in legal rules are based on the materials present within the legal system at the time the changes occur. Procedural characteristics are no less important, for the way in which cases are determined can shape the substantive law, so much so that the shape can remain even after the procedural features generating it have themselves disappeared. Institutional features – what we might broadly think of as legal culture – carry great weight too; the way in which the law adapts to changing situations is inevitably influenced by the way in which it is conceptualised, and by where the power to adjust or reform it is traditionally located.

In this chapter, therefore, we describe three fundamental features. First is the law of tort itself, where continental European systems were based substantially on the Roman lex Aquilia, with some variants from place to place, while English law had its own very distinct history. Secondly, the balance between judge and jurist was very different, again with a dividing line between the English common law and the continental systems within the Roman tradition. Thirdly, once again differentiating England from the continent was legal process and procedure, with the deep-seated historical division between the English system, based on original writs and trial by jury, and the Romano-canonical procedure, which formed the base of continental European legal systems.

[1] See below, pp. 179–182.

I The law of tort

A *The lex Aquilia and Roman law*

The lex Aquilia was a statute, enacted probably in the third century BC.[2] Only the first and third chapters survived into classical Roman law: the first gave a remedy for the killing of a slave or grazing animal, the third for other property damage. Understood literally, the lex Aquilia only applied to the direct infliction of injury, but the praetors provided analogous remedies where injury was caused indirectly, and the praetorian actions were further interpreted to give a remedy at least in some cases where there had been economic loss without actual damage, as where an animal or slave was allowed to escape from the control of its owner. Both chapters one and three of the lex had required that the killing or injury be done *iniuria*, wrongfully, but in the middle of the second century AD it was explained by one jurist, Gaius, that this was interpreted as meaning that it had to have been done either deliberately or blameworthily, *dolo* or *culpa*, an opinion repeated half a century later by Ulpian.[3] Blameworthiness was interpreted on a case-by-case basis,[4] but one particular example of blame or fault was to prove highly influential many centuries later, the failure to foresee and guard against what a careful person would foresee and guard against.[5] On the other hand, counterpoised against this external standard, it was said that a young child or a madman could not be liable under the lex, since no blame could be attached to those who were not in control of their minds.[6]

The Roman texts dealing with the lex Aquilia therefore left a number of issues unresolved:

1. What limits, if any, were there on the types of loss that would generate a claim under the lex Aquilia or its praetorian extensions?

[2] R. Zimmermann, *The Law of Obligations: Roman Foundations of the Civilian Tradition* (Cape Town: Juta, 1990), pp. 953–1017, with further references to the abundant literature.

[3] G.3.211; D.9.2.5.1. For the relationship between *culpa* and *iniuria* see in particular B. Beinart, 'The Relationship of *Iniuria* and *Culpa* in the Lex Aquilia' in A. Vogliano (ed.), *Studi in Onore di Vincenzo Arangio-Ruiz* (Naples: Jovene, 1953), vol. 1, 279; M. F. Cursi, *Iniuria cum Damno* (Milan: Giuffrè, 2002).

[4] S. Schipani, *Responsabilità 'ex Lege Aquilia': Criteria di Imputazione e Problema della 'Culpa'* (Turin: Giapichelli, 1969); G. Mac Cormack, 'Aquilian Culpa' in A. Watson (ed.), *Daube Noster* (Edinburgh: Scottish Academic Press, 1974), 201.

[5] D.9.2.31: 'Mucius dixit ... culpam autem esse quod cum a diligente provideri poterit, non esset provisum.' Cf Inst. 4.3.5.

[6] D.9.2.5.2.

2. Was *culpa* to be treated purely casuistically, or was some more precise definition possible?
3. To what extent were personal characteristics of the actor relevant to the assessment of *culpa*?
4. Was there any requirement of unlawfulness separate from that of blameworthiness?

Although the lex Aquilia was the principal source of later doctrine, the role of the law of contract was not insignificant. It was in this context that the Romans explored the varying standards of care that might be demanded of an actor.[7] In some circumstances, typically where he or she did not profit under the contract, a person might be liable only for deliberate wrongdoing, *dolus*, though the second-century jurist Celsus treated gross negligence, *culpa lata*, as being on a par with this. More commonly, a contractual party was liable for *culpa levis*, failing to take the care that would have been taken by a reasonable person, a *bonus paterfamilias*,[8] though in some circumstances, which were not clearly defined, the standard of care was related to the care that the actor took in the management of his or her own affairs, *diligentia quam in suis rebus*.[9] Normally there was no liability for mere accident, *casus*, though there may have been a form of strict liability, known as *custodia*, in some circumstances in which one person was looking after the goods of another.[10]

Alongside the lex Aquilia, the Romans identified a number of so-called quasi-delicts, which were destined to play a part in the later development of fault liability.[11] An innkeeper, shipmaster or ostler was strictly liable for the loss of a guest's goods;[12] the occupier of a house was liable if a passer-by, be it slave or free person, was killed or injured by something thrown or poured from his property, and subject to a fixed penalty if he allowed something to be placed or hung from his property in such a way that it was dangerous to passers-by;[13] and a judge was liable if he 'made a cause

[7] V. Arangio-Ruiz, *La Responsabilità Contrattuale in Diritto Romano* (Naples: Jovene, 1933); Zimmermann, *Obligations*, pp. 192–199.

[8] D.16.3.32.

[9] H. Hausmaninger, 'Diligentia Quam in Suis' in D. Medicus and H. H. Seiler (eds.), *Festschrift für Max Kaser zum 70. Geburtstag* (Munich: Beck, 1976), 265.

[10] Zimmermann, *Obligations*, pp. 193–195. Arguably, this was only the normal *culpa* standard with a reverse burden of proof: R. Robaye, *L'Obligation de Garde* (Brussels: Faculté Universitaire de Bruxelles, 1987).

[11] Inst 4.5. [12] Inst 4.5.3.

[13] Inst 4.5.1.

his own', with one text emphasising that this liability arose even if it was only the result of his own *imprudentia*.[14]

B From the glossators to natural law[15]

The medieval Civil lawyers who worked in the Roman tradition were substantially constrained by the Roman texts, though to a large extent they were able to manipulate these to bring about a measure of generalisation. The canon lawyers were not so constrained, and hence a greater degree of generalisation is visible there, though so far as compensation for the causation of loss is concerned, they followed closely the Civil law.[16] Finally, the lawyers of the sixteenth and early seventeenth centuries brought together the Civil-law and canon-law approaches, freeing themselves from the limitations of the Roman law. The development beyond Roman law can be seen at three principal points: the generalisation of an idea of recoverable loss; the concretisation of the idea of *culpa*; and a move towards the integration of the quasi-delicts into a general pattern of civil liability for wrongs.

As a result of the availability of the praetorian actions, Roman law already had the potential to generalise liability in terms of the blameworthy causation of any loss, though the extent to which it actually did so is problematic.[17] It was, therefore, not a large step for the medieval

[14] Inst 4.5.pr.; D.50.13.6. Exactly what the scope of this quasi-delict was remains controversial.

[15] G. Rotondi, 'Dalla Lex Aquilia all'Art 1151 Cod. Civ, Ricerche Storico-Dogmatiché' (1916) 14 *Rivistà del Diritto Commerciale* 942, 15 *Rivistà del Diritto Commerciale* 236 (also in G. Rotondi, *Scritti Giuridici* (Milan: Ulrico Hoepli, 1922), vol. 2, 465); H. Lange, *Schadenersatz und Privatstrafe* (Munich: Böhlau, 1955); Zimmermann, *Obligations*, pp. 1017–49; G. P., 'Responsabilità Extracontrattuale: Diritto Intermedio' in *Enciclopedia del Diritto* (Varese: Giuffrè, 1988), 1099; P. Cerami, 'La Responsabilità Extracontrattuale dalla Compilazione di Guistiniano ad Ugo Grozio' in L. Vacca (ed.), *La Responsibilità Civile da Atto Illecito nella Prospettiva Storico-comparatistica* (Turin: Giappichelli, 1995), 103; J. Hallebeek, 'Negligence in Medieval Roman Law' in E. Schrage (ed.), *Negligence* (Berlin: Duncker & Humblot, 2001), 74; B. Winiger, *La Responsabilité Aquilienne en Droit Commun* (Geneva: Helbing and Lichtenhahn, 2002); O. Descamps, *Les Origines de la Responsabilité pour Faute Personnelle dans le Code Civil de 1804* (Paris: Librairie Générale de Droit et de Jurisprudence, 2005), 35–43, 51–65, 68–93.

[16] S. Kuttner, *Kanonistische Schuldlehre von Gratian bis auf die Dekretalen Gregors IX* (Vatican City: Biblioteca Apostolica Vaticana, 1935), p. 246 note 1; H. Dondorp, 'Crime and Punishment: Negligentia for the Canonists and Moral Theologians' in Schrage (ed.), *Negligence*, pp. 101, 119–123. The central text of the developed canon law, *Decretum Gratiani*, X.5.36.9, is unequivocally general in its formulation: 'If loss is caused by your fault (*culpa*), it is right that you make amends for it.'

[17] Above, p. 53.

glossators to identify such a principle. It clearly seems to have been taken by the middle of the thirteenth century, when Accursius defined *damnum* as any reduction in wealth, *deminutio patrimonii*, and observed that the praetorian *actio in factum* was available where there was any wrongful causation of loss falling outside the ambit of the lex Aquilia.[18] One consequence of this was that an action now lay for bringing about the death of a free person, to the extent that this caused actual loss in the form of medical expenses or loss of expected earnings.[19] A corollary was that no liability would arise under this head in the absence of a genuine pecuniary loss: a person who was scarred or otherwise disfigured would have no claim to compensation as a result of this, except perhaps if the victim was a woman whose marriage prospects were thereby diminished.[20] And although the gloss itself conservatively retained the distinction between the direct action on the lex Aquilia and the praetorian actions,[21] the more practically oriented *Speculum Judiciale* of Gulielmus Durandus ran them together under its more general heading *de damno dato*, as well as bringing the main forms of quasi-delict under the same rubric.[22]

This process of generalisation did not prevent further exploration of the notion of loss. Hugo Grotius, probably following the French humanist Donellus, enumerated a set of protected interests: those arising from the nature of human beings – one's life, one's body, one's limbs, one's reputation, one's honour, and one's freedom – and those arising from their recognition in human society – from ownership, from contract, or by

[18] *gl iniuriae actio*, ad Inst. 4.3; *gl in factum actione*, ad Inst. 4.3.16; and for pre-Accursian texts see P. Rasi, 'L'Actio Legis Aquiliae e la Responsabilità Extracontrattuale nella Glossa' in G Rossi (ed.), *Atti del Convegno Internazionale di Studi Accursiani* (Milan: Giuffrè, 1968), vol. 2, 725, 740 note 43. But compare J. Hallebeek, 'Negligence in Medieval Roman Law' in Schrage (ed.), *Negligence*, pp. 74, 79–85, pointing towards a rather slower generalisation.

[19] *gl gloriae causa* ad D.9.2.7.4. For the development of this idea see R. Feenstra, 'Théories sur la Responsabilité Civile en Cas d'Homicide et en Cas de Lésion Corporelle avant Grotius' in R. Feenstra (ed.), *Fata Iuris Romani* (Leiden: Presse Universitaire de Leide, 1974), pp. 323–337; R. Feenstra, 'L'Actio Legis Aquiliae Utilis en Cas d'Homicide chez les Glossateurs' in J.E. Spruit (ed.), *Maior Viginti Quinque Annis* (Assen: Van Gorcum, 1978), 45–65.

[20] R. Feenstra, 'Réparation du Dommage et Prix de la Douleur chez les Auteurs du Droit Savant, du Droit Naturel et du Droit Romano-Hollandais' in B. Durand, J. Poirier and J.-P. Royer (eds.), *La Douleur et le Droit* (Paris: Presses Universitaires de France, 1997), 411, 411–412. The case of the unmarriageable woman is discussed by Jacques de Révigny: R. Feenstra, *Vergelding en Vergoeding*, 3rd edn by L. Winkel (Amsterdam: Kluwer, 2002), 36.

[21] Rasi, 'L'Actio Legis Aquiliae', pp. 741–743.

[22] *Speculum Judiciale, De Iniuriis et Damno Dato*, 2.11.

operation of law.[23] Grotius's most important follower, Samuel Pufendorf, was to go yet further:

> [The word *damnum*] implies all Hurt, Spoil, or Diminution of whatsoever is already actually our own; all Interception of what by a perfect and absolute Right we ought to receive, whether such Right be the original Gift of Nature, or whether it be allow'd us by human Institution and Law. And lastly, all Omission or Denial of any Duty, or Performance, which others by a perfect Obligation stand bound to pay us.[24]

The second point at which there was scope for development beyond the Roman texts was in the expression of the liability condition, *iniuria* and *culpa*.[25] This was the more difficult for medieval lawyers because of the variety of different contexts in which the issue arose – delictual, contractual, and quasi-delictual[26] – but two general trends are clearly visible by the seventeenth century. First was the eclipsing of *iniuria* by *culpa*, reflecting the move which had earlier been taken by Gaius and Ulpian. The beginnings of this are found already in the earliest glossators,[27] and it was substantially completed in the works of the sixteenth-century humanists such as Hugo Donellus and Spanish neo-scholastics such as Luis de Molina and Leonard Lessius.[28] In Grotius's *De Jure Belli ac Pacis*, wrongdoing, *maleficium*, is defined as 'any *culpa* whatsoever …'[29] Secondly, there was a tendency to assimilate delictual *culpa* to contractual, thereby producing a dalliance with the different standards of care which had been recognised by the Romans in the contractual context,[30] and making it

23 H. Grotius, *De Jure Belli ac Pacis*, 2.1.21. R. Feenstra, 'Grotius' Doctrine of Liability for Negligence', in Schrage (ed.), *Negligence*, 129 at pp. 140–144.

24 *De Iure Nature et Gentium*, III.1.3. Jean Barbeyrac, in his note to this passage, goes further still: 'It ought also further to be observed, that a Damage or Hurt may be done to the Soul by neglecting to inform the Mind, or regulate the Passions of such as we are obliged to instruct or reform, and much more by leading them on purpose into any Error or Vice from which we ought to restrain them.'

25 Above, p. 52.

26 Hallebeek, 'Negligence in Medieval Roman Law', pp. 85–98.

27 Rasi, 'L'Actio Legis Aquiliae', pp. 748–749. Telling is the shift visible between Petrus de Bellapertica (late thirteenth century) and Bartolus (mid-fourteenth century): for the former *culpa* was a *deviatio* from that which was required by law, for the latter a *deviatio* from that which was good. W. Engelmann, *Die Schuldlehre der Postglossatoren* (Leipzig: Duncker & Humblot, 1895, reprinted Aalen: Scientia Verlag, 1965), 17–20.

28 Donellus, *Commentariorum de Jure Civili*, Book 15 chapter 27 s.2 (in *Opera Omnia* (Florence, 1842), vol. IV col. 235); Molina, *De Delictis*, Disputatio 697 no. 4 (in *Opera Omnia* (Antwerp, 1615), p. 54; Lessius, *De Iustitia et Iure* (Paris, 1618), 2.7.6 ; B. Winiger, *La Responsabilité Aquilienne*, pp. 77–83.

29 *De Jure Belli ac Pacis*, 2.17.1.

30 U. Agnati, *Il Commento di Bartolo di Sassoferrato alla Lex Quod Nerva (D. 16,3,34)* (Turin: Giapichelli, 2004).

easier to put weight on the Roman quasi-definition of *culpa* as the failure to foresee and guard against what a diligent person would foresee and guard against,[31] and approximating this to the care which would have been taken by a *bonus paterfamilias* which was appropriate to the generality of contractual situations.

C *Ius proprium* and *ius commune*: the case of France

Over much of continental Europe the principles of Aquilian liability had come to be applied generally in practice well before the nineteenth century, either in the Middle Ages or in the sixteenth and seventeenth centuries. France, however, was an important outlier, where a tension remained between the framework of liability traceable back to Roman law and a framework based in French customary law.[32] The medieval texts, perhaps influenced by the developed Civil law, show a clear tendency to lay down a general principle that all patrimonial loss is recoverable where the defendant has committed an actionable wrong to the plaintiff. Beaumanoir's *Coutumes de Beauvaisis* provides a clear example: 'A person hurting or injuring another must pay his losses, which means the cost of the physicians and the expenditures of the injured person and the lost work days according to his job ... '[33] Unlike in Roman law, however, where the independent requirement of unlawfulness had effectively been eclipsed by the time of Justinian,[34] medieval customary law in France was strongly shaped by an underpinning structure of separate wrongs. To take again the example of Beaumanoir, we are presented with a list: murder, treason, homicide, rape, arson, theft, apostasy, sodomy, counterfeiting, poisoning, suicide, beating another, injuring another, offensive words, moving boundary markers, and so on.[35] So far as the liability condition is concerned, from as early as the thirteenth century works influenced by the Civil law show a movement towards a definition of fault in terms of failing to act as a reasonable person. In the *Liver de Jostice et Plet*, for example, the general principle is stated that a person who behaves

[31] D.9.2.31; above, p. 52. See for example Donellus, *Commentariorum de Jure Civili*, Book 15 chapter 27 s.2 (in *Opera Omnia* (Florence, 1842), vol. IV, col. 235–236).

[32] For what follows, see in particular Descamps, *Faute Personelle*; D. Deroussin, *Histoire du Droit des Obligations* (Paris: Economica, 2007), 639ff.

[33] F.R.P. Akehurst, trans., *The Coutumes de Beauvaisis of Philippe de Beaumanoir* (Philadelphia: University of Pennsylvania Press, 1992), s.841. This might merely be a starting point: Descamps, *Faute Personnelle*, pp. 218–222.

[34] Above, p. 52.

[35] Akehurst, *Coutumes de Beauvaisis*, ss.823–851.

as a *prodhome* and does as a *prodhome* ought to do avoids liability for causing harm;[36] and in the *Coutume d'Anjou* of 1437, fault – '*couppe*' – is defined in terms of the failure to recognise what all or most people recognise.[37] Alongside this, however, especially in the north of France, there continued to be found traces of an older form of liability uninfluenced by Roman law: in some places talion or the payment of fixed penalties for certain wrongs was not for a long time superseded by the calculation of compensation by reference to the victim's loss.[38] As well, for some writers liability remained purely objective, independent of the wrongdoer's state of mind or blameworthiness. In his fourteenth-century *Somme Rural*, Jehan Boutillier formulated a very general principle with no reference at all to fault: 'According to the law, none can be damaged or injured in any way whatsoever without being recompensed.'[39] Where such a principle of objective liability was found in customary laws, it was open to the wrongdoer to defend himself by showing that he had been acting in self-defence or under a material misapprehension of the circumstances or that the cause of the injury was the victim's own fault.[40]

The period between the sixteenth and the eighteenth centuries has been characterised in terms of a tension between general principles and casuistic analysis.[41] The process of generalisation was refracted sometimes through a lens of Roman law, sometimes through a lens of customary law, and sometimes through an amalgam of the two.[42] Perhaps as a consequence of the mingling together of the two different streams there were some advances in the law, such as the extension of compensation loss from purely patrimonial loss to losses that could not be quantified in precise financial terms, such as the loss of a marriage or the death of a loved one.[43]

36 P. Rapetti (ed.), *Liver de Jostice e Plet* (Paris: Documents inédits, 1859), 19.48.4.

37 C.J. Beautemps-Beaupré (ed.), *Coutumes et Institutions de l'Anjou et du Maine Antérieures au XVIe Siècle* (Paris: Durand and Pedone, 1877), s.410.

38 J.-M. Carbasse and F. Auzary-Schmalz, 'La Douleur et sa Réparation dans les Régistres du Parlement Médiéval (XIIIe-XIVe Siècles)', in Durand et al., *La Douleur et le Droit*, 423, 430; Descamps, *Faute Personnelle*, pp. 204–205.

39 L. Charondas le Caron (ed.), *Le Grand Coustumier et Practique du Droict Civil et Canon Observé en France Composé par M Jehan Boutillier* (Paris 1621), 1.37. See too P. Viollet, (ed.), *Les Établissements de Saint Louis* (Paris: Renouard, 1881), vol. 2, 123 (= livre 1, s.74).

40 Descamps, *Faute Personnelle*, pp. 252–254.

41 *Ibid.*, p. 265.

42 J. Gaudemet, 'Les Tendances à l'Unification du Droit en France dans les Derniers Siècles de l'Ancien Régime' in B. Paradisi (ed.), *La Formazione Storica del Diritto Moderna in Europa* (Florence: Olschki, 1977), vol. 1, 157.

43 Descamps, *Faute Personnelle*, pp. 302–303.

None the less, some tensions remained. Most significant was that between the Roman focus on fault and strict, objective liability associated with customary law. In his *Droit Commun de la France*, for example, François Bourjon describes the liability of the owner of a building for injury caused by a falling tile or chimney or the like without any reference to fault; he continues by saying that the liability is negatived if the fall was the consequence of some *force majeure*, such as an unusually violent wind, where the owner was not to blame.[44] The keepers of animals are described as being guarantors of any damage caused by their animals, so the owner of a dog is liable if it bites someone; but if the dog is goaded by another, it is that person who is liable rather than the owner since it was his fault and not the owner's.[45] Yet both of these situations are characterised as based on the owner's or keeper's lack of foresight. The owner of a house from which a fire has spread is liable for any damage that flows from it, unless the fire is caused by lightning since this constitutes a *force majeure* which cannot be imputed to him; similarly the owner of a carriage is guarantor of the acts of his coachmen, though this is loosely explained on the basis that he has chosen them.[46] In neither of these is fault directly relevant, yet both are distinguished from the case of general average, where part of a ship's cargo has been jettisoned in a storm and the loss has to be shared among all the cargo owners; here the action for contribution derives from a pure accident without any fault or negligence. Bourjon's treatment of liability brings out well the tension between general principle and specific provisions. Exactly the same is visible in Jean Domat's *Loix Civiles dans leur Ordre Natural*, where individual texts from Roman law are loosely structured around more abstract bases of liability.

While the casuistic approach framed around individual wrongs was to be swept away in the *Code Civil*, the tension between fault liability and strict liability was to remain and to play a very important part in the development of French law in the nineteenth and twentieth centuries.

II Codification in the nineteenth century[47]

Although the roots of the move towards codification are rather earlier, it was in the nineteenth century that the movement reached its peak. The

[44] F. Bourjon, *Droit Commun de la France* (Paris: Grangé, 1747), 6.3.6.

[45] *Ibid.*, 6.3.7 [46] *Ibid.*, 6.3.7.2, 6.3.8.

[47] For what follows we draw upon D. Ibbetson, 'Harmonisation of the Law of Tort and Delict: A Comparative and Historical Perspective' in R Zimmermann (ed.), *Grundstrukturen des Europäischen Deliktsrechts* (Baden-Baden: Nomos, 2003), 83.

first wave was heavily influenced by the natural law movement traceable back to Grotius and Pufendorf. By far the most significant of these codes was the French *Code Civil* of 1804,[48] which was to influence those of the Netherlands, Italy and Spain. The second wave, leading to the German BGB in 1896, was more heavily influenced by Roman law and pandectist legal science.

A France

Articles 1382–1386 of the French *Code Civil* were largely derived from Jean Domat's *Loix Civiles dans leur Ordre Naturel*, substantially reordered.[49] At the core of liability was the opening principle in the general rule of article 1382 (elaborated in article 1383), that all human acts giving rise to damage to another, oblige the person through whose fault it occurred to make compensation.[50] Article 1384 dealt with damage caused by things and by the acts of a range of other people, generalising a text of Domat dealing with the liability of occupiers for things thrown from buildings and adding to it a section taken from the *Code Rural* of 1791 imposing liability for others' delicts on a wide range of individuals. Article 1385 imposed liability for the acts of animals, and by article 1386 the owner of a building was made liable for injuries caused by it where this was the result of the failure of maintenance or by a flaw in its construction.

Given the reordering of the sources, we should not be surprised that there does not seem to be a single consistent theoretical position underlying articles 1382–1386.[51] Indeed, if we are to judge by the *travaux préparatoires*, there were two. For Treilhard and Tarrible, addressing the *Corps législatif*, all was explicable in terms of fault.[52] Straightforwardly,

[48] The first major code was the Prussian *Allgemeines Landrecht* of 1794, but since this was to be superseded by the BGB after the unification of Germany it can be left on one side for the purposes of the present work.

[49] A.-J. Arnaud, *Les Origines Doctrinales du Code Civil Français* (Paris: Librairie Générale de Droit et de Jurisprudence, 1969); B. Auzary-Schmaltz, 'Liability in Tort in France before the Code Civil: The Origins of art. 1382 ff. Code Civil' in Schrage (ed.), *Negligence*, 309, esp. at pp. 335–339.

[50] The relevant provisions of the Code (and the other codes dealt with in this section) are to be found in the Appendix to this book.

[51] A. Watson, *Failures of the Legal Imagination* (Philadelphia: University of Pennsylvania Press, 1988), 1–33.

[52] J.-G. Locré, *La Législation Civile, Commerciale et Criminelle de la France* (Paris: Treuttel and Würtz, 1828), vol. 13, pp. 31–32, 57–59 (also in P. Fenet, *Recueil Complet des Travaux Préparatoires du Code Civil* (Paris: Videcoq, 1836), vol. 13, 452–491, esp. pp. 475–477 and 488).

articles 1382 and 1383 were explained on the basis that liability should be based on *dolus* or *culpa*; in the absence of either of these any injury was accidental and the loss flowing from it had to be borne by the victim. Article 1384 was likewise explained in these terms: a father, employer or the like had a responsibility to oversee his children or employees, and if they acted outside the acceptable limits of behaviour, then he was at fault for his lack of control. So too articles 1385 and 1386, though it was not at all clear that liability depended specifically on the fault of the owner of the building.[53] In complete contrast to Treilhard and Tarrible, in his *rapport* to the *Tribunat*, Bertrand de Greuille took a different approach, beginning with the fact that injury had been caused to the victim and then asking to whom this injury could be imputed.[54] Considering article 1382, therefore, he explained that once it had been established that some person's act had caused the loss, it was just to make him liable for that loss if it had stemmed from his feebleness or imprudence. Superiors should be liable for the acts of their dependents since they took the benefit from the labour and had shown confidence in them by delegating the work to them. It would not be just that the victim of this misplaced confidence should bear the consequences of it; and to allow redress against the superior gave a greater guarantee that the victim would in fact receive compensation. The owner of an animal should be liable because of his failure properly to supervise it, and because of the general principle that nothing belonging to one person should injure another with impunity. The same with buildings: it followed from the 'incontestable truth' that one man's property should not injure another's that the owner of a building should be liable for loss caused by its ruin in so far as it stemmed from lack of maintenance or a fault of construction.

Bertrand de Greuille's theoretical stance was more closely in accordance with the way that the law had been oriented before the enactment of the Code – in particular it is noteworthy that the earlier draft of Cambacérès had made no mention of fault, 'celui qui cause un dommage est tenu à le réparer, quel que soit le fait qui y donne lieu'[55] – and with a precise reading

[53] Though note the proposed amendment to what became article 1386, replacing the words *par une suite de défaut d'entretien ou par le vice de sa construction* with *par sa faute*, not on the grounds that the text as it stood imposed liability on a person who was not at fault, but because it might be interpreted restrictively as covering only these two particular cases of fault: Locré, *Législation*, vol. 13, p. 19; Fenet, *Recueil Complet*, vol. 13, p. 455.

[54] Locré, *Législation*, vol. 13, pp. 40–44; Fenet, *Recueil Complet*, vol. 13, pp. 476–477.

[55] J.J.R. de Cambacérès, *Projet de Code Civil* (1794), art. 745. See too J. Carbonnier, *Droit Civil, iv: Les Obligations*, 22nd edn (Paris: Presses Universitaires de France, 2000), 369.

of the Code: in article 1382, for example, it is the act which causes loss to another that triggers potential liability, and the *faute* that identifies who is the appropriate person to bear that liability. On the other hand, the repeated references to fault and allied criteria reveal a cast of mind clearly moving in the direction of fault-based liability as formulated by Treilhard and Tarrible. Though the language of the Code was not remotely clear, there was little room for doubt about the direction in which it was looking and the commentators of the nineteenth century focused sharply on fault as the basis of all liability. At the same time, however, it contained within itself the potential for later lawyers to discover forms of strict liability.

B Austria

The Austrian Code of 1811 (the ABGB) had no such ambiguity. The opening articles of its section on delict laid down the fundamental principle that liability depended on fault (*Verschulden*), with the corollary that in the absence of such fault no liability would arise: there had to be an illicit act or omission, 'illicit' being defined in terms of deliberate wrongdoing or of conduct marred by ignorance, inattention, or lack of the necessary diligence.[56] As if to emphasise this, there was a formal presumption that the injury had been caused without fault unless the victim could prove the contrary.[57] Unlike in the *Code Civil*, liability for the acts of third parties was explicitly based on the fault of the employer in knowingly employing an unsuitable person, *culpa in eligendo*.[58] Similarly, again in contrast with the *Code Civil*, liability for animals was explicitly made dependent upon fault.[59] The only hints of strict liability were found in direct analogues of the Romans' quasi-delicts: the strict liability of innkeepers and carriers for the misdeeds of their servants;[60] the strict liability of occupiers for things poured or thrown from their houses.[61] The Austrian Code formed

[56] ABGB, Arts. 1294, 1295, 1306. Further explanations of what constitutes fault are found in articles 1297, 1299 and 1300. The theoretical background and its basis in natural law is explained in H. von Zeiller, *Abhandlung über die Principien des Allgemeinen Bürgerlichen Gesetzbuches* (Vienna, 1816–1820; reprinted Vienna: Manz, 1986), 172–174; and see H.P. Benöhr, 'Ausservertragliche Schadenersatzpflicht' (1976) 93 *Zeitschrift der Savigny-Stiftung für Rechtsgeschichte (Romanistische Abteilung)* 208, 224–226, 233–242.

[57] ABGB art. 1296. [58] ABGB arts. 1314, 1315.

[59] ABGB art. 1320. [60] ABGB art. 1317.

[61] ABGB art. 1318; and note especially art. 1319, dealing with the Austrian administrative mechanism paralleling the Roman liability for *res positae vel suspensae*, and art. 1341, dealing with the complaints procedure which had come to supersede the Romans' liability against the *iudex qui litem suam fecit*.

the basis for the codes of the pre-unification Italian states, but articles 1151–1155 of the post-unification *Codice Civile* of 1865 were a direct translation of articles 1382–1386 of the French *Code Civil.* In terms of wording, therefore, they retained its ambiguities; and within a few years of their enactment the Italian courts began explicitly to apply strict liability for the acts of animals.[62] Liability, it was said, stemmed from the principle of reason and justice that loss should not go uncompensated; if there was any suggestion that fault was in fact necessary, then there was an irrebuttable presumption that the owner was at fault.[63]

C *Spain*

Spanish law too was strongly influenced by the French *Code Civil*, but the existence of a strong principle of liability only for fault in the thirteenth-century *Siete Partidas* made it easier to neutralise the hints of strict liability found in France. Hence, the *Código Civil* of 1889 subtly reworked the general principle of article 1382 to bring it into line with the mainstream of liability for fault: the person who by act or omission causes damage to another by fault or negligence is obliged to repair the damage caused.[64] Despite the very close similarity of wording to the equivalent provision of the *Code Civil*, fault is here clearly a characteristic of the liability-generating act, and not, as it arguably was in France, the appropriate criterion to identify the proper defendant. The same shift of emphasis is visible in the provision providing for imposition of liability for the acts of third parties: where the French code laid down that parents, schools and artisans could avoid liability for the acts of their children, pupils or apprentices by showing that they could not have prevented the harm (article 1384), the Spanish equivalent provided for exoneration by showing that the care of a *bonus paterfamilias* had been taken to prevent the damage.[65] The shift towards fault is similarly visible in the provision relating to liability for animals: the draft code of 1851 provided for liability in terms rather similar to the French, though with the proviso that no liability would arise if the victim was personally at fault; thirty years later the

[62] *Giurisprudenza Italiana* 1879.1.2.386.

[63] See the discussion in G. Giorgi, *Teoria delle Obbligazioni del Diritto Moderno Italiano*, 2nd edn (Florence: Cammelli, 1924–27), vol. 5, 592–614, esp. at p. 609.

[64] Art. 1902. A similar approach is found in art. 1900 of the projected code of 1851: D.F. Garcia Goyena, *Concordancias, Motivos y Comentarios del Código Civil Español* (Madrid: Sociedad Tipográfico-Editorial, 1852), vol. 4, 252–258.

[65] *Código Civil*, art. 1903.

Código Civil – adopting a model already found in Latin America – had expanded the proviso to exclude liability for *force majeure* as well.[66]

The general trajectory of the later nineteenth-century codes rooted in the French tradition was towards an express focus on fault as the basis of liability, sometimes with a reversed burden of proof, largely scouring away the leaning towards strict liability visible behind the *Code Civil* itself. It was only in Italy, where the Code of 1865 was a literal translation of the French, that any serious vestige of liability independent of fault could be constructed with any degree of ease. Even in Scotland, with its double basis in the common law and the Civil law, fault was established as the governing principle of liability for reparation by the middle of the nineteenth century, building on the foundations laid down by the institutional writers from Stair onwards.[67] Increasing weight came to be put on the principled maxim *Culpa tenet suos Auctores* and more generally on fault-based reasoning as a justification for the imposition of liability.

D The Netherlands

The only substantial exception to this move of natural law codes towards a purely fault-based rule was articles 1401–1405 of the Dutch *Burgerlijk Wetboek* (the BW) of 1838.[68] With one exception, this was a straight translation of the equivalent provisions of the *Code Civil*. The exception was article 1401, which added a requirement that the defendant's act should have been unlawful: Every *unlawful* act which causes damage to another makes the person whose fault caused the damage liable to make compensation (emphasis added). Behind this, no doubt, was the influence of the

[66] *Código Civil*, art. 1905; 1851 draft art. 1902. Compare the Argentine *Código Civil*, art. 1128 (1869). More sophisticated was the Chilean code of 1855, which provided for strict liability in the case of ferocious animals (with some exceptions) and fault liability otherwise: *Código Civil* arts. 2327, 2326 (and see the illuminating notes on the various drafts of this provision in M.L. Amunátegui, *Obras Completas de Andrés Bello* (Caracas: Ministerio de Educación, 1951), vol. 13, 914–915).

[67] G. MacCormack, 'Culpa in the Scots Law of Reparation' (1974) 19 *Juridical Review (NS)* 13; H.L. MacQueen and W.D.H. Sellar, 'History of Negligence in Scots Law' in Schrage (ed.), *Negligence*, 273; D. Visser and N. Whitty, 'The Structure of the Law of Delict in Historical Perspective' in K. Reid and R. Zimmermann, *A History of Private Law in Scotland* (Oxford University Press, 2000), vol. 2, 422.

[68] A. Hol, 'Fault in Legal Doctrine in the Netherlands' in N. Jansen (ed.), *The Development and Making of Legal Doctrine* (Cambridge University Press, 2010), 164 at pp. 165–166; E. J. H. Schrage, 'Negligence in the Discussion during the Preparation of the Dutch Civil Code of 1838', in Schrage (ed.), *Negligence*, 391.

text of the lex Aquilia,[69] with its requirement that the loss should have been caused *iniuria*. As a consequence, Dutch law had the potential to expand the range of liability beyond simple fault into other areas of wrongfulness such as improper interference with trade.

E Germany[70]

Before the unification of 1871, the German territories were politically fragmented, as was their law. Against that background, two broad groups may be identified. First were those where codification had occurred: Bavaria (1756), Prussia (1794), Austria (1811) and Saxony (1865), to which there has to be added the Rhineland territories in which the French *Code Civil* applied. Outside these regions, the law that applied was the *ius commune*, as it had developed into the *usus modernus pandectarum* in the seventeenth and eighteenth centuries, based transparently on Roman law. The codes were all rooted in natural law thinking, and hence contained general clauses imposing liability for loss caused by fault. The *usus modernus pandectarum* had a similar fault-based rule, but channelled through the lex Aquilia with its ambiguous reference to unlawfulness and with a more casuistic approach to liability which was in contrast with the general clauses of the natural-law codes. These two approaches were reflected in doctrinal literature. For Johann Christian Hasse, writing within the Roman-law tradition, the general clause was just too broad; instead there had to be, as well as fault, some unlawful act.[71] Other writers expressly agreed with this, but at the same time got close to the acceptance of a general principle of recovery by suggesting that an act leading to damage was in itself unlawful in the absence of some recognised excuse. This instability is found in Windscheid's *Pandektenrecht*; and since Windscheid was the prime mover behind the German Civil Code (BGB), that instability carried forward into the debates which led up to the codification. In practice, though, extensions to the core of Aquilian liability for physical injury were achieved by piecemeal legislation. Similarly, islands of strict liability were created through legislation; particularly important here from the point of view of later law was the Prussian Railways Act of 1838, giving compensation independent of fault to the victims of railway accidents. That said, judges could in practice impose forms of strict liability

[69] Above, p. 52.
[70] W. Ernst, 'Negligence in 19th Century Germany' in Schrage (ed.), *Negligence*, 341; N. Jansen, 'Developing Legal Doctrine: Fault in the German Law of Delict' in *Doctrine*, 96.
[71] J.C. Hasse, *Die Culpa des Römischen Rechts* (Kiel 1815; 2nd edn, Bonn: A. Marcus, 1838).

themselves, for example when an *actio negatoria* was brought to deny a right to interfere with one's enjoyment of property.[72] Moreover, despite the dominance of the fault principle as a matter of rhetoric, by the 1870s arguments were being heard that it was outdated and should be replaced by some other principle more suited to an industrial society.

The relevant provisions of the BGB effectively fossilised this background. Paragraph 823 contained the carefully delineated general clause, based on negligently or deliberately causing harm but preventing too great a spread of liability by defining the interests whose infringement was treated as wrongful: life, body, health, freedom, property, 'or other right'. Other forms of wrongfulness were recognised in the form of breaches of statutory provisions (§ 823 II), but compensation was only to be awarded if there was fault. Most tellingly, perhaps, § 831 imposed liability on an employer for the acts of his employees only if he had failed to take ordinary care in the choice of the employees, the provision of tools, or the superintendence of their work.

F English common law[73]

To understand the law in England in the middle of the nineteenth century it is necessary to look back six centuries earlier. By the 1250s, the principal action to claim compensation for wrongs was the writ of trespass. Although at its base 'trespass' meant simply 'wrong', and was therefore in effect coextensive with the modern 'tort' or 'delict', the writ of trespass was divided into three sub-forms – trespass to land, trespass to goods, and trespass to the person – and in all of these it was essential to allege that the wrong was done forcibly and in breach of the King's peace. By the 1360s it was clear that this was too limiting, and that there were forms of actionable wrongdoing which did not fit cleanly into this straitjacket. The courts therefore developed an alternative, more open-ended, way of formulating a claim, which came to be known as trespass on the case (or, more simply, the action on the case). In this form, all the plaintiff had to do was briefly to state the facts which he claimed had occurred, to assert that these constituted wrongful conduct on the part of the defendant and that as a result of that he had suffered loss, and to seek a remedy. There was no need for any formal allegation of force or breach of the King's peace,

[72] Below, p. 143.

[73] D. Ibbetson, *Historical Introduction to the Law of Obligations* (Oxford University Press, 1999), 39–70.

and no theoretical limit to situations which could potentially be brought within the scope of the action. Within a few decades – by 1390 at the latest – trespass on the case had come to be seen as a form of action wholly distinct from the older general trespass.

In 1850 the duality between trespass and the action on the case was still fundamental to the structure of tortious liability, with trespass still divided into its original three sub-forms. The action on the case, however, had developed somewhat. In the fifteenth and sixteenth centuries there had crystallised out a number of distinct torts, which remained in formal terms actions on the case: conversion (effectively English law's action to claim moveable property, though framed as an action claiming damages for interference with it), defamation and nuisance (interfering with the enjoyment of land). In the eighteenth century, almost certainly borrowing from Samuel Pufendorf and other natural lawyers of the previous decades, lawyers had come to identify a principle of liability for negligence within this residuary body of innominate actions on the case, without affecting the nominate torts:

> Every man ought to take reasonable care that he does not injure his neighbour; therefore when a man receives hurt thro' default of another, tho' the same were not wilful, yet if it be occasioned by negligence or folly the law gives him an action to recover damages for the injury so sustained ... However it is proper in such cases to prove the injury was such as would probably follow from the act done.[74]

By 1850 this principle was generally recognised as a major source of liability, and the action on the case for negligence had begun to eat away at the older action of trespass: litigants by now had the choice to frame their actions in case rather than in trespass if they chose to do so. Nonetheless, despite the growing dominance of this principle of negligence liability, the action on the case still retained the potential to recognise new situations of liability independent of it.

There was no uniform approach to liability across the field of actions of trespass and case. In trespass, on the face of it, liability was strict, but it was accompanied by such a substantial range of defences that in practice fault of some sort almost invariably lay at the base of it. The action on the case for negligence was, clearly, based on negligence, defined by 1850 as the failure to take the care which would have been taken by a reasonable man, but there were other varieties of actions on the case in which

[74] F. Buller, *An Introduction to the Law of Trials at Nisi Prius* (London: Woodfall and Strahan, 1767), 35–36.

different standards were applied. Liability in conversion, defamation and nuisance, and in some innominate situations, was strict, while at the other extreme, in the action on the case for deceit, liability only arose if there had been deliberate wrongdoing.[75] There was room for a considerable measure of ambiguity: it was held in the Court of Queen's Bench in 1846 that a person who kept a dangerous animal with knowledge that it had a propensity to bite was strictly liable if it did so, without any need to allege that he had been negligent in the keeping;[76] yet, sitting rather awkwardly with this, the court remarked that 'the negligence is in the keeping'.[77]

G *Fault and unlawfulness, fault and non-fault*

There is no doubt that by the middle of the nineteenth century the fault principle was treated as near-axiomatic throughout the countries studied. At the same time, it was accompanied in some places – most notably Holland and Germany – by an additional requirement of unlawfulness traceable back to the Roman lex Aquilia. It had been expunged by the natural law tradition, but even in those places where there was a code based on natural law the heritage of Roman law was sufficiently strong that the unlawfulness principle still had the capacity to revive. It was probably only in England, as a result of its separation from Roman law, that it had no part at all to play. As well, for all the strength of the fault principle, in every system there were elements of liability independent of fault. One of the features of the law of the later nineteenth and twentieth centuries is that the different positioning of these elements in different systems was an important factor in shaping the way in which legal developments occurred.

III **Judges and jurists**

A Learned lawyers and the *communis opinio doctorum*

From as early as the end of the Republic, Roman law had developed as a rational science, in which men with a particular form of learning strove to identify 'true' rules of law by the operation of reason. Although this legal science fell away after the beginning of the third century, its precepts were preserved in Justinian's *Corpus Iuris*. Of particular importance was

75 *Pasley v. Freeman* (1789) 3 TR 51, 100 ER 450.
76 *May v. Burdett* (1846) 9 QB 101.
77 *May v. Burdett* (1846) 9 QB 101 at p. 112.

the text in the Codex which provided that judgments should be given in accordance with the laws rather than by reference to comparable fact situations: *non exemplis sed legibus iudicandum est.*[78] That the doctors of law in the medieval universities should themselves have claimed to be able to identify the rules of (Roman) law is hardly surprising, but from the thirteenth century there developed in the city courts of northern Italy a judicial practice of consulting learned doctors and deciding cases in accordance with the opinions of these experts.[79] This practice was consolidated as learned opinion crystallised the proposition that in some circumstances an expert opinion was binding on the judge deciding a case, and even in situations where there was no such formally binding force, a judge who followed an expert opinion came to be effectively protected from liability for misapplying the law. Legal practice and learned law were in this way largely married together.

It was not a large step to take from treating the opinions of experts as substantially determinative of a legal issue before a judge to treating at least some written works as having authority in their own right. The Accursian gloss had such a status in Italian courts,[80] and from the fourteenth century certain individual jurists' writings were recognised as sources of law, quite explicitly so in some Italian statutes. Alongside this, by the end of the fourteenth century, in legal practice particular weight was attached to the *communis opinio doctorum*, the dominant view of jurists.[81] Judges would normally follow this, and if they failed to do so they were at risk of liability for having delivered a false judgment; so too were legal scholars expected to have regard to it in their *consilia* (advice given to litigants or courts), however much they ignored it in their more theoretical writings.[82] In these ways the products of legal science came to play a central part in legal practice, but in doing so they lost their scientific character: their importance lay in their authoritative status, not in the validity or strength of the reason that lay behind them.

The dominant position of legal scholars was underscored across continental Europe in the late fifteenth and sixteenth centuries, as university-

[78] C.7.45.13.

[79] J.P. Dawson, *The Oracles of the Law* (Ann Arbor: University of Michigan Law School, 1967), 138–147; L. Lombardi, *Saggio di Diritto Giurisprudenziale* (Milan: Giuffrè, 1967), 124–164.

[80] Lombardi, *Saggio di Diritto Giurisprudenziale*, pp. 112–115.

[81] *Ibid.*, pp. 164–183.

[82] Marianus Socinus, *Consiliorum* IV, c 8 no. 15 (cited by Lombardi, *Saggio di Diritto Giurisprudenziale*, p. 145 note 125), referring to Jason de Mayno and Philippus Decius as having given consilia *contra communem*.

trained lawyers came to supplant as judges men with a grasp primarily of customary law.[83] What was once described as the 'Reception of Roman Law' is now more generally analysed as the intellectualisation of legal practice, one aspect of which was the greater use in courts of the rules and principles of Roman law and Canon law as they had been developed in the medieval universities. It is impossible to read the collections of decisions of superior courts right across continental Europe, with the exception of the Balkan territories in the far south-east and Scandinavia, without being struck by the ubiquity of citations to the international literature of the learned laws; and even after the substantial renationalisation of the laws in the seventeenth century, scholarly lawyers in the universities continued to have a dominant influence on the practice of the courts.

Within the continental tradition, therefore, there were close links between the law of the universities and legal practice. Alone or in groups, legal scholars might give advice to judges and litigants; works of individual jurists might have a degree of authority in themselves; and the *communis opinio* of learned lawyers might be treated as a conclusive or near-conclusive statement of the law.

England was completely different. Although Roman law was taught in the universities from around 1200, the common law developed almost wholly in isolation from them. From around the middle of the thirteenth century, English law was being taught in London, focused around the courts at Westminster.[84] The teaching was basic and orientated towards legal practice, and it was supplemented by observation of lawsuits in the central courts themselves. In the fourteenth century there appeared the Inns of Court, originally perhaps hostels for lawyers in London for the short law terms, which took on an educational function as junior lawyers learned from senior ones.[85] The common law developed at this time as the custom of lawyers,[86] the direct equivalent of the *communis opinio doctorum* of the Civil law except that the *doctores* were legal practitioners rather than scholars and there was only tradition, not text, on which they had an opinion. Without any formal text, and without any scholarly profession independent of legal practice, the legal revolution of the

[83] F. Wieacker, *A History of Private Law in Europe*, trans. Tony Weir (Oxford: Clarendon Press, 1995), 91–126.

[84] P. Brand, 'Courtroom and Schoolroom: The Education of Lawyers in England Prior to 1400' (1987) 60 *Historical Research* 147.

[85] S.E. Thorne, 'The Early History of the Inns of Court' (1959) *Graya* 79; J.H. Baker, *The Third University of England* (London: Selden Society, 1990).

[86] J.H. Baker, *The Law's Two Bodies* (Oxford University Press, 2001), 59–90.

sixteenth century led not to the dominance of university-trained lawyers or the incorporation of learned law into legal practice but instead to the dominance of the most senior legal practitioners, the judges. By the early seventeenth century at the latest the common law had the practice of following precedents, deriving authoritative rules from previous decisions; continental lawyers, it is true, developed similar ideas, but in England there was no text of equivalent authority to the *Corpus Iuris* with the result that there was nothing to counterbalance the weight of judicial decisions. English law began to be taught in the universities in the 1750s, but it was not before the middle of the nineteenth century that robust scholarship in English law began to be produced in any field, and tort scholarship was noticeably meagre. By now the die had been cast, with academic writings having very little authority attached to them, so that even a scholar of the calibre of Sir Frederick Pollock was constrained by the decisions of the courts and hamstrung in the degree of theorisation that was open to him.

IV Process and procedure

The final feature of the pre-1850 law to which attention needs to be directed briefly is the process and procedure for the legal resolution of tort claims. Throughout continental Europe, Civil procedure was based on the Romano-canonical procedure of the Middle Ages.[87] This was in essence a written procedure (though oral aspects remained very late in Scandinavia): the claimant formulated his claim and the evidence he would be adducing to support it; the defendant formulated his defence together with further evidence on which he would be relying. Predetermined questions were put to witnesses by judges or commissioners appointed by them and the answers recorded; written testimony was presented to the court, and on the basis of this the judges reached their decisions. By contrast, in the English common law actions were begun by writs (or equivalent means of initiating litigation) which might be very stereotypical; this was followed by the parties pleading to issue, in tort actions very commonly by the defendant simply denying liability. The case was then heard by judge and jury. The judge decided on the legal sufficiency of the pleadings, with a power to reserve difficult points to be decided by all the judges of the

[87] A. Engelmann et al, *History of Continental Civil Procedure* (Boston: Little Brown, 1927, reprinted New York: Kelley, 1969). Essentially the same procedure was adopted in the English Court of Chancery, but not in the common law courts.

court sitting as a single body (each court had only a relatively small number of judges). Subject to this, the jury decided whether or not the defendant was liable.

The great difference between England (and, by 1850, Scotland) and continental Europe, therefore, was that in the former cases were tried by judge and jury and in the latter by judge alone. This gave a very different flavour to English proceedings by comparison with those taking place elsewhere. In formal terms, it was particularly significant in shaping the embryonic tort of negligence. The core question, whether the defendant had in fact taken the care which would have been taken by a reasonable person in the circumstances, fell to be decided by the jury, but it was for the judges to say whether liability could have arisen on the alleged facts since these were visible on the face of the pleadings. The jury's question was strongly resistant to any further degree of definition, whereas by contrast the judges' questions were the subject of increasingly detailed analysis. The tort of negligence, as it was beginning to develop in the middle of the nineteenth century, was structured in terms of a detailed catalogue of duty situations, all of which led on to the same question (assuming it was held that the defendant did owe a duty to the plaintiff), whether reasonable care had been taken in the circumstances. There is a very clear difference here from continental European practice, where lower-court judges would make findings of fact largely addressing the question whether the defendant had been at fault, without having to separate out the assessment of the defendant's conduct and the circumstances in which that conduct had occurred.

A further procedural feature in some systems – notably France, Italy and Spain – was that civil liability might fall to be established in criminal proceedings. We may take France as the leading example.[88] Medieval procedure did not allow a clear distinction to be drawn between criminal and civil procedure where relatively minor wrongdoings were concerned. In both the initiative was taken by the injured party, and in both the normal result was the payment of some monetary recompense to the victim.[89] Ordinances of 1498 and 1539, consolidated in 1670, strengthened

[88] In Spain, the development occurred in the middle of the nineteenth century under the influence of Joaquín Francisco Pacheco (*El Código Penal* (Madrid: Tello 1867, reprinted 2000), 279) and incorporated into the *Código Civil* as article 1092. In Italy the courts' practice developed independently as part of the medieval *ius commune*, though its modern adoption was probably the result of French influence: G. Salvioli, *Storia della Procedura Civile e Criminale* (Milan: Hoepli, 1927), 369–372; V. Manzini, *Trattato di Diritto Processuale Penale*, 6th edn by G.D. Pisapia, (Turin: Utet, 1967), vol. 1, 373–375.

[89] J.-M. Carbasse, *Histoire du Droit Pénal et de la Justice Criminelle*, 2nd edn (Paris: Presses Universitaires de France, 2006), 180–205. Descamps, *Faute Personnelle*, pp. 204–213.

the inquisitorial role of the judge and public prosecutor in criminal cases; the victim might continue to play a part in the suit and recover compensation, but now he did so as a *partie civile* rather than as accuser.[90] A criminal court, though, might legitimately apply different criteria in determining whether a defendant was criminally or civilly responsible: in his *Institutions du Droit François*, Claude Serres gave prominence to a case of 1719 in which the *Parlement* of Toulouse had required a lunatic to make civil reparation notwithstanding that he was not subject to penal liability.[91]

This distinction between criminal and civil procedure had an analytical dimension too. From the sixteenth century, writers had begun to distinguish between those wrongs which were appropriate to the former and those which were appropriate to the latter. The former could be categorised as crimes or delicts, the latter as quasi-delicts.[92] Hence Jean Domat treated wrongs which were *ni crimes ni délits* as part of the civil law, with crimes and delicts (which were tantamount to the same thing) as part of public law. This was a valuable distinction to draw, since undesirable conduct might be sanctioned by both penal and civil actions.[93] However, it came to have an effect within the civil law itself. Since criminality was associated with intention, the division between delict and quasi-delict could approximate roughly to that between intentional and unintentional wrongs;[94] it was in this form in which it was stated in Pothier's *Traité des Obligations*, though shorn of its roots in the division between criminal and civil wrongs.[95] In truth, though, this was a distinction without a difference, leaving its mark on terminology alone.[96]

90 A. Esmein, *History of Continental Criminal Procedure* (Boston: Little Brown, 1913, reprinted New York: Kelley, 1968), 143. For the working out of the details see J. Imbert, *La Practique Judiciaire tant Civile que Criminelle* (Paris: La Société, 1624), 3.1.3–10.

91 C. Serres, *Institutions du Droit François* (Paris: Caveller, 1753), p. 581.

92 Descamps, *Faute Personnelle*, pp. 273–288.

93 This applies equally to the modern law, where criminal law may relieve the pressure for tortious remedies to be made available. See below, pp. 89–90.

94 See J. Cujas, *ad Inst* 4.5 no. 1, in *Opera Omnia* (Paris, 1658), 1.245–246, contrasting *culpa* and *delictum* (though recognising the ambiguous status of actions on the lex Aquilia). The association between quasi-delict and liability for *imprudentia* goes back to the glossators: Hallebeek, 'Negligence in Medieval Roman Law', p. 85 note 42.

95 R.-J. Pothier, *Traité des Obligations* (Paris: Debure, 1764), section 116.

96 It is for this reason that in the present work we prefer to use the term 'tort' rather than 'delict' to describe civil wrongs.

3

Homogeneity in legal development: products and medical liability

In some fields the track of legal development over the last century-and-a-half appears substantially homogeneous. Although each system has remained largely distinct, they have moved along tracks which have been more or less parallel and they have ended up in very similar positions. The changes have not always occurred at the same time. In part, they have come as a response to external factors which have occurred at different moments. In part, they have depended on capricious local factors, such as the chance nature of the individuals who have been able to influence the law at any time and place. Changes have not always taken an identical form, since at any moment each legal system has had its own particular rules, principles, values and institutional structure against the background of which changes have occurred. But these differences aside, it is possible to paint a coherent picture of convergent legal development across Europe.

In this chapter we look at two areas of homogeneity in rather different ways. First is the field which we today think of as product liability, now shifted outside the main tort law regime as a result of the European Product Liability Directive of 1985[1] as integrated into the different legal systems of Europe. This we examine in big-picture terms, stressing the similarities which are seen within systems and noting, in passing, differences in the timing of changes visible in the development of the different systems. The second topic is the liability of medical practitioners to the victims of faulty treatment. Here we focus at a more microscopic level, concentrating on the reasons why changes occurred at different times against the background of a similar long-term development. For reasons of space, and of comprehensibility, the focus here is on the comparison of only two countries, England and France. The second section, with its concentration on detail, is inevitably considerably longer than the first.

[1] Council Directive 1985/374/EEC of 25 July 1985 on the approximation of laws, regulations and administrative provisions of the Member States concerning liability for defective products, OJ L 210, 7 August 1985, 29 ('The Product Liability Directive').

I Product liability

Liability for injuries caused by things supplied by one person to another provides a very good example of an area in which there has been substantial homogeneity of development across Europe. The topic is commonly described as 'Product Liability', but it is better to avoid putting too much weight on that terminology at the start of our period. However, the use of this terminology or something very close to it has, in the last half-century, been an important factor in bringing about the very homogeneity which is observed.

A Contract and tort

In the middle of the nineteenth century, all of the legal systems studied treated cases of this sort as a matter of contract, in particular of the contract of sale. In those systems whose roots lay in Roman law, the claims of the disappointed buyer were of two sorts: an action to rescind the contract or to obtain damages reflecting diminution in value where a thing had a latent defect which had not been disclosed by the seller to the buyer, and more generally an action for damages where the seller had known of a defect and failed to disclose it.[2] Reflecting its different history, English law was slightly different. It solved the problem of defective things by incorporating into contracts of sale implied warranties of quality, breach of which would be actionable without proof of knowledge or fault. In practice, although the legal frameworks were different, the practical working of English law was largely the same as in those systems more heavily influenced by Roman law.

Because of the operation of the rules of privity of contract and their equivalents, it followed that, in all the systems studied, the claim would always be against the immediate supplier, and there was no general claim against the manufacturer as such. As well, the claim would normally have to be brought by the buyer of the product, who might not always be the person who had suffered the injury.[3] However, piecemeal exceptions were made to these rules.[4] Mass injuries, or the fear of mass injuries, heightened the sense that there was a need to protect consumers. The response,

[2] S. Whittaker, 'Introduction to Fault in Product Liability' in *Products*, 1, 11.

[3] S. Whittaker, 'The Development of Product Liability in England' in *Products*, pp. 51, 58–60.

[4] *Ibid.*, pp. 67–68, citing especially *Frost v. Aylesbury Dairy* [1905] 1 KB 608: buyer recovered his out-of-pocket expenses for caring for his wife who died due to infected milk.

however, was not to expand private-law rights; the preferred route was regulation, as was found in the English legislation from the Food, Drink and Drugs Act of 1872 and the Food and Drugs Act of 1875 to the Public Health (Regulations as to Food) Act of 1907.[5]

Behind all of this there lay a core belief that contract was the appropriate framework within which claims of this type should be dealt with, even when as a matter of legal form it would, or should, have been possible to construct a non-contractual claim against a manufacturer. Perhaps more importantly, though, there was very little pressure to have a generally available action against the manufacturer who was not the immediate supplier. A chemical compound might commonly be manufactured by the person who had sold it; products made by others and supplied to individual consumers would commonly not carry much risk of causing injury; before liability insurance developed in the late nineteenth century, small manufacturers of machinery might not be able to internalise the cost of injuries flowing from their negligence, particularly where there was a low risk but the injury caused was likely to be substantial – or at least it was plausible for manufacturers to argue that it was so; many of those suffering injury from badly constructed machines did so in the course of their employment, and there were commonly legal barriers to claims between employee and employer as well as alternative social mechanisms for providing compensation or financial support for those who had been injured.

B The twentieth century

Around the beginning of the twentieth century, in most jurisdictions there was some shift towards the better compensation for victims of injuries caused by defective products. This was not uniform, and the mechanisms used were varied, depending on the devices that were available within each legal system.

In Germany, the expansion of liability was brought about through the law of delict, perhaps because the first case that arose, in the Stuttgart *Oberlandesgericht* in 1902, was one in which a contractual claim might not

[5] J. Phillips and M. French, 'Adulteration and Food Law, 1899–1939' (1998) 9 *Twentieth Century British History* 350. The trigger for the 1907 Act was the moral panic following revelations of the acute lack of hygiene in Chicago's meat-packing industry, which appeared in a popular novel, *The Jungle* by Upton Sinclair: 1081 Hansard (HL) col. 1063, 22 August 1907.

have lain.[6] Paragraphs 823ff of the BGB, formulating liability in terms of a general principle of fault liability and a catalogue of protected interests, were easily applicable to the situation in which a manufacturer could be shown to be at fault and the victim had suffered personal injury or property damage. The law of contract might just as well have been used to bring about this expansion, given the BGB's recognition of contracts for the benefit of third parties, but since German law had no rule of mutual exclusivity of contract and tort there was no strong reason to favour this route, and the tighter limitation period in contractual litigation militated against it. A contractual route would moreover have been problematic where the injured party was a bystander with no direct or indirect contractual link with the manufacturer, and in the *Newcastle Disease* case[7] of 1968 a unitary approach of treating all product liability cases within the law of delict was preferred to a fragmented approach of using contractual liability in cases where this was possible and delictual liability where it was not.

In England, the seeds of a general remedy in tort against the negligent manufacturer had been sown as early as 1869,[8] but despite the support of Frederick Pollock, the leading academic writer on the subject, the courts steadily weakened the authority of this decision. Increasingly in the early decades of the twentieth century it was stressed that the law of tort should not be expanded in such a way as to undermine the restrictive ambit of contractual liability – the so-called contract fallacy – with the result that the liability in tort of manufacturers was steadily weakened. This tendency was reversed by the House of Lords in the Scottish case of *Donoghue v. Stevenson* in 1932,[9] holding that a negligent manufacturer might be liable to the ultimate consumer despite the lack of contractual privity between them. There is some reason to suspect that this litigation was in fact being orchestrated by the defendant manufacturer, operating against the background of conflicting Scots decisions:[10] as manufacturing enterprises had

[6] G. Wagner, 'The Development of Product Liability in Germany' in *Products*, pp. 114, 118. The case involved a workmen's compensation insurer suing a manufacturer on behalf of a worker who had been injured by a defective motor-powered saw. It is unlikely that German law would have found there to be a contract between the manufacturer and the employer for the benefit of a third party (the worker), because the worker may not have been identifiable at the time of the contract.

[7] BGHZ 51, 91, 93ff; Wagner, *Products*, pp. 123–124.

[8] *George v. Skivington* (1869) LR 5 Exch. 1; D. Ibbetson, 'George v Skivington' in C. Mitchell and P. Mitchell (eds.), *Landmark Cases in the Law of Torts* (Oxford: Hart, 2010), 69.

[9] [1932] AC 562.

[10] For the background, see W.W. McBryde, 'Donoghue v. Stevenson. The Story of the "Snail in the Bottle" Case' in A.J. Gamble (ed.), *Obligations in Context* (Edinburgh: Green,

grown so that costs could be more easily internalised, and now that liability insurance was generally available, the interests of manufacturers were served by there being clear rules rather than unclear rules which might capriciously work in favour of them and their competitors. Furthermore, very shortly afterwards the rule of *res ipsa loquitur* was applied to such situations, thereby putting the burden of proof onto the manufacturer to show a lack of negligence once a clear inference of negligence could be made from the circumstances.[11]

The Dutch development was not dissimilar. Although adopting the provisions of the French Code on delict in most respects, articles 1401 and 1402 of the BW of 1838 had imposed a general liability for fault only where there had been an *unlawful* act, reverting to the framework of the Roman lex Aquilia.[12] At first there was some dispute as to whether unlawfulness was an additional condition alongside fault, but in 1919 the Hoge Raad, in the *Lindenbaum* case, softened the notion of unlawfulness so that it encompassed any situation of behaviour which was contrary to good morals.[13] The context of the *Lindenbaum* decision was very different from product liability – unfair competition – but the principle in that case was of wider application. Hence in the *Zootjes* decision of 1933, it was held that behaviour constituting a breach of contract fell within this broad definition of unlawfulness.[14] In his note on the decision, E. M. Meijers, the leading Dutch scholar of the period, expressly linked this case to the earlier *Lindenbaum* decision.

The development in France was rather different. The scope of liability expanded along two main routes, neither of which involved the use of the general principle of article 1382 as a means of imposing liability on manufacturers.

First, French law had already in the first part of the nineteenth century weakened its ideas of contractual privity, allowing a purchaser to bring an *action directe* against a person other than his or her immediate supplier, thereby allowing a claim against a manufacturer provided the other conditions of liability in contract were satisfied.[15] Alongside this, in

1990), 13. Note the view of Lord Normand, counsel for the defenders, at p. 25, that they should not have appealed to the House of Lords but rather gone to proof of the facts.

11 *Grant v. Australian Knitting Mills Ltd* [1936] 1 AC 85: Whittaker, *Products*, pp. 74–75.

12 A. Hol, 'Fault in Legal Doctrine in the Netherlands' in *Doctrine*, pp. 164, 165.

13 *Lindenbaum v. Cohen*, HR 31 January 1919, (1919) NJ 161.

14 *Zootjes v. Loos*, HR 6 April 1933, (1933) NJ 881.

15 S.1820.1.171; J.-S. Borghetti, 'The Development of Liability for Products in France' in *Products*, 87, 94.

due course the requirement of knowledge of the defect within the general action on sale was muted, it being presumed whenever the vendor was acting in a professional capacity.[16] This expanded contractual liability, in conjunction with the French rule of *non cumul* which prevented the use of a delictual action where a contractual claim was available, meant that the scope for the use of a delictual claim as had occurred in Germany, England and the Netherlands was substantially narrower in France. Furthermore, Demogue distinguished between obligations to use one's best efforts (*obligations de moyens*) and obligations to achieve an outcome or result (*obligations de résultat*). The former would be breached only by fault. With this sophistication within contract, obligations to achieve product safety could be classified by the courts as 'obligations of result', so there was little interest in using the fault provisions of the Code relating to delict as a way of protecting purchasers and those for whose benefit the purchaser was contracting.[17]

Secondly, within the law of extra-contractual responsibility, from the 1890s there was a gradual rediscovery of the strict liability of the keeper of a thing which caused injury under article 1384, paragraph 1.[18] Together with the greater protection which had been afforded to workers in 1898 (although the right of action against the manufacturer as opposed to the employer was preserved), these combined together to relieve any pressure that there might have been to impose liability on blameworthy manufacturers under article 1382 of the *Code Civil*.

But these legal mechanisms did not cover the whole of the ground. As well, from the 1930s it was held that the sale of a defective thing by a professional might, in itself, constitute *faute* sufficient to trigger liability under the general principle of article 1382. Thus in one example, a worker injured by a machine which had been badly constructed could bring an action against the blameworthy manufacturer.[19] In the 1960s this line of cases developed so as to create a wider delictual liability for injuries caused by defective products.[20] It is important to recognise that these

[16] See in particular Cass. civ. 22 July 1931, *Condé c Air Liquide*, Gaz. Pal 1931.2.683. Contrast Gaz. Pal. 1926.1.102, where the claim failed because it was based specifically on the defendant vendor's contractual duty.

[17] A. Tunc, 'La Distinction des Obligations de Résultat et des Obligations de Diligence', JCP 1945.I.449.

[18] Cass. civ. 16 June 1896, *Oriolle, Guissez et Cousin c Teffaine*, S. 1897.1.17, note Esmein; D. 1897. 1.433, concl. Sarrut, note R. Saleilles.

[19] Borghetti, *Products*, p. 95.

[20] *Ibid.*, p. 96.

developments all took place rather haphazardly within the case-law of the courts, with piecemeal influence through the cases' academic annotations; it was only at a late stage in the process that doctrinal writing, most notably an article by Henri Mazeaud published in 1955, began to catch up and impose some ordered coherence on the law by bringing together the available contractual and extra-contractual claims.[21]

The routes by which these similar results were reached, therefore, differed from system to system, but the trajectory of development was very similar. Each system treated the problem on its own terms, autopoietically, using the legal materials available within that system; but at the same time each can be seen as responding to more or less the same changes in the environment in which it was functioning. In social and intellectual terms, the first few decades of the twentieth century marked a shift towards a feeling that individual victims should be better protected against the consequences of the negligence of manufacturers,[22] and the pro-consumer decisions reached by the courts fitted seamlessly against this background. It is, however, noteworthy too that a number of the pivotal cases were not straightforward cases of injured consumers, but involved injured (or killed) workers, where compensation for the victims was already provided under the relevant workmen's compensation provisions; in these cases, the true plaintiffs were not necessarily the victims themselves or their families, but insurance companies attempting to pass on their losses to the negligent manufacturers.[23] It may be, therefore, that the trigger for some, perhaps most, of the litigation – the cause of reaching the tipping point – was circumstances internal to the insurance market at the relevant time. A third factor cannot be ignored: it is telling that the central decisions in France, England and the Netherlands took place at almost exactly the same time, in 1931, 1932 and 1933 respectively, and while it is unlikely that the *Condé* decision had any influence on *Donoghue v. Stevenson* in Britain, foreign law might have provided a pointer for the *Zootjes* decision in the Netherlands.

Whatever the reason, although the legal frameworks in Germany, England, the Netherlands and France by this time conduced towards the

[21] 'La Responsabilité Civile du Vendeur-Fabricant', *Revue trimestrielle de droit civil* 1955, 611.

[22] See, e.g. J.-L. Halpérin, 'The Process of Codification Applied to the Law of Delicts' in *Ideas*, pp. 167, 184.

[23] This is clearly the case in the German 1902 decision (above, n. 6), the French *Condé* decision (above n. 16), and the Dutch *Zootjes* decision (above n. 14).

imposition of a potentially rather strict liability on manufacturers, there is little evidence that these remedies were in practice used to any significant extent. Injuries arising in an industrial context were already well covered by the general law and by the specific regimes of workmen's compensation: where injuries occurred outside this context we may suspect that the cost of obtaining legal advice and bringing an action – without any help from a trade union or other workers' protection society – were too high for it to be normally worthwhile initiating an action for compensation. Nor was there any political will to alter this situation: in pre-war and post-war society there were other obvious priorities. In effect, the law stood still.

Italy and Spain, despite their Codes being based on the French Code (the Italian being to all intents and purposes identical to it), were more conservative. In Italy, although the case-law occasionally followed French precedent, it commonly took a restrictive approach to liability, adopting neither the French *action directe* nor its presumption of knowledge; nor did it habitually apply the general principle of fault liability found in article 2043 of the 1865 Code. It was only where the manufacturer had been guilty of a crime that liability would regularly be imposed independent of contract.[24] Doctrinal writers, almost unanimously, approved this restrictive approach; the one notable exception was Gino Gorla, who in 1937 advocated the adoption of an approach based on French law.[25] The developments which were taking place in France and Germany were well known, and it may well be that the failure to follow a similar track was the result of a more or less conscious decision.[26] With that in mind, we might reasonably suspect that the justification for the conservatism of the law articulated by some (Italian) scholars in the second quarter of the century, that it was desirable to give protection to emergent industrial enterprises, reflected a more widely held view. The situation in Spain was very similar, if perhaps yet more conservative. As in Italy, liability was invariably channelled through the provisions governing the contract of sale in the 1889 Code, without the *action directe* and the presumption of knowledge which had broadened liability in France; and extra-contractual liability would arise only where the defendant's conduct was criminal.[27] In both

[24] N. Coggiola, 'The Development of Product Liability in Italy' in *Products*, 192, at pp. 198–201.

[25] *La Compravendità e la Permuta* (Turin: UTET, 1937), nos. 121, 170.

[26] Coggiola, *Products*, p. 194.

[27] M. Martín-Casals and J. Solé Feliu, 'The Development of Product Liability in Spain' in *Products*, 234, at pp. 237–238.

countries we may see the relatively undeveloped state of the law as a parallel to the conservative contractarianism found elsewhere in the nineteenth century, time-displaced as a result of the later industrialisation of the economies in Italy and Spain.

C *Catalysts for the development of product liability*

The developments towards a greater sensitivity towards victims, which were already visible in the more economically advanced states, were consolidated more generally from the 1960s. Two principal interlocked themes are visible, one internal to the law and one external: internally, there was a marked increase in the influence of American law; externally, there were a number of high-profile disasters where drugs or other products were used with catastrophic consequences.

From the 1940s, building on the decision of Traynor J in *Escola v. Coca Cola Bottling Co of Fresno*,[28] the American Supreme Court began to impose strict liability for injuries caused by defective products. This was not merely a matter of stricter liability being imposed; as well, the cause of action was seen to lie in the fact that the product was defective and not in the wrongful conduct of the manufacturer or supplier. The closer relationship between American and European lawyers in the post-war period meant that these developments became known in Europe; particularly important were writings of Gino Gorla in Italy and Werner Lorenz in Germany, both of whom had spent time as Visiting Professors in the United States. However, although these works raised awareness of what was happening in America, they had no direct effect on the law.[29]

More important were the disasters that occurred. Public opinion was concentrated by the birth defects caused by the drug Thalidomide/Contagen in England, Germany and the Netherlands, where proof of negligence on the part of the manufacturers was problematic;[30] while in Italy and Spain the trigger was the mass injuries caused by the use of contaminated colza oil.[31] While it was only in Spain that this gave rise directly to

[28] 24 California Reporter 2nd series 453, 461 (1944). The other members of the court preferred to analyse the case on the basis of *res ipsa loquitur.*

[29] J. Bell, 'The Relevance of Foreign Examples to Legal Development' (2011) *Duke Journal of Comparative and International Law* 431, 440–442.

[30] Whittaker, *Products*, p. 77; Wagner, *Products*, p. 139; Giesen, 'The Development of Product Liability in the Netherlands' in *Products*, pp. 158–159.

[31] Coggiola, *Products*, pp. 223–224; Martín-Casals and Solé Feliu, *Products*, pp. 251–256.

consumer protection legislation, the *Ley General para la Defensa de los Consumidores* of 1984,[32] elsewhere in Europe it created a climate within which there was pressure for a regime of liability which was not dependent on the proof of negligence. France was not affected by any such scandal, but there was no need for any such stimulus to a wider liability principle, since from the nineteenth century it already had a precociously strong leaning towards protecting victims.[33]

In the 1960s and early 1970s, in Italy, Germany and the Netherlands steps were taken in the direction of liability without fault by reversing the burden of proof of negligence, but the main channel for change was the enactment of the Product Liability Directive in 1985. Jacques Ghestin, one of those responsible for the Directive, emphasised the importance of the American law of product liability in the thinking behind this, though an alternative explanation that it reflected the general acceptance of the earlier French approach was also given.[34] Although the justification given for having a pan-European principle, that it avoided the distortion of competition by the existence of different liability regimes, was not especially convincing, it was generally welcomed. Its dominant feature was the focus on the injury caused by the product coupled with the attribution of liability for that injury to producers, suppliers or importers into the European Union, a marked contrast with the earlier focus on the wrongdoing of the manufacturer or supplier coupled with legal presumptions or procedural rules to avoid the difficulties caused by an inability to prove fault. The post-1985 law, as incorporated into national legal systems, is a law of product liability rather than of manufacturers' liability. The trigger of the Product Liability Directive made it possible for legal systems whose traditions had focused on negligence or fault as the basis of liability to extract the liability for injuries caused by defective products out of the mainstream of liability in negligence or its equivalents and to establish it as a heading of liability *sui generis*, and hence making it free of any need to conform with the general principles of liability applicable in other fields.

[32] Martín-Casals and Solé Feliu, *Products*, p. 246.

[33] France did have a consumer scandal involving the poisoning of bread flour at Pont St. Esprit, which was one of the leading cases which endorsed the expansion of the liability of the professional seller towards consumers: see Nîmes, 25 April 1960, D. 1960, 725, note Savatier, on appeal Cass. civ. 19 January 1965, D. 1965, 389.

[34] Borghetti, *Products*, p. 98.

II Medical negligence in England and France[35]

A Introduction

Looked at from a pan-European point of view, the development of liability for medical negligence in the century-and-a-half since 1850 is similar to the development of product liability.[36] The only major difference is that there was nothing equivalent to the Product Liability Directive, and hence the law of the European Community and European Union played no part in imposing a measure of harmonisation in the latter part of the twentieth century. Therefore it has been possible for the Nordic countries and France to develop specific compensation schemes distinct from the normal rules of fault liability largely applicable elsewhere.

At first, there was no suggestion that any special rules applied to medical practitioners. They were liable only if they were at fault. In general, in the nineteenth century, a relatively low standard of care was demanded of them, with the result that fault was difficult to prove. Courts were reluctant to challenge professional medical opinion about appropriate treatment. A change in approach is perhaps visible in the early twentieth century, but it was difficult for plaintiffs, and for the courts, to identify what a doctor had done wrong in using the new, complex technical apparatus that was becoming available. Through the second half of the century the law was increasingly plaintiff-friendly, with far higher standards being demanded of doctors and compensation becoming more easily available. The costs of this, though, were not borne by the doctors themselves, but either by public health services or by insurers. At the same time, works were being written which treated medical liability as a distinct field. France appears to have had a few theses before 1939, but it is the theses of Emile Arrighi de Casanova[37] and Emile Kornprobst[38] and the lectures of René Savatier[39] in the period 1946 to 1948 that marked the intellectual search for principles identifying a distinctive field of study. German, Austrian, Spanish

[35] This section is based largely on the chapters by W. Swain, 'The Development of Medical Liability in England and Wales' and by S. Taylor, 'The Development of Medical Liability and Accident Compensation in France' in *Medical*, chs. 2 and 4, supplemented by our own researches. Much of the primary source material from England is taken from the *British Medical Journal*, which reported many cases not found in the Law Reports.

[36] See Hondius, 'Introduction' in *Medical*, together with the national chapters in the volume.

[37] *La Responsabilité Médicale et le Droit Commun de la Responsabilité Civile* (Aix: Éditions provençales, 1946).

[38] *La Responsabilité Médicale: Origines, Fondement et Limites* (Paris: Baillière, 1947).

[39] *La Responsabilité Médicale* (Louvain: Centre d'études Laennec, 1948).

and English discussions date from the 1940s or 1950s, though everywhere the great growth in literature on the subject occurred only in the 1980s. There were, of course, differences of detail, in particular the use of different legal categories (contract, tort, administrative law, regulations) at different times and in different places, but these did not undermine the substantially homogeneous core of liability for fault.

As with product liability, too, there was cross-border knowledge of changes in the law relating to medical care. English cases were known in France;[40] German developments were discussed in England;[41] one of the earliest works in Spanish touching on the subject was a translation of an Italian book.[42] American law was widely known too, but for European writers it was seen more as an example of what should be avoided rather than a model which should be followed.[43]

This development took place against a very similar pan-European background. Changes in medical science and techniques were not national; on the contrary, the use of new vaccines and drugs spread quickly, as did technological advances such as X-rays and the use of antiseptics in treating wounds. Changes in healthcare, and in particular the growth of hospitals in which teams of specialists combined together to cure patients, can similarly be seen as a European phenomenon (and not just European, of course) rather than a set of local ones. In addition, reflecting the consumer movement which influenced the shifts in product liability, from the middle of the twentieth century there was a European patients' rights movement.

At a more detailed level, though, the picture is more granular. Change did not occur everywhere at the same time, and local conditions militated against or in favour of the law moving in some particular direction. Above all, individuals made a difference, whether as judges, academics or legislators. It is not practicable to undertake comparative analysis of several systems simultaneously at this level of detail, so in the rest of this

[40] Until 1914 the Sirey reports contained a section dealing with foreign case-law.

[41] For example, E.J. Schuster, 'National Health Insurance in England and Germany' (1912) *Journal of the Society of Comparative Legislation* 11, esp. pp. 24–25.

[42] A. Montel, *Problemas de la Responsabilidad y del Daño*, trans. Juan Roca (Alcoy: Editorial Marfil, 1955).

[43] P.C. Weiler, H.H. Hiatt, J.P. Newhouse, W.G. Johnson, T.A. Brennan and L.L. Leape, *A Measure of Malpractice* (Cambridge, Mass.: Harvard University Press, 1993), 2–6 note that medical liability costs began to rise sharply in the late 1960s. This is illustrated by a rise in the premiums paid by an average doctor in New York from $360 (at 1990 prices) in 1949 to $1000 in 1965 and to $7,500 in 1975.

chapter we examine the development of medical negligence in England and France only.

B *The nineteenth century*

In neither England nor France were doctors and other medical practitioners immune from legal liability for incompetence before 1800, but in each country the nineteenth-century development was substantially grounded on a decision taken in the 1830s.[44] In England the foundation was provided by the observations of Tindal C.J. in *Lanphier v. Phipos*:

> Every person who enters into a learned profession undertakes to bring to the exercise of it a reasonable degree of care and skill. He does not undertake if he is an attorney, that at all events you shall gain your case, nor does a surgeon undertake that he will perform a cure; nor does he undertake to use the highest possible degree of skill.[45]

The equivalent foundation in France was the opinion of Procureur-Général Dupin in *Thouret Nourey c Guigne*. After citing, inter alia, the earlier writings of Domat and Pothier, Dupin stressed that liability was not restricted to situations where the fault of the doctor (or other professional) lay in the performance of a purely mechanical task, and continued:

> It is not a matter of being more or less extensively competent, more or less brilliantly talented, more or less reliable, but only of guaranteeing against carelessness or omission, thoughtlessness, and a crass ignorance of things which one ought necessarily to know and practise in one's profession.[46]

The parallels between the two statements are very marked: a doctor is not required to be a genius, but he is required to live up to a reasonable professional standard. This constitutes a common spine when dealing with

[44] For medical liability before this see A. Trebuchet, *Jurisprudence de la Médecine* (Paris: Baillière, 1834), 183–188; J.W. Willcocks, *The Laws relating to the Medical Profession* (London: J. & W.T. Clarke, 1830), 105–110 (noting that in practice actions had been brought against surgeons and apothecaries but not against doctors). A review of Willcocks's work appeared in French, written by 'A.L.P.' and published in Geneva: British Library, 640.f.32 (8).

[45] (1838) 8 C & P 475, 479, 173 ER 581.

[46] S. 1835.1.401: 'Il ne s'agit pas de capacité plus ou moins étendue, de talent plus ou moins brilliant, plus ou moins solide; mais seulement de la garantie contre l'imprudence, la négligence, la légèrité, et une ignorance crasse de choses qu'on devait nécessairement savoir et pratiquer dans sa profession.' In part the French argument for non-liability depended on the distinction between *officiers de santé* and qualified doctors, the former being expressly made liable for accidents when not supervised by a doctor: art. 9, Law on Medicine of 19 Ventôse An XI (10 March 1803).

medical liability for the rest of the nineteenth century, and both cases continued to be cited well into the twentieth.[47] Both cases, too, can be seen as representing an 'establishment' view of the proper scope of liability.

Some actions against doctors would be straightforward, but others would raise questions of the appropriateness of medical or surgical practice. In such cases, in both countries the evidence of experts might be heard. This had been the practice in England since at least 1767,[48] and in the second quarter of the nineteenth century it was stressed that they should only be testifying as to matters of science and not as to matters of opinion;[49] it was for the jury to decide what weight to give to the evidence and how to assess the defendant's behaviour.[50] This was all established without significant controversy. Matters were different in France. The issue had arisen in 1830 in the *Hélie* case, an action against a doctor who had been assisting at a difficult childbirth and in the course of the delivery had broken both of the child's arms.[51] The *Tribunal Civil* of Domfront approached the Académie Royale de Médecine for an opinion. A commission was set up; this delivered an inconclusive report, but a second commission came down clearly in favour of the doctor. Notwithstanding this, the court gave judgment for the plaintiff. The decision was criticised strongly in the *Gazette des Tribunaux*, and the opinion expressed there was adopted by Adolphe Trébuchet in his *Jurisprudence de la Médecine*, which appeared in 1834.[52] *Hélie* clearly implied that, where there was a difference of opinion between experts, it was for the court to make up its own mind what the doctor should have done. In other words, before treating a patient the individual doctor had to decide not merely which strand of expert opinion was the best, but more importantly which strand of expert opinion would be thought best by the court that might eventually sit in judgment on his conduct. In reaction against this, as the principle of liability became settled after 1835, the French courts came to stress that

[47] France: A. Lacassagne, *De la Responsabilité Médicale* (Lyon: Stirk, 1898), 7, referring to the *rapport* of Dupin as the standard statement of doctrine. In England *Lanphier v. Phipos* is still cited as the fundamental source for the liability of professionals: Michael Jones (ed.), *Clerk and Lindsell on Torts*, 20th edn (London: Sweet & Maxwell, 2010), para. 10.02.

[48] *Slater v. Baker* (1767) 2 Wils. 359, 95 ER 860.

[49] *Campbell v. Rickards* (1833) 5 B. & Ad. 840, 846, 110 ER 1001, 1003 per Denman CJ.

[50] *Carter v. Boehm* (1766) 3 Burr. 1905, 1917, 97 ER 1162, 1168; *Lovatt v. Tribe* (1862) 3 F. & F. 9, 176 ER 5; *Rich v. Pierpont* (1862) 3 F. & F. 35, 176 ER 16.

[51] Dalloz, *Répertoire de Jurisprudence Générale*, vol. 39, s. 129 note.

[52] A. Trébuchet, *Jurisprudence de la Médecine, de la Chirurgerie et de la Pharmacie en France* (Paris: Baillie, 1834), 193–207.

they would not examine questions of scientific judgment, i.e. situations where scientific opinion was divided, taking a view diametrically opposite from that which had activated the Domfront court.[53]

In purely formal terms, therefore, there was a difference between English and French law in that in the former a doctor might be liable notwithstanding that he had acted properly according to one strand of medical opinion, whereas in the latter he could not be. Outside the legal domain proper, a result similar to the French was reached in England: it was said that in disciplinary proceedings before the General Medical Council (established in 1858) a doctor should not be regarded as having been neglectful provided he had acted in accordance with some strand of medical opinion.[54] Why then was English law not tipped into adopting the French rule? The answer appears to be twofold. Most obviously, there was at first no *cause célèbre* like the *Hélie* case which triggered dissatisfaction with the English rule. Secondly, by the time that negligence claims against doctors became relatively frequent, in the 1890s, a substantial number were channelled through the Medical Defence Union (MDU), which had been founded in 1885 to protect doctors against the costs of legal claims against them.[55] Here the practice was to defend cases very robustly (and very successfully) from the start;[56] and where all or most doctors were members of the MDU it might have been difficult for a plaintiff to find anyone who would act as an expert witness against a fellow practitioner.[57] Moreover, in particular as the MDU began to provide insurance from the first decade of the twentieth century, it operated as an agent to settle cases rapidly where it was thought that the plaintiff's claim was well founded.[58] Speculative litigation of the sort which might have triggered a change in

[53] Besançon 18 December 1844, S. 1845.2.602.

[54] R.G. Smith, *Medical Discipline: The Professional Conduct Jurisdiction of the General Medical Council, 1858–1990* (Oxford: Clarendon Press, 1995).

[55] The Medical Defence Union was not the only medical protection society, but it was the most important and its solicitor, Mr William Hempson, became the leading medical lawyer of the day.

[56] R. Forbes, *Sixty Years of Medical Defence*, 2nd edn (London: Medical Defence Union, 1955), 49; C. Hawkins, *Mishap or Malpractice?* (Oxford University Press, 1985), 40–41; *British Medical Journal*, 24 May 1902, 1284. For the explosion of negligence complaints from the mid-1890s, see Hawkins, *Mishap*, pp. 42–43.

[57] See *Willams v. Ward*, *British Medical Journal*, 24 August 1901, 487, where it was said that a Welsh miner was unable to find a single doctor in Wales who was willing to testify for him. Note also p. 505, where the case is characterised in terms of the union of doctors being pitted against the union of mineworkers.

[58] In 1949 it was reported that of the 69 negligence complaints serious enough to pass to solicitors in that year, 39 had been withdrawn, 16 settled, 11 successfully fought in court,

the formal English rule was very effectively discouraged: plaintiffs had to cover their own costs while those of the defendants were covered by the MDU, and defendants were represented by a tenacious lawyer with huge experience in medical work while the plaintiffs would not be.[59] There was insufficient pressure from within or outside the legal community to bring about a legal tipping point.

C *The standard of liability*

In England nothing occurred to displace the rule articulated in *Lanphier v. Phipos*. Although a doctor whose act brought about death would be guilty of manslaughter if he had been guilty of gross negligence, this had no effect on the rule of liability for simple negligence which applied in civil claims: the two systems of liability were completely distinct.[60] That said, in non-formal texts it was occasionally stated that a medical practitioner should be liable for gross negligence. If anything, the negligence principle was strengthened by the passing of the Medical Act in 1858, setting up the General Medical Council. The effect of this was to draw a clear line between the qualified doctor and the unqualified quack; there was a presumption that the former knew what he was doing, so that the proof of any negligence on his part was correspondingly more difficult.

The situation was very different in France, where criminal and civil liability were more closely related. Articles 319 and 320 of the *Code Pénal*, dealing with *homicide* and *blessures involontaires*, imposed criminal liability on a person who killed or injured another through 'maladresse, imprudence, inattention, négligence ou inobservation des règlements' (incompetence, carelessness, lack of attention or failure to respect (legal) rules), essentially the same as the *faute* and *negligence* of articles 1382 and 1383 of the *Code Civil*.[61] Moreover, the system of *parties civiles* meant that

and only two unsuccessfully defended: *British Medical Journal*, 1 October 1949, 752. Of the 267 negligence claims passed to solicitors between 1896 and 1905, only two were unsuccessfully defended: Forbes, *Sixty Years of Medical Defence*, p. 51.

59 In discussion, Lord Bingham recollected that in the 1960s doctors were surprised to lose actions when they were sued.

60 It was not until 1968, even, that a conviction in a criminal court was held to be conclusive in a subsequent civil action: Civil Evidence Act, s. 11. For a clear and early example of the distinction, see Willcocks, *The Laws relating to the Medical Profession*, p. 86 (criminal liability for gross negligence), p. 105 (civil liability by reference to the general and ordinary knowledge of the profession, or the attention which a professional man of ordinary discretion might be reasonably expected to show).

61 Similarly, art. 1320 made involuntary wounding an offence under the same conditions.

criminal courts might be in a position to award damages to the victim; or, in other words, a criminal court might have at its disposal a wide range of penal and compensatory remedies. Since the liability rule was the same, it was held by the Cour de cassation in 1855 that an acquittal in a criminal case would automatically exclude civil liability; it was not open to the civil court to re-open the issue which had already been determined by the criminal court.[62] This decision was strongly criticised by Victor Marcadé,[63] and in 1866 the rule was reversed.[64] Although the same formal test was applicable in the civil and criminal tribunals, there was a continuum of blameworthiness and the judge in the criminal court might look for a greater level of fault than his counterpart in the civil court; hence, it was now said, the acquittal in the criminal suit was not conclusive of the civil.[65] Within the civil courts themselves there was a comparable lack of sharpness: it was stated in the 1860s that where there was a question of liability for a professional failure, as opposed to a situation where the alleged wrong was a non-professional one which happened to have occurred in the course of giving treatment, liability would only arise for *faute lourde*,[66] but any suggestion that what was required was a serious fault was rapidly scotched by its being treated on a par with culpable negligence, obvious lack of skill, and failing to follow the rules appropriate to the treatment being given.[67] What was important, if anything, was that the fault should have been clearly established rather than that it should have been serious in itself.

In formal terms English law required only that the plaintiff show on the balance of probabilities that the doctor had failed to take reasonable care. The standard of care was uncontroversial. It was stressed that there was no guarantee of a cure nor any requirement that the defendant should have had a very high level of expertise, though this was counterbalanced by the oft-repeated statement that the standard might in practice vary according to the circumstances, so that a doctor in a wealthy part of London might

[62] Cass. civ. 7 March 1855, D. 1855.1.81.

[63] V. Marcadé, *Revue Critique de Jurisprudence* (1855) 658.

[64] Cass. civ. 9 July 1866, D. 1866.1.334.

[65] Cass. civ. 27 January 1869 and 21 December 1868, D. 1869.1.169, note Griolet; Cass. civ. 7 March 1874, D. 1874.1.398; Cass. civ. 15 April 1889, D. 1890.1.136; Req. 31 May 1892, D. 1892.1.381; Cass. civ. 30 November 1898, D. 1899.1.74, note Sarrut; Req. 31 October 1906, D. 1910.1.511.

[66] Metz 21 May 1867, D. 1867.2.110; more generally Colmar 10 July 1850, D. 1852.2.196.

[67] Trib. civ. Gray 29 July 1873, D. 1874.5.436; A. Sourdat, *Traité Générale de la Responsabilité*, 3rd edn (Paris: Librairie Générale de Jurisprudence, 1876), § 677 *bis* (not in 2nd edn). Sourdat does require there that the faute is '*certaine et caracterisée*' (*ibid.*).

be expected to have greater knowledge and skill than an ordinary country practitioner and therefore might be found negligent where the country doctor would not be. So far as the burden of proof is concerned, the formal rule was clear, that the plaintiff needed to prove his claim on the balance of probabilities. However, the practice by the start of the twentieth century was to say that a verdict should only be given against a doctor if the claim had clearly been made out.[68] The direction given to the jury by Bucknill J in *Shaw v. Wood* is eloquent: they 'must be absolutely sure that the plaintiffs had made out their case before they could find in their favour; if they had a doubt or anything short of positive certainty the defendant was entitled to their verdict'.[69] In practice, therefore, the law in France and England was to all intents and purposes the same, despite the different verbal formulations in the two systems.

In the years around 1900, the formal rule relating to the standard of care in French public law shifted from *faute lourde* to *faute ordinaire*, though the rate of change differed from one public service to another.[70] This was no more than a verbal shift, and involved no change in the allocation of substantive responsibility. The tipping point was not brought about by any perceived pressure to impose liability on doctors where it had not existed before, therefore; the explanation for the change is external to the law of torts, in the organisation of the medical profession. In 1858, the same year as the English Medical Act was passed, there was founded the *Association Générale des Médecins de France*, followed by a number of more specialised or more localised medical unions.[71] The *Association Générale* had as its main aim the protection of doctors, both through the provision of pensions and sickness benefits and through the extirpation of competition from pharmacists, nuns and priests, and – increasingly – from the *officiers de santé* who had been established in 1804 as a lower rank of medical practitioners.[72] The latter campaign culminated in the abolition of the rank of *officiers de santé* in 1892, and the consequent unification of

[68] *Fursteneau v. Tomlinson*, *British Medical Journal*, 16 August 1902, 496; *Wood v. Bailey*, *British Medical Journal*, 24 June 1905, 1408; *Trinder v. Bridle*, *British Medical Journal*, 1 August 1908, 295; *Stranger v. Wood*, *British Medical Journal*, 27 February 1909, 570.

[69] *British Medical Journal*, 27 February 1909, 570.

[70] M. Hauriou, *La Jurisprudence Administrative de 1892 à 1929* (Paris: Sirey, 1929), vol. 1, 530–540.

[71] J. Léonard, *Médecins de l'Ouest au XIXe Siècle* (Paris: Champion, 1978), 1003–83; *Shaw v. Wood*, *British Medical Journal*, 27 February 1909.

[72] O. Faure, *Histoire Sociale de la Médecine* (Paris: Economica, 1994), 67–75. While doctors were qualified by virtue of their formal medical education, *officiers de santé* were qualified by apprenticeship and were permitted to undertake only a limited range of tasks.

the medical profession.[73] As had happened in England thirty years earlier, the medical man was now presumed to be competent, and the case-law moved explicitly into line with the ordinary negligence standard applicable to other professionals, reflecting Roman law and the dominant doctrinal approach of the late nineteenth century.[74] This explanation of why doctors should be treated like other professionals is made clear in the note of Mérignhac to *Chini c Cocconi*.[75] There remained the issue of the relationship between criminal and civil fault, allied to the practical question of the effect of a criminal acquittal on subsequent civil proceedings. Here, in the second decade of the century, criminal law moved into line with the newly articulated civil rule: any *faute* was sufficient, its gravity being relevant to the measure of punishment rather than the fact of liability, so that the fact of acquittal by the criminal courts on the grounds of lack of fault once again became conclusive in the civil courts.[76]

Around 1900, in both England and France, there occurred two major changes in the provision of medical care. First, there was a greater availability of medical services to the relatively poor. The history of this went back well into the nineteenth century. In England, the Poor Law Amendment Act of 1834 provided for free medical treatment for inmates; and between 1861 and 1901, perhaps following the example of Germany, there was a 14.6 per cent increase in the number of doctors.[77] In France the *loi* of 7 August 1851 expanded the role of *hospices*, which had taken over the provision of healthcare from religious foundations at the time of the Revolution.[78] These *hospices* could appoint doctors, surgeons and pharmacists under article 18 of the *loi* of 31 October 1821, but it was not until 1893 that French practice began to follow that of Germany and

[73] J. Léonard, *La Médecine entre les Savoirs et les Pouvoirs* (Paris: Aubier-Montaigne, 1981), 284–298.

[74] Aix 22 October 1906, D. 1907.2.41, note Mérignhac (constructing a history of the point back to 1895), S. 1909.2.321, note Perreau; G. Baudry-Lacantinerie, *Précis du Droit Civil* (Paris: Sirey, 1926), vol. 2, § 1349; F. Laurent, *Principes du Droit Civil Français*, 3rd edn (Brussels: Bruylant, 1878), vol. 20, nos. 444ff; Sourdat, *Traité Générale de la Responsabilité*, §§ 652ff. The relevance of the ordinary fault standard is emphasised in Cass. civ. 29 November 1920, DP 1924.1.103, affirming Req. 21 July 1919, DP 1920.1.30, note Denisse (which provides a good summary of the earlier case-law), but contrast Paris 16 January 1913, 1913.2.237, which required *faute lourde*.

[75] D. 1907.2.41.

[76] Cass. civ. 18 December 1912 and 12 June 1914, D. 1915.1.17; Cass. civ. 15 January, 24 April and 30 December 1929, D. 1930.1.41, note Savatier.

[77] E.P. Hennock, *The Origin of the Welfare State in England and in Germany, 1850–1914* (Cambridge University Press, 2007), 247–249.

[78] *Loi* of 22 Vendémiaire An II (1793), art. 18; *loi* of 16 Vendémiaire An V (7 October 1796).

England.[79] These developments of the late nineteenth century were one aspect of the greater protection being provided for workers, typified by the legislation of 1898 in England and France.[80] Sometimes treatment was provided and paid for by employers, sometimes by trade unions or similar bodies, and eventually by the state. Outside this, as a matter of charity some doctors or surgeons might treat for free those who could not afford their services. In the first decade of the twentieth century, the surgeon Mary Thorne set aside one day a week to operate on poor women in central London. More normally, however, such medical services would have to be paid for. Where such services were paid for, either directly by the poor or indirectly, this brought about an upsurge in litigation about doctors' negligence, not primarily because the poor were taking the initiative in suing but because they were counter-claiming for negligence when the doctor was suing to recover his (or occasionally her) fees.

Alongside these social changes, medical science experienced a major upheaval towards the end of the nineteenth century. In particular, the work of Louis Pasteur in France and Joseph Lister in England brought about a major revolution in the effectiveness of medical treatment, recognising the centrality of bacteria in the causation of disease, pioneering practices to reduce the risks of infection in surgical operations and childbirth, and triggering the introduction of new treatments for old diseases.[81] The new science created a fissure in the profession, between those who willingly adopted the modern methods and those who were suspicious of them and clung to their old-fashioned ways of doing things, with the latter being more vulnerable to legal action. Expectations of doctors changed, sometimes unreasonably: there was a belief that they should be able to effect a cure, and a greater willingness to blame them if they did not. It was now easier to argue that there had been fault where a practitioner was unaware of developments which had been publicised in the medical literature. This was the background to the formation of the Medical Defence Union in England – legal actions were being brought against doctors, unjustifiably so in the eyes of the profession, and they needed expert defence[82] – though it was only in the mid-1890s that the

[79] G. Pécheyran, *L'assistance Médicale en France et la Loi du 15 Juillet 1893* (Paris: Chevalier-Maresq, 1899), 3–14.

[80] See M. Lobban and J. Moses, 'Introduction', in *Ideas*, pp. 12–13.

[81] B. Latour, *The Pasteurization of France*, trans. A. Sheridan and J. Law (Cambridge, Mass.: Harvard University Press, 1988); W. Bynum, *Science and the Practice of Medicine in the Nineteenth Century* (Cambridge University Press, 1994).

[82] Hawkins, *Mishap*, p. 20. And see *British Medical Journal*, 14 October 1903, 1083, suggesting (from the doctors' point of view) that juries were too inclined to find against medical men.

number of actions began to rise steeply. In France, the distance between doctors' perceptions of themselves and their treatment by the legal system was stark. In 1894 the Académie de Médecine petitioned – unsuccessfully – that doctors should be excluded from the application of article 1382 of the *Code Civil*, and hence be wholly immune from civil liability;[83] at the same time the medical establishment was up in arms against the successful prosecution of Dr Lafitte for bringing about an abortion, when in their view the expert evidence produced to the court tended to show his innocence.[84] Perhaps more telling was the *Laporte* case,[85] where a young doctor was called out at night to assist at a particularly difficult childbirth. He had failed to equip himself with the proper instruments, his manipulation of the instruments he did have (a hammer, a mattress needle and a pair of scissors) was clumsy (the expert witnesses described him as not having operated with the prudence and ability which were desirable), and the mother died as a result of lesions caused by him. On the basis of this interpretation of the evidence he was convicted by the Tribunal de la Seine of *homicide involontaire* contrary to article 319 of the *Code Pénal*, though his conviction was later overturned on appeal on the basis that he was acting in an emergency and had had no opportunity to seek assistance from a doctor with more experience.

D *The twentieth century*

By the middle of the twentieth century healthcare had changed enormously from what it had been at the start of the century. Technology had become increasingly dominant. Any complex procedure with a risk of causing injury would be carried out in a hospital rather than at home, commonly involving a team of specialists rather than a single practitioner. The nature of hospitals had changed: whereas in the nineteenth century they were places where the sick went to die, those suffering from

83 Lacassagne, *Responsabilité Médicale*, p. 5; at p. 3 the whole issue of medical liability is described in terms of the friction between doctors and magistrates. For a similar suggestion in England, drawing the parallel with the immunity of barristers, see *British Medical Journal*, 16 June 1906, 1433.

84 Latour, *Pasteurization of France*, p. 128. See for example (1894) 20(2) *Progrès Médical* 273; (1894) 32 *Annales d'Hygiène Publique et de Médecine Légale*, 349; *Gazette Médicale de Paris*, 15 September 1894, p. 40, 13 October 1894, p. 490; (1894) *Archives Générales de Médecine*, 632.

85 Paris 4 March 1898, S. 1898.2.90, D. 1898.2.449; Taylor, *Medical*, p. 78. Its contemporary importance for the understanding of medical negligence is noted by Lacassagne, *Responsabilité Médicale*, p. 3.

infectious diseases were kept apart from the rest of the community, and the infirm might be kept, after the First World War they increasingly became places where the sick and injured went with the hope of treatment and cure.[86] The hospitals themselves had shifted from being charitable institutions providing unequivocally beneficial services to a local community to being far more like emanations of the state. This was especially so in England after the formation of the National Health Service in 1948, but in France, too, state-run rather than private hospitals were the norm. It followed that such reluctance as there might have been beforehand to bring actions for negligence had been eroded away, for there was no obvious link between the value of any compensation recovered and a diminution of the resources of the hospital.[87] Moreover, this development changed the whole doctor–patient relationship away from an intensely personal one in which the patient was seeking help to a more distant one in which the patient had an expectation that the treatment would be successful. Economic factors, also, changed the legal landscape: as well as the hospitals having apparently deep pockets, by now doctors were invariably insured, and in England the introduction of the state-funded legal aid scheme in 1949 made it far easier for the less well off to initiate lawsuits. In France, too, limited assistance in bringing a claim was available, and there was a ceiling on lawyers' fees. Changes in the courts' approach to vicarious liability added to the depersonalisation of medical litigation: in 1942 it was held, contrary to previous decisions, that a hospital authority was liable for the act of a radiographer working there, and this volte-face was consolidated by the decision of the Court of Appeal in *Cassidy v. Ministry of Health* in 1951.[88] The establishment of vicarious liability did not, however, relieve the doctors of personal liability: there were good practical reasons for joining them as co-defendants, and judges could (and at least in the 1940s did) apportion liability between them and the hospital.[89] In

[86] For the transformation in medical care as an aspect of the war effort, see A. Hardy, *Health and Medicine in Britain since 1860* (Basingstoke: Palgrave, 2001), ch. 2.

[87] It is noteworthy that in England right up to the beginning of the Second World War (and perhaps later too) negligence actions against doctors were still primarily generated by counter-claims against actions by doctors for their fees: *British Medical Journal*, 8 October 1938, 757. Most of these involved medical treatment of the relatively poor, for whom the fees could seem astronomically high. Private treatment of these people almost totally disappeared after 1948; thereafter negligence claims were actively initiated by the disgruntled patient.

[88] *Gold v. Essex County Council* [1942] 2 KB 293; *Cassidy v. Ministry of Health* [1951] 2 KB 343.

[89] Cf *Lister v. Romford Ice and Cold Storage Co. Ltd* [1957] AC 555, upholding the legality of this; but see G. Gardiner, 'Lister *v* The Romford Ice and Cold Storage Company, Ltd.

France, liability was primarily contractual,[90] either because the patient was paying (and being reimbursed by medical insurers) or because medical services were bought on their behalf and they were third parties benefited by the contract. This meant that there was no reason to expand the rules of vicarious liability in order to make hospitals liable for the wrongs of doctors.[91] The hospital became an institution and not just a place within which independent medical practitioners performed surgery and the like, so alongside its vicarious liability for the acts of negligent doctors and nurses there was the possibility of direct liability of the hospital if there were inadequacies in its workings.

These changes had little effect on the formal rules of liability. The English rules were the same in the middle of the twentieth century as in the middle of the nineteenth, with the same cases being cited as authority: the doctor had to take the care which would be taken by a reasonable professional man in his position. The situation in France was essentially the same, though slightly more complex. It was held in 1936[92] that, as a matter of private law, the liability of a doctor to a patient was contractual since there was a contract between them in place; the duty under the contract was an *obligation de moyens*, so that the doctor was only liable for a failure to take reasonable care. The *non cumul* rule therefore excluded the operation of articles 1382 and 1384 of the *Code Civil*. So far as article 1382 was concerned this was a purely technical point, but the exclusion of article 1384 meant that the strict liability for injuries caused by things – by now becoming significant in the road traffic context and elsewhere – had no place in doctor–patient cases. Article 1384, however, was held in 1968 to apply where the doctor's duty was owed to someone other than the patient,[93] and it was argued by Savatier, and subsequently recognised by the courts, that the appropriate contractual duty vis-à-vis the doctor's equipment was an *obligation de sécurité*, i.e. a duty of strict liability:[94] to

(Report of the Inter-Departmental Committee)' (1959) 22 *Modern Law Review* 652, to the effect that it was by then very rare in practice.

[90] Below, p. 102.

[91] P. Giliker, *Vicarious Liability in Tort* (Cambridge University Press, 2010), 63.

[92] Cass. civ. 20 May 1936, *Nicolas c Mercier*, DP 1936.1.88, concl. Matter, rapp. Josserand; Taylor, *Medical*, p. 80. It should be noted that conclusions in this case follow the academic opinions of Professor Josserand who was the reporter judge in the case. This is a good example of the interplay between academic and judicial roles at the time. See also Cass. civ. 15 June 1937, *Le Bail c Le Janne*, and 1 July 1937, *Ménart c Desplats*, S.1938.1.5.

[93] Cass. civ. (1) 1 April 1968, *X c Y*, D.1968.653, note Savatier.

[94] *Ibid.*, presaged by R. Savatier, 'Sécurité Humaine et Responsabilité Civile du Médecin' D. 1967 chr. 35, 42; Rouen, 7 February 1984, *Hanocque c Herbet*, Gaz. Pal. 1984.1.262. See J. Penneau, 'Réforme de la Responsabilité Médicale' (1990) RIDC 525, 532–534.

have held otherwise would have meant that a higher duty was owed to a patient's relatives, and to others who might be affected, than to the patient him- or herself, an obviously unpalatable conclusion. A similar *obligation de sécurité* was later applied to the provision of infected blood for transfusions.[95] The division between public and private law in France meant that cases against public hospitals and the doctors working in them fell into the former category and would potentially be treated differently from purely private law cases, with a lower standard of care being applied; but already in 1935 it was decided that ordinary fault was sufficient to ground liability for non-professional failings,[96] and in 1992 public law finally fell into line with private law in all medical cases, liability being imposed for the failure to take reasonable care.[97]

However, in the years after 1945 in each country there was a very substantial rise both in the number of actions for medical negligence, and also in their success rate, so much so that in England the issue was raised in Parliament in 1953.[98] Two years later, Eddy pointed to the very steep rise in compensation payments made by hospitals in the first five years of the existence of the National Health Service, from £7,500 in 1948/9 to £23,000 in 1950, £38,000 in 1951, £106,000 in 1952, and £153,000 in 1953. Concerns expressed in professional journals at the time show that doctors' personal liabilities were rapidly increasing too. Although the French statistics are less easy to interpret, everything points to the same trend having occurred there.[99]

Although the formal rule of liability for negligence remained through the second half of the twentieth century, there remained a question of what constituted fault. Here the two systems diverged markedly in the 1950s and1960s, gradually moving together after about 1980. In France there was a tendency towards the finding of fault on relatively slim grounds, moving towards an explicit recognition of strict liability in serious cases

[95] CE Ass. 26 May 1995, *Consorts Nguyen, Jouan, consorts Pavan*, Lebon 221. The same result of strict liability had earlier been reached by treating the patient as a third-party beneficiary of the contract between the supplier and the hospital: Cass. civ. 17 December 1954, *Centre Nationale de Transfusion Sanguine* c *L*, D. 1955.269; JCP 1955.II.8490, note Savatier.

[96] CE Sect. 8 November 1935, Lebon 1019.

[97] CE Ass. 10 April 1992, *Epoux V*, AJDA 1992, 355, concl. Legal.

[98] HC Deb. vol. 514 col. 75*W* (23 April 1953). On what follows in this paragraph see J.C. Eddy, *Professional Negligence* (London: Stevens, 1955), 79–81; R. Heilbron, 'When is a Doctor Negligent?', *British Medical Journal*, 28 December 1957, 1540; J.G. Fleming, 'Developments in the English Law of Medical Liability' (1959) 12 *Vanderbilt Law Review* 633.

[99] Taylor, *Medical*, p. 85 note 88.

in the 1990s, whereas in England at first a relatively low standard of care was demanded of doctors, with a reversal in the French direction occurring after 1981.

In England, the early twentieth-century approach of favouring the defendants in medical cases reasserted itself. In particular, Denning LJ influentially reversed what was felt (by doctors at least) to be the pro-patient bias which was developing by re-emphasising that doctors should not be liable for every little mistake. His most eloquent statement of this was in *Hatcher v. Black*:

> [The plaintiff's] counsel had compared her case to an accident on the road or in a factory. That was the wrong approach, because on the road or in the factory there would be no accidents if everyone used proper care. In hospital, where people who were ill came for treatment, there was always a risk no matter what care was used. It would be wrong, and bad law, to say that simply because a mishap occurred, the hospital and the doctors were liable, and it would be disastrous for the community. It would mean that a doctor examining a patient or a surgeon operating at the table instead of getting on with his work would be for ever looking over his shoulder to see if someone was coming up with a dagger. An action for negligence against a doctor was like a dagger which could wound his reputation as severely as it could his body. The jury must not find a doctor negligent simply because one of the risks inherent in an operation had actually taken place, or because in a matter of opinion he had made an error of judgment. A doctor was only negligent when he had fallen short of the standard of reasonable medical care, when he deserved censure.[100]

Two years later McNair J extra-judicially stated that this represented the current practice of the courts.[101] A similar pro-doctor leaning is visible in Scotland at this time. In *Hunter v. Hanley*,[102] although rejecting the suggestion that there was a formal rule that a doctor should only be liable for gross negligence, Lord President Clyde held that liability would arise only if the defendant had adopted a course 'which no professional man of ordinary skill would have taken if he had been acting with ordinary care', further stressing that there was a heavy onus on the plaintiff.[103]

Hunter v. Hanley and *Hatcher v. Black* were the two principal authorities relied on by McNair J in *Bolam v. Friern Barnett Hospital Management*

[100] *British Medical Journal*, 10 July 1954, 105. See also The Times, 29, 30 June, 1, 2 July 1954, [1954] CLY 2289. For similar views, less eloquently expressed, see *Roe v. Ministry of Health* [1954] 2 KB 66, 86–87.

[101] Mr Justice McNair, 'Medical Responsibility in Hospitals' (1956) 24 *Medico-Legal Journal* 129.

[102] [1955] SC 200. [103] [1955] SC 200, 206.

Committee.[104] The principal question here was whether the doctor had been negligent in his treatment of the patient. Medical opinion differed. McNair J directed the jury that the fact that some doctors would have acted differently from the defendant was not in itself sufficient to justify a finding that he had been negligent. That the direction in *Bolam* was capable of two interpretations was immediately recognised by Montrose.[105] On the one hand there was the utterly unexceptionable analysis that the mere fact that other professionals might have acted differently from the defendant was not in itself sufficient to show that he had been negligent. On the other was the more questionable interpretation, that the defendant would necessarily not have been negligent if he had acted in accordance with some strand of recognised professional opinion.

The precise status of *Bolam* in the two decades after it was decided is ambiguous. It was incorporated into textbooks without comment, and so far as can be judged from reported cases, it was hardly cited either in argument or by judges even where we might expect it to have been.[106] The Scots decision in *Hunter v. Hanley* was relied upon, though producing what was later described as a twisted version of the *Bolam* rule,[107] and it is possible that it existed as a weapon in the armoury of defence counsel without leaving any trace in the reports. More likely, though, is that it was effectively ignored because it had no real function: its focus was on the way in which the jury ought to evaluate expert evidence, and as jury trial disappeared (it was already very uncommon in 1957) there was no necessity for judges to deal with this. What was important, simply, was their evaluation of whether the doctor had failed to live up to an appropriate standard of competence, and it did not need any formal rule for the assessment of evidence to achieve this. The traditional rule of liability for failing to take the care which would have been taken by a competent professional remained unchanged, therefore, though the interpretation of what constituted a failure to live up to the appropriate standard of care

[104] [1957] 1 WLR 582.

[105] J. Montrose, 'Is Negligence an Ethical or a Sociological Concept?' (1958) 21 *Modern Law Review* 259; cf. Fleming, 'Developments in the English Law of Medical Liability', at 641–642.

[106] See for example the judgment of Sachs LJ in *Hucks v. Cole* (1968) as reported in (1993) 4 *Medical Law Review* 393, with the comments of Margaret Puxon QC. It is noteworthy that the judgment of Sachs LJ was only published after the so-called *Bolam* principle, that a doctor should not be liable if he or she was following any recognised medical practice, had become controversial: Swain, *Medical*, pp. 43–46.

[107] Margaret Puxon QC, note to *Chapman v. Rix* (1960) (1994) 5 *Medical Law Review* 239, 249.

probably leant in favour of the doctor: Lord Denning MR was quite open about this,[108] and the Pearson Commission noted in 1978 that doctors were less likely to be held liable than were other professionals.[109]

By the 1970s attitudes to negligence liability in England had changed considerably. In *Nettleship v. Weston*,[110] a road traffic case, the Court of Appeal brought to the surface the non-moral nature of negligence liability, and the moral principle behind negligence liability for more than two centuries was supplanted by a more policy-based approach in *Home Office v. Dorset Yacht Co.*[111] and *Anns v. London Borough of Merton*,[112] underpinned by a predominantly victim-orientated sentiment. These changes in the perception of liability had their effect on the courts' approach to medical negligence. A rhetorical shift is at first visible in their judgments, pointing to the very high standards demanded of doctors (and other professionals), without there being any change in the rules or (apparently) in their application. In substantive terms, the turning point in the law came about through two decisions of the House of Lords, *Whitehouse v. Jordan*[113] and *Wilsher v. Essex Area Health Authority.*[114] In the first of these the House of Lords disapproved of the approach of Lord Denning MR in the Court of Appeal, where it had been suggested that no liability should be imposed for an error of judgment. This was perhaps little more than a linguistic trick dependent on the boundary between errors of judgment and negligent conduct, but *Wilsher v. Essex Area Health Authority* was more substantial. Here it was held that the proper standard of care to be legally demanded of a doctor was not to be determined by the experience and skill of the defendant himself or herself, but by the level of expertise and skill which could reasonably be expected of a doctor doing the work that the defendant was doing. Hence, a junior doctor could be held liable if he or she fell below the standard expected of a more senior doctor when

[108] Lord Denning, *The Discipline of Law* (London: Butterworths, 1979), 237–245, saying explicitly that doctors were only liable for gross negligence.

[109] Royal Commission on Civil Liability and Compensation for Personal Injuries (Cmnd. 7054, 1978), vol. 1, para. 284, noting that only 30–40% of medical negligence claims were successful, compared with 86% of other negligence claims; S. McLean, 'Negligence – A Dagger at the Doctor's Back?' in P. Robson and P. Watchman (eds.), *Justice, Lord Denning and the Constitution* (Farnborough: Gower, 1981), 99.

[110] [1971] 2 QB 691; R. Bagshaw, 'The Development of Traffic Liability in England and Wales' in *Traffic*, p. 41.

[111] [1970] AC 1004.

[112] [1978] AC 728; D. Ibbetson, 'The Tort of Negligence in England' in *Doctrine*, pp. 64–65. J. Bell, *Policy Arguments in Judicial Decisions* (Oxford University Press, 1983), 43–53.

[113] [1980] 1 All ER 650 (CA); [1981] 1 WLR 246 (HL).

[114] [1988] AC 1074.

doing work that would normally be done by such a person. Moral blameworthiness had no part at all to play: the standard of care depended in effect on the reasonable expectations of the patient.

Parallel to this de facto lowering of the level of care that might be treated as negligent, the *Bolam* principle, that a doctor who followed a recognised practice would not be negligent even if there were others who thought and acted differently, underwent a transformation. Instead of being a largely ignored approach to the interpretation of expert evidence, it became a rule of substance that a doctor who had followed any approved practice – even if approved only by a small minority – would not be regarded as having been negligent. As put by Lord Scarman in *Maynard v. West Midlands Regional Health Authority*, it was not for the judge to prefer one branch of medical opinion over another.[115] This approach was subsequently deprecated in *Bolitho v. City and Hackney Health Authority*,[116] where it was strongly emphasised that it was part of the function of the judge to decide whether a practice adopted by the defendant was reasonable, not merely to see if there were other professionals who thought it was reasonable. However, the precise effect of this shift remains unclear: the fundamental point remains, that in practice it will frequently be impossible for the judge to determine whether the expert evidence presented on one side is preferable to that presented on the other.[117]

The development of the law in France is rather easier to sketch. As in England, the starting point was a formal adherence to the standard of reasonable care with a tendency to interpret what was reasonable in the interests of the patient.[118] Already in the 1930s in some situations this interpretation of fault was moving the law in practice in the direction of strict liability: when, for example, a surgeon left a swab in a patient,[119] or when X-rays were administered at a level greater than was strictly necessary even though all proper precautions were taken.[120] An inference of fault in cases such as these was unexceptionable, but by the early 1960s similar inferences were being made in more questionable circumstances. In *A c X*[121] the Cour de cassation upheld the judgment of the Paris Cour d'appel against a doctor who had injected his patient in the carotid artery

115 [1984] 1 WLR 634, 640. 116 [1998] AC 232. 117 Swain, *Medical*, pp. 44–45.

118 J. Penneau, *Faute et Erreur en Matiére de Responsabilité Médicale* (Paris: Librairie Générale de Droit et de Jurisprudence, 1973), 101–105; Taylor, *Medical*, 82–84.

119 Paris 29 October 1934, *Chagnon c C*, Gaz. Pal. 1934.2.905; Tribunal civil de la Seine 4 July 1939, *M c LeVaguières*, Gaz. Pal. 1940.1.63.

120 Paris 17 July 1936, *D c F*, DH 1936.498.

121 Cass. civ. 19 June 1962, JCP 1962.IV.110.

in such a way that some of the liquid had settled in the tissues and partially incapacitated her. It was argued that the mishap had been caused by the patient jerking her head, but the expert evidence was that this should not have been sufficient to push the needle off its course. On the facts, the conclusion that the doctor was at fault seems reasonable; but it was justified on wider grounds than were necessary, that the injection would necessarily have been successful if the proper procedures had been followed. In effect, a presumption of fault was being applied simply because the injury had occurred. Coupled with attempts to use article 1384 as a means of imposing strict liability, culminating in the strict (contractual) *obligation de sécurité* for the doctor's equipment after the late 1960s, there was a clear movement towards the raising of the level of care required of doctors, verging into strict liability. In addition, again favouring the compensation of injured patients, from 1965 the French courts reduced the need for full proof of causation by imposing a form of proportionate liability based on the loss of a chance of recovery or of not being harmed.[122]

From the end of the 1980s this tendency towards stricter liability became yet more marked.[123] In both the administrative and civil courts a presumption of liability was imposed where a patient contracted a bacterial disease while in hospital,[124] and the administrative courts (though not the civil) introduced strict liability for *aléas thérapeutiques*, i.e. situations in which harm was directly caused by the medical treatment rather than by the patient's illness.[125] This development fitted with the traditional French administrative law idea of a fault in the service rather than the fault of an individual for whom the service was responsible.[126] Alongside the tightening of liability by the courts, there were moves to reform by legislation. The suggestion that there should be a no-fault system was first moved by André Tunc in 1966. After a number of tentative sallies through the latter decades of the century, the French Government eventually put forward its own proposals, which were enacted in 2002.[127] This law largely put into

[122] Cass. civ. (1) 14 December 1965, *Z c A*, JCP 1966.II.14753, note Savatier.

[123] Taylor, *Medical*, pp. 89–98.

[124] Taylor, *Medical*, p. 90: CE 9 December 1988, *Cohen*, Lebon 431; CE 1 March 1989, *Bailly*, *Responsabilité civile et assurances* 1989, no. 199.

[125] CE 9 April 1993, *Bianchi*, Lebon 127, concl. Daël.

[126] See M. Hauriou, *La Jurisprudence Administrative*, vol. 1 (Paris: Sirey, 1929), 532–533, tracing the first use of the term in the conclusions of Romieu to CE 21 June 1895, *Cames*, S. 1897.3.33, and in case-law to CE 1 July 1904, *Nivaggioni*, Lebon 536. The liability of public hospitals is discussed in terms of fault of the service at this time.

[127] *Loi* of 4 March 2002, *relative aux droits des maladies et à la qualité du système de santé*, as amended by the *loi* of 30 December 2002. For the history of these developments, see

statutory form the changes which had gradually been introduced over the previous thirty or forty years, and introduced a streamlined system for awarding compensation to victims of medical treatment governed by the strict liability regime whether the injury suffered was defined as serious. However, outside these situations the traditional analysis in terms of fault remains, albeit with the tendency towards a high standard of care and the operation of presumptions in favour of the patient.

Although the trajectories of development in England and France were similar, therefore, there were differences in point of detail. In particular, while in France the leaning towards liability continued without a break, in England it was interrupted by a pro-doctor phase between about 1953 and 1980; and in France there was no equivalent to the *Bolam* test's protection for doctors who had followed a recognised strand of medical practice. The differences cannot be attributed to variations in the structures of healthcare, since the two countries were very similar: in both places it could be assumed that the defendant was either an insured doctor or a hospital. So far as the former is concerned, we can attribute the pro-doctor phase in England largely to the dominant role of Lord Denning, whose personal view this reflected. This would not in itself have been enough, of course; in addition, it was important that his opinion could be justified by saying that it was better to focus expenditure on healthcare on the curing of the sick rather than on compensating those who had been injured as a result of risks which were inherent in the whole system. The counter-justification, that the victims of medical misfortune should not be treated differently from those who had suffered injuries on the roads, for example, was no less strong; but it was not so strong as to make Lord Denning's conservative position untenable. It was only when English law moved into its very generally strong pro-plaintiff phase in the tort of negligence around 1980 that the tipping point was reached and the approach of the courts flipped into favouring the position of patients rather than of doctors. At the same time, there was a growing willingness to challenge the privileged position of doctors in relation to medical decisions.[128] In France there was no such dominant pro-doctor figure, and the rule of strict liability for things found in article 1384 of the *Code Civil* and applied most noticeably in the context of road traffic gave a gravitational weight to arguments in favour of no-fault liability which were absent from

C. Evin, 'L'indemnisation des Accidents Médicaux' [2001] *Revue Générale de Droit Medical* 71.

[128] See I. Kennedy, 'What is a Medical Decision?' in I. Kennedy, *Treat Me Right* (Oxford University Press, 1988), 19, 29–31 (a lecture given in 1979).

English law. The latter difference, the absence of an equivalent to *Bolam* in France, is explicable in terms of the difference in trials in the two countries. In England, at least at first, trial might be by jury, and the *Bolam* test was specifically focused on the way in which the jury should be directed when there was conflicting expert evidence given on behalf of plaintiff and defendant. In France, article 302 of the Code of Civil Procedure 1806 provided for only a single court-appointed expert, so clashes of expert evidence could not occur; and since there was no jury it was always a matter for the court to determine what weight it should give to the opinion of the expert, conscious of the possibility that there was a risk that he or she might feel a sense of professional solidarity with the defendant and so lean in favour of the doctor.

E Consent

The greater understanding of the aetiology of disease in the late nineteenth century had little or no effect on the formal rules of liability in either France or England; its real influence was on the way in which fault was assessed within the legal process. But the changes which occurred in medical science in the late nineteenth century involved more than a better understanding of disease and better surgical techniques. There were as well technical breakthroughs, such as the development of X-ray machines and the introduction of radiotherapy. These did have substantial consequences for the nature of legal liability. The problems are well illustrated by two parallel decisions, *Smith v. Pare* in 1904[129] and *Chini c Coconni* in 1906.[130] In the former, the patient suffered from cancer, which was treated with X-rays and high-frequency electric current. When the doctor sued for his fees, the defendants counter-claimed on the basis that there had been negligence in the use of the X-rays, as a result of which the patient had been burned. Lawrance J directed the jury that they should decide first whether or not she had consented to being treated with X-rays, and secondly whether the treatment had been carried out properly. The jury found that there had not been proper consent and that the treatment had been negligently carried out, and judgment was given against the doctor. A similar factual problem occurred in *Chini c Coconni*,[131] heard on appeal in Aix. The plaintiff had injured his leg at work in 1899 and was referred

[129] The Times, 10, 11, 12, 13 May 1904; *British Medical Journal*, 21 May 1904, 1227.

[130] D. 1907.2.41, note Mérignhac (referring specifically to the problems of radiography).

[131] Aix 22 October 1906, D. 1907.2.41 note Mérignhac.

to the defendant doctor. Although it should have been perfectly possible to determine the nature of the injury by using traditional methods, the defendant preferred to use his new X-ray machine to see what it could do. In what the court described as a neglect of all prudence, he subjected the plaintiff to too great a number of sessions of too great a length and failed to take proper account of the technical aspect of the use of the machine; the plaintiff suffered burns. We can identify three issues here. First was the question of causation, whether it had been shown that the defendant's conduct had brought about the burns. On the facts of the case this was not too difficult since the experts' opinion was that there was nothing else that might have done so.[132] Secondly, was it shown that the defendant was at fault in not having acted with the circumspection demanded by the medical knowledge of 1899, a time when far less was known about the side effects of the machine than in 1906? This was more difficult, but on the facts the court was able to say that the conduct was clearly blameworthy by the standards of 1899. Thirdly, and most easily, the court was able to point to the defendant's fault in not warning the plaintiff of the extent of the risks that he was running in allowing himself to be X-rayed repeatedly.

The focus on consent in these two cases is telling. There was nothing strange, of course, in the requirement that the patient should (normally) have consented to the treatment; what was new was the way in which it was being brought into the foreground in cases which were more naturally analysed in terms of improper treatment. It is not difficult to understand why this occurred. In cases involving modern technology or new surgical practices, patients were not in a good position to know whether the doctor had acted improperly, nor to predict whether a court would do so: in cases in England it was not uncommon for jurors to disagree, necessitating a new trial.[133] Whether or not there had been consent was a matter which lay more straightforwardly within the patient's own knowledge, and was a simpler question of fact for the court. It would be wrong to see this as a very early move in the direction of patients' autonomy; it was far more a practical way of getting round what would otherwise have been

[132] A more problematic case, where the court had to decide whether the plaintiff's injury was caused by her pre-existing condition or by the defendant's fault, was D. 1919.2.73 (2nd case).

[133] For a very good example, where the issue at the heart of the case was whether two doctors were at fault in not having sent the patient to be X-rayed, see *Southern v. Skyrme and Thomas*, *British Medical Journal*, 16 December 1905, 1620, 1 December 1906, 1607, 8 December 1906, 1673.

difficult issues of proof. Although from the point of view of the doctor the role of consent was the same in England and France – it was incumbent on him to get the consent of the patient – it functioned slightly differently in the two legal domains.

In England, consent was principally relevant to the lawfulness of the treatment; its absence or insufficiency would make the doctor or surgeon liable in the tort of trespass (or battery). However, from as early as the 1870s the formerly distinct torts of trespass and negligence were beginning to run together, and the claim in an action in negligence might turn out to be based on a failure to obtain a proper consent.[134] Questions might arise as to whether an apparent consent was valid, for example where it had been given by a minor or obtained by fraud, but cases hinging on this were very unusual.[135] There was also room for disagreement as to whether consent had been obtained, and a risk that a lack of consent had not been effectively communicated to the doctor or surgeon. This came to a head in *Cull v. Chance*[136] in 1932, where a letter from a patient's doctor to a hospital, informing them that the patient did not consent to an operation, was negligently mislaid in the hospital. Both the hospital and the surgeon were held liable, the latter only condemned in nominal damages. In the wake of this, the Medical Defence Union introduced standard forms which could be used in hospitals, to be signed by the patient or the person responsible for him or her.[137]

Similar issues arose in France: the consent had to be valid and properly evidenced, and it was not enough for the doctor simply to say that he had acted in the interests of the patient.[138] However, since claims against medical men were all channelled through article 1382 of the *Code Civil*, the patient's consent was legally just one matter to be taken into account in determining whether the doctor or surgeon was at fault. It could therefore be bundled up with other circumstances rather than kept separate as in England. This had particular consequences in cases of cosmetic surgery, where it was said that the full and free consent of the patient might not be

[134] *Maddocks v. Wilson*, *British Medical Journal*, 5 February 1927, 265; *Hatcher v. Black*, The Times, June 29, 30, July 1, 2 1954.

[135] *Crier v. Hope and Currie*, *British Medical Journal*, 17 March 1906, 655 (question of fraud). The issues were discussed by the Medico-Legal Society, under the presidency of Atkin LJ, in 1925: *British Medical Journal*, 2 May 1925, 842, 850.

[136] The Times, 15, 16, 17, 18 June 1932; *British Medical Journal*, 25 June 1932, 1195.

[137] Hawkins, *Mishap*, pp. 181–183, citing the MDU Annual Report for 1933.

[138] Tribunal civil de la Seine, *L c Chavorin*, 16 May 1935, D. 1936.2.9, note Dubois; on appeal, Paris 11 May 1937, DH 1937.340, Gaz. Pal. 1937.2.379.

sufficient to exonerate the defendant, even where the procedure had been carried out faultlessly, since the risks attending it outweighed the minimal benefits to be gained. Hence, radiographers who caused burns while attempting to remedy minor facial disfigurements for young ladies were required to compensate them:[139] it was their *faute* to have undertaken such a dangerous procedure, even at the request of the women themselves. The result of these cases was, effectively, that the risks of cosmetic surgery lay wholly with the person conducting it. This undesirable result was in practice reversed in 1931, in a case where an operation to improve the appearance of the not-shapely-enough legs of a model went wrong.[140] Then, it was said, the consent of the victim should not simply be disregarded in assessing the defendant's fault, but the greater the dangers the more explicit the warnings of them had to be. This perhaps went too far in respecting the wishes of the patient, since there was an element of public policy (*ordre public*) in play too; hence the consent of the patient to a sterilisation operation was not in itself sufficient to exonerate the doctor.[141]

Although the English and French law relating to consent at this period had different foci, as a result of the different structuring of tortious liability in the two systems, there is a sense of their moving in the same direction. In France a medical practitioner was liable if he had done the wrong thing, even with consent. In England, however, it was said that a doctor or surgeon would not be liable if he had done the right thing – if an operation was clinically necessary – even if he did not have consent; provided, that is, he did not have the express dissent of the patient.[142]

The 1930s and 1940s saw a more general tightening up of the rules relating to consent in French law, a development which occurred in the wake of the greater emphasis on the autonomy of the patient as a human

[139] Paris 26 June 1919, D. 1919.2.73; Cass. civ. 29 November 1920, D.1924.1.103. Note that in the former case the experts had had to determine what constituted proper use of the machine at the time of the injuries, several years previously (they decided that it had been used properly).

[140] Paris 12 March 1931, *Le Guen c Dujarrier*, D. 1931.2.141, note Loup, S. 1931.2.129, note Perreau.

[141] Crim. 1 July 1937, S. 1938.1.193, note Tortat; R. Savatier, *Traité de la Responsabilité Civile en Droit Français* (Paris: Librairie Générale de Droit et de Jurisprudence, 1939), no. 786.

[142] See most clearly *Maddocks v. Wilson*, *British Medical Journal*, 5 February 1927, 265: a surgeon who had operated on a woman without gaining her consent defended himself by claiming that he had acted in her best interests. The jury, bringing in a verdict in favour of the surgeon, added a rider that operations should not take place without the consent of the patient, to which Wright J added 'if it can be avoided'. The practical position was captured by Wright J: a doctor who operated without consent bore the risk of satisfying the jury that he had done the right thing in the circumstances.

being in the Code of Ethics (*règlement de déontologie médicale*) drafted in 1930 and published in 1936 by the Confédération des Syndicats Médicaux Français, subsequently incorporated in the formal Code adopted by the Ordre des Médecins in 1947.[143] The principal decision here was the *Teyssier* case, in the Cour de cassation in 1942,[144] where a surgeon was held liable to a patient on whose arm he had operated on the grounds that he had not explained the 'exact nature' of the operation nor properly informed him of the risks involved, even though the operation was one which was objectively beneficial to him. This got close to introducing a doctrine of informed consent, though it was only in 1988 that the details of this began to be fleshed out, first in the context of biomedical research and then more generally.[145]

In England, by contrast, the nature of the consent was hardly touched upon; it all depended on the circumstances. The position was accurately summarised by Lord Nathan in 1957:

> To be an effective answer to a claim for assault the patient's consent must be fully and freely given. In ordinary circumstances, therefore, the medical man, before obtaining consent, should give his patient a fair and reasonable explanation of the nature of the operation or treatment proposed, of its probable effects and of any unusual risks involved in it; for where an inadequate or misleading explanation has been given there is a danger that the apparent consent obtained will be held to be ineffective.[146]

Development beyond this was bedevilled by the lingering legacy of the trespass-negligence distinction. So far as trespass was concerned, it was held in *Chatterton v. Gerson* that the doctor would avoid liability provided that he or she had informed the patient 'in broad terms' of the nature of the procedure intended; there was here no requirement at all of informed consent.[147] The effect of this was to marginalise the tort of trespass, and instead to put weight on the tort of negligence. Here there was room for a more nuanced approach to the responsibility of the doctor, but it was

[143] Médecin de France, 12 October 1936, 948–949; June 1947, 1080; R.A. Nye, 'Médecins, Éthique Medicale et État en France, 1789–1947' (2006) *Le Mouvement Social*, 19, 32–36. (See also www.conseil-national.medecin.fr/article/introduction-aux-commentaires-du-code-225, last visited 8 December 2011.)

[144] Req. 28 January 1942, DC 1942, 64, cf. Req. 30 November 1938, DP 1939.1.49, note Savatier; B. Hoerni and J.P. Bouscharain, 'Arrêt Teyssier de la Cour de cassation, 28 janvier 1942: Quelques Remarques sur une Décision "Oubliée"' (2001) 35 *Histoire des Sciences Médicales* 299–304.

[145] *Loi* 88-1138, 20 December 1988 (on which see D. 1989 chr. 167).

[146] Lord Nathan, *Medical Negligence* (London: Butterworths, 1957), 168.

[147] [1981] QB 432.

channelled through the ordinary rule determining the standard of care required of the doctor. This approach was confirmed by a majority of the House of Lords in *Sidaway v. Governors of Bethlem Royal Hospital*,[148] expressly refusing to adopt the approach found in some American states of imposing on the doctor a duty to disclose to the patient all the circumstances and risks which might have been thought relevant by a 'prudent patient' in order to exercise a free and informed choice, subject to a right to withhold information which would have been psychologically seriously detrimental to the patient if it had been revealed.[149] So long as the standard of care was the *Bolam* standard, the effect of this was to leave it in the hands of the individual doctor to decide what should be disclosed, provided that the decision was one that would be supported by some group of respectable medical practitioners,[150] and even after the decision of the House of Lords in *Bolitho* great weight was still put on the views of such professionals.[151] The important changes which have happened since *Sidaway*, therefore, are changes in what constitutes good medical practice, as evidenced by the detailed guidance given by the General Medical Council emphasising the obligation to give to patients the information they want or need to know.[152] This was reflected in the decision of the House of Lords in *Chester v. Afshar*, where it was accepted that a failure to warn a patient of a small (1–2 per cent) risk of a serious side effect of a back operation constituted a breach of the doctor's duty of care in negligence.[153] The change in the understanding of the doctor–patient relationship since *Sidaway* is clearly visible. Lord Steyn followed the approach of Lord Woolf CJ in *Pearce v. United Bristol Healthcare NHS Trust*,[154] saying that the doctor was under a duty to inform the patient of any significant risk which would affect the judgment of a reasonable patient, effectively following the prudent patient test of *Canterbury v. Spence*.[155] Lord Walker stressed

[148] [1985] 1 AC 871.

[149] *Canterbury v. Spence*, 464 Federal Reporter 2nd series 772 (1972).

[150] For a pre-*Bolam* case, see *Hatcher v. Black*, The Times, 29, 30 June, 1, 2 July 1954, where a doctor who had lied to his patient about the risks inherent in an operation was said to have done exactly what a wise doctor would have done, and was duly acquitted of negligence by the jury.

[151] Above, p. 101.

[152] *Consent: Patients and Doctors Making Decisions Together* (2008), available at www.gmc-uk.org/static/documents/content/Consent_2008.pdf (accessed 11 September 2010). See generally M. Jones, *Medical Negligence*, 4th edn (London: Sweet & Maxwell, 2008), ch. 6.

[153] [2005] 1 AC 184. The principal issue in dispute in the case was whether causation was established; this is not relevant to the present discussion.

[154] [1999] *Personal Injury and Quantum Reports* 53.

[155] [2005] 1 AC 184, paras. [15]–[16].

the human right of the patient to make her own decision, reflecting the focus on personal autonomy in the dissenting speech of Lord Scarman in *Sidaway*;[156] while Lord Hope, though not explicitly following the *Canterbury v. Spence* test, emphasised the fundamental requirement that it was for the patient to make the decision whether to undergo the operation, a requirement necessitating that she should have been informed of the risks she was running.[157] Although there remains some lack of clarity on the law, the practical consequence of the decision in *Chester v. Afshar* is well summed up in the Department of Health's guidance to medical practitioners: 'it is advisable that healthcare professionals give information about all significant possible adverse outcomes and make a record of the information given'.

156 [2005] 1 AC 184, para. [92].

157 [2005] 1 AC 184, paras. [55]–[56].

4

Doctrinal divergence: roads and industrial nuisances

I Introduction

The previous chapter looked at examples of homogeneity in the development of legal systems. The principal common features of the two situations examined were that the social and technological backgrounds against which the systems operated were largely similar, that there were no system-specific rules which were brought into play as product liability and medical negligence crystallised out as defined areas of law, and that there was a flow of legal information across national borders. There was close similarity in the content of legal development, even though it has to be recognised that the changes did not necessarily occur at the same time.

This chapter focuses on two situations where legal rules appear to have diverged from each other, at least in formal terms: liability for road traffic accidents and relations between neighbours in the context of industrial development. The former provides both a long-standing example of divergence and one which shows significant differences between jurisdictions over time, while the latter shows less change in terms of the legal rules themselves but divergence in the way in which tort law and property law related to each other. The social and technological backgrounds are the same – the rise of motor car use and industrial development – though the timing of these varied considerably from place to place, and there was knowledge of what was happening in different legal systems. The major distinctions between these two fields and those examined in the previous chapter are that here there were significant system-specific rules in existence before 1850 and that in both fields the law of tort has played only a subsidiary role.

II Roads

A *The social context*

The problem of road accidents arose with the rapid acquisition of motor cars. The Benz was driven first in 1886, and motor car ownership grew

Table 1: *Motor vehicles in use (thousands)*

	1906	1914	1925	1938	1950	1960	1970
France	26.3	108	821	2269	2150	7180	15645
Germany*	11.3	64.4	254.6	1656	888	5192	14979
Italy		24	117.6	372.6	571	2451	11085
Netherlands		4	31	144	231	779	2902
Spain					172	450	3119
Sweden		3	79.6	219.6	346.5	1324	2448
UK	32	265	913	2527	3290	7015	13209

* West Germany from 1945.

Source: B.R. Mitchell, *European Historical Statistics 1750–1975*, 2nd revised edn (London: Macmillan, 1981), Table G6.

rapidly thereafter. Large scale production was developed from 1895, with France taking the lead. (Legal restrictions on speed and usage in force in England until 1896 hampered the development of the market.[1]) In 1895, there were 350 cars on the road in France and 75 in Germany[2] but the industry grew rapidly, especially because of the introduction of Ford factories in Europe.[3] Speed also increased from 10 m.p.h. in 1886 to 40 m.p.h. in 1901. Table 1 shows the rapid growth in motor vehicles on the roads. The 1920s saw a rapid increase in production and prices fell and so ownership was no longer confined to the elite.

[4] Car production declined markedly because of the economic recession in the early 1930s, but it picked up after the Second World War. The rate of road deaths rose markedly from the 1920s until the 1970s.[5]

1 See M. Ruiz, *One Hundred Years of the Motor Car 1886–1986* (London: Willow Books, 1985), 15.

2 *Ibid.*, p. 16. 3 *Ibid.*, pp. 22 and 51.

4 *Ibid.*, p. 46; O. von Gadow, *Die Zähmung des Automobils durch die Gefährdungshaftung* (Berlin: Duncker & Humblot, 2002), 52–53. S. Bowden also points to the growth of hire purchase as a means of funding car purchase in the 1920s onwards: 'The New Consumerism' in P. Johnson (ed.), *Twentieth Century Britain* (London: Pearson, 1994), 242 at p. 254, recording that in Germany and Italy 75% of purchases were by hire purchase, compared with 60% in Britain and 50% in France.

5 J.J. Leeming, *Road Accidents. Prevent or Punish?* (London: Cassell, 1969), 19, Table 1 shows 96 deaths in motor vehicle accidents per million of the population in 1946, rising to 144 per million in 1961, whereas the death rate in other kinds of accident remained fairly constant (261 per million in 1946 and 242 per million in 1961). France had 90.4 deaths

So the twentieth century was the period of rising ownership and rising numbers of accidents. The contours of the issues were established very quickly, but the pace of development was varied. Spain was very slow in developing and rural countries such as Sweden and the Netherlands saw the growth in motor vehicles mainly after the First World War, whereas urban countries such as France, Germany and the UK saw earlier development of motor car usage. This was most likely because rural roads were not good, nor was there an effective distribution arrangement for petrol in the early years.

The place of tort liability and the parties to tort actions were quite quickly established, even if some issues remained to be resolved more satisfactorily later. There were four main categories of personal injury victims: drivers, gratuitous passengers (typically family members), paying passengers, and other road users (especially pedestrians and cyclists). Only the paying passengers would be able to find a remedy in contract, so tort was the main legal vehicle of redress for those who had suffered injury. So far as defendants are concerned, because the car was a luxury item, many of the first owners were able to employ a driver or chauffeur; hence each legal system had to determine whether the driver or the owner of the vehicle could be responsible for injuries caused by the vehicle.

The legal issue was not new. Roads in towns were congested even in the eighteenth century, and this led to collisions between carriages and injury to pedestrians. There were substantial numbers of pedestrian injuries before trains and cars were invented, and it may be that water transport was more hazardous still.[6] The advent of the train and the motor car increased the risks significantly. Whereas stagecoaches could travel quickly and sometimes overturned, the novelty of railway accidents in

on the roads for every billion kilometres travelled in 1970 but only 8.2 in 2007 (see www.statistiques-mondiales.com/accidents.htm, last visited 28 November 2011). For German statistics see von Gadow, *Die Zähmung des Automobils*, pp. 41–46.

[6] Leeming, *Road Accidents*, p. 22, Table 3 sets out the following death rates in Britain per million of the population:

Type of Accident/ Date	1863–70 Males (Females)	1891–1900	1931–38	1963
Railway	71 (5)	59 (4)	20 (2)	9 (1)
Road	124 (19)	90 (17)	235 (76)	204 (74)
Drowning (water transport)	214 (37)	151 (27)	58 (12)	30 (7)
Total	409 (61)	300 (48)	313 (90)	243 (82)

the nineteenth century and then car accidents in the twentieth was the markedly higher speed of the vehicles and the greater complexity of their mechanisms. This gave rise to five problems:

1. The scale of the accidents – more people might be injured, especially in a railway accident.
2. The speed of the events might make it difficult for witnesses to see reliably what had happened and to provide sufficient evidence.
3. Many of the causes of accidents, particularly those involving cars, would not be just the vehicle, but the environment within which it was travelling: the road surface, the lighting and the weather.[7]
4. The complexity of the mechanisms would make it harder for the conscientious railway company or car owner to ensure that the vehicle was safe before it was used. Was that person really to blame if an injury occurred? Given the novelty of the technologies used in vehicle manufacture, there were bound to be features of the car itself which either contributed to the injury or did not prevent it happening. The dichotomous nature of litigation did not capture this feature fully and help with the apportionment of responsibility.
5. The person responsible for the railway or vehicle would often not be the driver. (The coachman became the chauffeur, and many delivery vehicles were owned by firms.[8]) There needed to be legal mechanisms to ensure that the victim was able to recover compensation from the major person responsible for the activity.

These problems highlighted two legal difficulties. First, is the natural focus of tort law on the driver appropriate? Secondly, how is the claimant going to prove fault or causation when the major evidence is in the hands of the defendant?

B *The place of tort litigation*

1 Tort law and insurance

In 1970, Tunc wrote: 'In France, as in all other industrialized countries, tort liability in the automobile accident field has become a mere infrastructure. In practice, insurers compensate for damages.'[9] The position he

[7] See von Gadow, *Die Zähmung des Automobils*, p. 49.

[8] *Ibid.*, pp. 113–114.

[9] Department of Transportation, *Comparative Studies in Automobile Accident Compensation* (Washington: Dept. of Transportation, 1970) (hereafter *Comparative Studies*), 6.

described of tort playing a subsidiary role was of long standing. Writing in the same collection, Pfennigstorf stated that most accident victims never had to rely on tort damages for compensation. Even as early as 1909, the combination of workmen's compensation, social insurance, and medical and hospital provision ensured that the victim had an immediate recourse to support for personal injuries following an accident.[10] Even in Sweden, where full state medical cover only existed from 1955, there was a substantial voluntary and state provision available from long before then.[11] In some particularly serious motor accident cases, tort might provide some additional compensation for personal injury, but its principal area of application was compensation for property damage. Social insurance and state medical care remain important today, but private insurance is the dominant feature in the compensation landscape.

Private insurance is ubiquitous. It has come to operate together with the tort system in three different ways. First of all, tort law affects insurance, since it provides the framework of liabilities within which insurance operates and, in particular, within which the burden of losses is shifted between funds that provide compensation. But, secondly, the insurance system can also operate with de facto liability rules different from those found within the tort system: in particular, where the investigation of fault is difficult and costly it can be more efficient for insurers to operate 'knock-for-knock' agreements within which victims' insurers compensate losses without any investigation whether someone else might have been to blame. Thirdly, insurance companies wield a good deal of power and hence constitute a highly effective lobby group for and against change in tort law.

Private insurance is not the only mechanism of compensation operating together with tort law. The range of mechanisms for providing compensation can be best seen from the point of view of different victims of road traffic accidents. Whoever the injured party was, by the middle of the twentieth century medical treatment would commonly be available under state-funded schemes. Those injured at work (and travelling to or from work) might fall within the workmen's compensation schemes established in many industrialised countries by 1900 or soon after; in Germany in 1968 about a third of all road accidents were estimated to occur while driving to work,[12] and an Oxford survey in 1968 found that employers

[10] W. Pfenningstorf, 'Analysis of the German Auto Accident Compensation System' in *Comparative Studies*, 33 at p. 37.

[11] See J. Hellner 'Analysis of the Swedish Auto Accident Compensation System' in *Comparative Studies*, 115 at pp. 116–119.

[12] Pfenningstorf, *Comparative Studies*, p. 51.

would nearly always give sick pay to employees, even if the traffic accident injuries occurred outside the hours of employment.[13] Fare-paying passengers would typically be compensable in contract (or in some places tort) on a similar basis to railway passengers. Pedestrians and cyclists falling outside the workers' compensation schemes would be less well protected – hence it was for these groups that a strict tortious liability of drivers was introduced in the Netherlands in 1924.[14] Behind all this there lay insurance: personal loss insurance at first, and increasingly in the twentieth century liability insurance taken out by the motorist. Compensation provided by insurers, even when they were not legally liable, reduced the number of uncompensated victims. As a result, in 1970 Tunc reported a survey suggesting that 95 per cent of pedestrians received compensation, even though only 30 per cent were legally entitled to it.[15] Hellner considered that a similar difference between the tort law position and the actual compensation of pedestrians existed in Sweden at that time.[16]

Private liability insurance was available from the early days of the motor car, but it took some time to become widespread practice.[17] Compulsory motor insurance was gradually introduced across Europe before the European Convention of 1959 covered all countries.[18] The gaps in this cover where the (identified) driver was uninsured were met by funds contributed to by insurers (Britain 1946, France 1951, Germany 1955); in some cases, these became statutory schemes. As Hellner put it, by 1970 most compensation was coming from social insurance, supplemented by private insurance (including motor vehicle liability insurance).[19] Tort was then the final and limited supplement. The widest variety between legal systems lay not in tort, but in the rules on subrogation, enabling one source of funding to obtain reimbursement for compensation paid to another. The availability of recourse by one fund against another, e.g. a social insurance fund against a motorist's liability insurer, did generate

[13] D.R. Harris, 'Analysis of the British Auto Accident Compensation System' in *Comparative Studies*, 65 at p. 89.

[14] C. van Dam and G. van Maanen, 'The Development of Traffic Liability in the Netherlands' in *Traffic*, pp. 132–133.

[15] A. Tunc, 'Analysis of the French Auto Accident Compensation System' in *Comparative Studies*, 1 at p. 7.

[16] *Comparative Studies*, p. 135.

[17] Von Gadow, *Die Zähmung des Automobils*, p. 48 reports that only a third of German cars had liability insurance in 1905, and the position in England was similar: see B. Supple, *The Royal Exchange Assurance* (Cambridge University Press, 1970), 232–237 and 429–433.

[18] Sweden 1929, Britain 1930, Germany 1939, France 1958.

[19] *Comparative Studies*, p. 143.

tort cases and sometimes, notably in France, litigation was protracted and difficult in this area.[20] The existence of alternative modes of compensation reduced the likelihood of claims in tort; moreover, rules requiring the offsetting of collateral benefits might well dissuade victims from bringing tort actions if they had to bring into account the compensation already received from social or workmen's insurance. This was the case in France from 1928,[21] for example, and in England from 1948.[22] Even where no account had to be given, there were two features which militated against tort litigation. The first was cost. Even in 1970, the cost of litigation was noted to be significant in Britain, France, Germany and Sweden.[23] This would dissuade victims (or their insurers) from bringing actions unless very substantial sums were being recovered. The second was that insurers had their own arrangements for settling most cases. In France, from the mid-1960s there was a scheme for settling small claims not involving person injury.[24] In Sweden, most claims and measures of damages were determined by a traffic insurance board; this did not bind the victim, but its recommendations were followed in 98 per cent of cases.[25] Estimates in 1970 were that 0.7 per cent of accident cases went to court in Sweden and under 2 per cent in England.[26] Even where the existence of insurance did not preclude litigation by the victim or the insurer, in practice this seems very rarely to have occurred. This has implications for the judicial development of tort law. On the whole, it was only atypical test cases that would be presented to the courts to resolve key issues, such as the liability for gratuitous passengers, or the liability of owners if they were still in the car with a driver permitted by them to drive.

2 The development of liability rules

In all of the legal systems studied, fault provided the core starting point for the establishment of tortious liability by the end of the nineteenth century. In most systems this had been incorporated into the text of the civil code, but even where there had been no codification there was a strong ideological pull in the direction of fault. This was only the core, however,

[20] Tunc, *Comparative Studies*, pp. 11–12.

[21] *Ibid.*, p. 11. P.-A. Rosenthal, in *Ideas*, pp. 258–259, notes the loss-shifting occurring from workmen's compensation to social insurance after the latter was set up in 1928.

[22] Law Reform (Personal Injuries) Act 1948, s. 2; Workmen's Compensation Act 1897, s. 6 provided that the employer could recoup compensation from a tortfeasor.

[23] Tunc, *Comparative Studies*, p. 13, p. 58; Harris, *ibid.*, pp. 88–89, 145.

[24] Tunc, *Comparative Studies*, p. 4 note 2.

[25] Hellner, *Comparative Studies*, p. 139.

[26] *Ibid.*, p. 145; Harris, *Comparative Studies*, p. 97.

and different systems knew different exceptions to the principle. Strict liability for injuries caused by trains had been introduced in Prussia in 1838 and adopted elsewhere in Germany, eventually being generalised in the Imperial Law on Liability of 1871. The Prussian law was followed in the Netherlands in 1859, though here there was considerable scholarly criticism of the way in which the statutory rule departed from the normal fault principle.[27] In France, strict liability under article 1384 was imposed in relation to boilers and trains in 1896, but initially this was explicitly not applied to cars.[28] (Strict liability had been applied to boilers in administrative law in 1895.) In England, strict liability had been imposed for the escape of dangerous things in 1868,[29] generating a rule whose boundaries were distinctly uncertain. It was against this chequered background that the rules of liability for injuries caused by cars were developed in the twentieth century.

Perhaps the most important precursor was the law relating to injuries caused by animals. Here a distinction was typically drawn, very clearly so in France and Germany, between where accidents were caused by horses and by horse-drawn vehicles. The basic position was that when the horse was being driven by a coachman, then the horse was considered to be only a tool in the hand of a human being and the injury was not the act of the animal. [30] The standard applied here was that owed by the ordinary coachman. By contrast, where the horse was not under human direction, but merely bolted on its own, the injury was considered to be that of the horse.[31] The same applied where the action was that of the horse alone, but human carelessness other than driving gave rise to the conditions causing harm, e.g. overloading of the wagon being drawn by the horse which bolted.[32] Although the liability of the keeper of the animal under the French Civil Code was not initially considered to be based on fault, in the course of the nineteenth century an opinion arose that it should be considered as a presumption of fault which could be displaced by showing that the keeper had not been negligent. (In Germany, this idea fitted

[27] S. Lohsse, 'The Development of Traffic Liability in Germany' in *Traffic*, pp. 80–90; van Dam and van Maanen, *Traffic*, pp. 118–119.

[28] Req. 22 March 1911, DP 1911.1.354, rejecting art. 1384 as a basis for liability and attributing responsibility to fault of the driver.

[29] *Rylands v. Fletcher* (1868) LR 3 HL 330.

[30] RG 21 March 1892, RGZ 29, 120 (before the BGB); RG 6 February 1902, RGZ 50, 180 (applying § 833 BGB). See H. Dernburg, *Das bürgerliche Recht des Deutschen Reichs und Preussens* (Halle: Buchhandlung des Waisenhauses, 1905), 746–747.

[31] RG 20 February 1902, RGZ 50, 219.

[32] Dernburg, *Das bürgerliche Recht*. See also cases below, n. 34.

the similar notion that the fault principle underpinned liability of an employer or other people.[33]) After years of conflicting case-law and doctrinal writing, this view was rejected in 1885 both in France and Germany in relation to animals.[34] Liability of the keeper for animals could only be displaced by showing positively a *force majeure* or act of the victim or of a third party. This duty of the owner was owed both to the coachman as well as to third parties.[35]

We can identify two aspects to the development of motor car liability: the imposition of liability on persons other than the driver of the car, and a shift towards strict or no-fault liability for personal injuries. The former of these was easier, involving making the driver or owner/keeper prima facie liable subject to a defined range of defences indicating a lack of fault; the latter was more challenging, since it involved a complete departure from fault-based thinking. The trajectory of both of these is consistent across Europe, but the means adopted varied from system to system, depending substantially on the pre-existing materials which each system had to work with.

In principle, liability might have been expected to have been imposed on the driver of the vehicle, the person through whose fault the accident occurred. However, since vehicles were expensive, at least in the first fifty years, many drivers would be chauffeurs for others rather than owning their own cars and would not be particularly wealthy. Vicarious liability was a tool for passing liability on to the person best able to bear it. Further considerations applied as car ownership became more widespread. By this time insurance was common, eventually compulsory, but it was the owner of the vehicle rather than the driver who would have taken out the policy; hence the imposition of liability on him or her was an effective route to enable the victim of an accident to get the benefit of the policy. Legal systems can be seen to have adopted two different strategies to achieve this end, either imposing new rules or manipulating existing ones. In Germany and Sweden, where the normal rules of vicarious

[33] See *ibid.*, pp. 710–712 and 746.

[34] RG 11 December 1885, RGZ 14, 316; Recueil Sirey 1897.4.18 (appeal from Rhineland based on art. 1385 French *Code Civil* in force in that territory; Cass. civ. 27 October 1885, S. 1886.1.33, rapport Michaux-Bellaire; G. Viney and A. Guégan-Lécuyer, 'The Development of Traffic Liability in France' in *Traffic*, p. 60. See also Req. 23 December 1879, S. 1880.1.463. Note that the principle of fault re-entered through the 1908 statute amending the BGB in relation to domestic animals: see J. Scherpe, 'Germany' in *Professions*, ch. 6.IV, even though it had been rejected in favour of stricter liability in the Commission creating the BGB.

[35] See RG 11 December 1885, RGZ 14, 316; Cass. civ. 9 March 1886, S. 1886.1.244, rapport Dareste.

liability were narrow and dependent on the master having failed to take care in the selection or supervision of the servant, the matter was dealt with by legislation in the first decade of the twentieth century. In Sweden, legislation of 1906 created liability for the fault of the driver, which the owner or driver could otherwise have avoided.[36] In Germany, a law of 1909 imposed liability on the operator of the car, not the driver, though this was modelled more on the existing liability for trains.[37] It is clear that the problem of owners making use of § 831 BGB to escape liability by showing that the employee was carefully chosen and supervised was a particular concern.[38] Articles appeared as early as 1899 on the topic and a number of leading lawyers at the 26th *Deutscher Juristentag* in 1902 spoke in favour of reform by applying the strict liability under the 1871 railway legislation to motor vehicles.[39] The more limited basis of liability under the 1909 law was a compromise resulting from pressure on the legislature by the motoring lobby.

Where normal vicarious liability rules involved simply a transfer of liability from servant to master, as in England, the employer of the negligent driver would be liable on general principles and there was no need for a legislative solution. There were still difficulties, though, where the driver was not an employee; here the courts expanded ideas of agency so as to make the insured owner liable when the car was being driven by a non-employee for the benefit of the owner.[40] The French law on liability

[36] See S. Friberg and B. Dufwa, 'The Development of Traffic Liability in Sweden' in *Traffic*, pp. 203–204. The position in ordinary law had to be remedied by legislation in the case of railways: *ibid.*, pp. 191–192.

[37] Lohsse, *Traffic*, pp. 93–95 and cf. pp. 81 and 86–87. Swedish legislation on railways began in 1886, though it was not quite so far reaching as the German equivalents: Friberg and Dufwa, *Traffic*, pp. 191–192.

[38] Von Gadow, *Die Zähmung des Automobils*, pp. 43–44 and RG 28 March 1904, *Juristiche Wochenschrift* 1904, 288.

[39] See Pfenningstorf, *Comparative Studies*, p. 35 citing Schriftführer-Amt der Ständige Deputation (ed.), *Verhandlungen des Sechsundzwanzigsten Deutschen Juristentages* (Berlin: Guttentag, 1903), vol. 1, pp. 27–55 and vol. 3, pp. 163–207; R. Millauer, *Die Haftung des Automobilhalters nach geltendem Recht und das zukünftige Rechs-Automobilgesetz unter besonderer Berücksichtigung des bisher ergangenen Rechtsprechung* (Stuttgart: Hess, 1909), p. 93. Von Gadow, *Die Zähmung des Automobils*, pp. 115–121 gives an account of the development of the 1909 Law, and especially on pp. 115–116 discusses the role of Karl Hilse in Berlin academic circles and in the 1902 Juristentag as a prime mover in attempting to have liability for motor vehicles as strict liability for dangerous things, by way of analogy with railways.

[40] R. Bagshaw, 'The Development of Traffic Liability in England' in *Traffic*, p. 48. See for example *Ricketts v. Thomas Tilling Ltd* [1915] 1 KB 644 (unauthorised driver); *Jefferson v. Derbyshire Farmers Ltd* [1921] 2 KB 281 (unauthorised action by employee); *Pratt v.*

for things followed the provisions of article 1385, imposing liability on the 'keeper' of the thing, who would generally be the owner.[41] In French public law, without a similar legislative provision, the general provisions of vicarious liability were applied, and the driving of a vehicle was considered a *faute de service*, rather than a *faute personnelle*, thus giving rise to state liability.[42]

There was nothing inevitable about this development, in which systems with narrow fault-based vicarious liability rules adopted legislative solutions to make car owners liable, while those with broader principles of vicarious liability or with strict liability for things simply used their existing mechanisms. In Spain article 1903 of the *Código Civil* imposed liability, inter alia, on employers for the wrongs of their workers, with the proviso that the employer could exonerate himself by showing that he had taken the care of a *bonus paterfamilias* in the selection and supervision of the worker.[43] The Spanish situation was, therefore, equivalent to that in Sweden and Germany, but it was not until 1995 that the legislature intervened to affix liability on the owner of a vehicle, despite having been urged to do so before this.[44] From the 1950s, though probably not before,[45] the courts minimised the significance of the requirement that the employer have been at fault by holding 'for social convenience' that very strong proof of lack of fault was needed to rebut the presumption of fault embodied in article 1903 of the *Códgio Civil*, and in general ways were found to impose liability on owners – who were likely to be insured by this time – under article 1903 or under the general principle of fault in article 1902. None the less, the lateness of the courts' intervention, and a fortiori that of the legislature, is striking. Why should it have been that the tipping point reached in Germany and Sweden in the first few years of the twentieth century

Patrick [1924] 1 KB 488 (owner not driver); Paul J. Taylor, *Bingham and Berryman, Motor Claims Cases*, 12th edn (London: LexisNexis, 2008), ch. 6. For the problems with the law on vicarious liability, see D.W. Elliott and H. Street, *Road Accidents* (Harmondsworth: Penguin, 1968), 198–201.

[41] Cass. ch. réunies 2 December 1941, *Connot c Franck*, DC 1941.1.369, 402.

[42] See TC 8 February 1873, *Blanco*, DP 1873.3.20 concl. David (a carriage accident); CE Ass. 28 July 1951, *Laruelle et Delville*, Lebon 464; *Revue de Droit Public* 1951, 1087, note Waline.

[43] In this respect the Spanish law was identical to that of the French *Code Civil*, but in Spain there was no equivalent to the strict liability for things of the French Civil Code, art. 1384.

[44] I. Gonzalez Pacanowska, 'The Development of Traffic Liability in Spain' in *Traffic*, pp. 185–186.

[45] The first case seems to have been STS 24 March 1953, RJ 1953\913.

was not reached in Spain until much later – nearly a century in the case of the liability of the car owner, and fifty years to establish a presumption of fault? We may point to two principal reasons. First there was the relatively low rate of car ownership in Spain before the middle of the twentieth century, coupled with the relatively low level of industrialisation. Secondly, but no less importantly, nineteenth-century Spanish law knew nothing like the Prussian/German railways laws of 1838 and 1871, or the Swedish law of 1886 which made the operator liable for the driver's negligence without proof of fault in selection or supervision. There was no seed around which the wider principle of owners' liability could crystallise. Instead, liability for car accidents followed the general moves in Spain towards objective fault as a way of getting close to strict liability. Presumptions of fault and treating breaches of administrative regulations as fault were devices in this expansion of the scope of fault liability.[46]

The second aspect of the twentieth-century European development was the shift in the direction of strict liability for personal injuries. While all systems moved in the same direction in the course of the century, they used a variety of mechanisms: reversals of the burden of proof, something which was already well known in some contexts in the various civil codes; strict liability for things; the formal enactment of strict or no-fault liability; a victim-orientated understanding of what constituted a failure to take reasonable care. Each step taken involved the making of choices from the available menu of options. The result was a range of different structures of liability rules.

In England, the formal rules of liability at the end of the twentieth century were identical to those at the end of the nineteenth: the defendant was liable if and only if he or she had failed to take reasonable care in all the circumstances. The rule was exactly the same as that framed by judges, before the motor car had been invented, to deal with injuries caused by horses and carriages, and which had been applied already to railway trains.[47] The fact that the rule remained static over this period does not mean that it was simply never questioned. In *Wing v. London General Omnibus Company*[48] in 1909 it was argued that where a bus skidded on a road surface which was greasy from rain the case could be analysed within the tort of nuisance, where a rule of strict liability might

[46] See M. Martín-Casals and A. Ruda, 'The Development of Legal Doctrine in Spanish Tort Law' in *Doctrine*, pp. 200–203.

[47] Bagshaw, *Traffic*, pp. 38–39. [48] [1909] 2 KB 652.

have applied. The Court of Appeal rejected this, holding that liability could only arise within the tort of negligence, and hence only where it was proved that the driver had been negligent. Looking back on this decision three-quarters of a century later, Spencer commented, 'In some ways, the decision that the use of a motor-vehicle on the highway involves fault rather than strict liability is the most significant event in the history of the law of tort this century.'[49] Similarly, in the 1920s it was argued that since there was a statutory requirement that a car should 'be in such a condition as not to cause, or to be likely to cause, danger to any person on the motor car or on the highway', it followed that where a car was not in such a condition the owner should be liable to anyone who suffered injury as a result of the defect, without any requirement to prove fault. Again, this argument was rejected by the Court of Appeal and the fault principle reinforced.[50] This has remained the law, explicitly and strongly restated in *Snelling v. Whitehead* in 1975 and *Mansfield v. Weetabix* in 1996.[51] Behind this, however, although there was consistency in the formal rule that the defendant was required to take reasonable care, by about 1970 there were indications that the standard of reasonable care demanded had in fact become very high.[52] Meanwhile, outside the courts, there were arguments that a no-fault system of compensation for road accidents should be introduced, with proponents including the most influential legal academic of the time, Arthur Goodhart, and the Lord Chief Justice, Lord Parker.[53] The Pearson Commission, too, recommended in 1978 that a system of no-fault liability for road accidents should be introduced, but nothing came of this. On the one hand there were concerns that changes in this direction would increase the costs of motoring; they were therefore politically unpalatable at a time when a general election was impending. On the other, those who supported more radical change in tort law generally were unwilling to support a limited change which would have favoured one group of accident victims and not others. Similar reasons lay behind the foundering of

[49] J.R. Spencer, 'Motor Cars and the Rule in *Rylands v. Fletcher*: A Chapter of Accidents in the History of Law and Motoring' [1983] *Cambridge Law Journal* 65, 79.

[50] *Phillips v. Britannia Hygienic Laundry Co. Ltd* [1923] 2 KB 832; Bagshaw, *Traffic*, pp. 40–41.

[51] *Snelling v. Whitehead* (1975) [1998] RTR 385; *Mansfield v. Weetabix* [1998] 1 WLR 1263. It is noteworthy that *Snelling v. Whitehead*, despite being a decision of the House of Lords, was not reported at the time.

[52] *Nettleship v. Weston* [1971] 2 QB 691; *Roberts v. Ramsbottom* [1980] 1 WLR 823.

[53] P. Bartrip, 'No-Fault Compensation on the Roads in Twentieth Century Britain' [2010] *Cambridge Law Journal* 263. Proposals for no-fault liability were being made as early as the 1930s.

later proposals for the formal implementation of a no-fault scheme. The move towards strict liability, therefore, took place behind the façade of fault; the inertial weight of the negligence principle was too strong for the judiciary of the second half of the twentieth century to displace,[54] and there was insufficient political will for any formal change in the law.

At the opposite extreme was Sweden. In all of the systems, the developments of the law occurred against the background of the growth of insurance, and in particular the imposition of rules of compulsory insurance. But in Sweden the role of insurance was dominant.[55] Already in the first decades of the twentieth century, it had moved towards the introduction of a system of compensation for the victims of road accidents outside the normal framework of tort liability, encapsulated in statutes of 1906 and 1916. However, although the framework was different, liability was still based on fault, though with a reverse burden of proof. In effect, there was a presumption of liability unless the defendant could show that the plaintiff's injury had been caused neither by a defect in the vehicle nor by the fault of the driver. Compulsory insurance by the owner was introduced in 1929, and the first attempt to restructure the whole of the law relating to traffic accidents within the framework of insurance law was made in 1938. This came to nothing, but after the Second World War there was a major thrust towards the reform of the law in the Scandinavian countries. So far as the reform of road traffic law was concerned, the dominant figure was the Swedish Ivar Strahl, whose ideas influenced debates in the United States in the 1950s, channelled through Ehrenzweig.[56] The thrust of the recommendations of the reform committee on road traffic was that compensation should be channelled through insurance without any reference to tortious fault. The victim should have a direct claim against the insurer, hence allowing the driver/owner to recover and not just those injured by him or her. The exceptions contained in the 1916 statute (no liability where the car was stolen, or where the damage was not caused by a defect in the vehicle or the fault of the driver) were to be abolished, so that liability was separated from fault. Nonetheless, even against the background of enthusiasm for reforming the law in order to achieve socially desirable results, the bill proposing the changes did not succeed.

[54] The judges in *Snelling v. Whitehead* and *Mansfield v. Weetabix* (above note 51) were not opposed to the granting of better protection to the victims of road accidents, but believed this was a matter for the legislature rather than the judiciary.

[55] Friberg and Dufwa, *Traffic*, pp. 203–222.

[56] See in particular I. Strahl, 'Tort Liability and Insurance' (1959) 3 *Scandinavian Studies in Law* 199.

It was not until 1974 that the proposals were resurrected, significantly on the initiative of the insurance industry and taking into account the movement towards liability without fault in the USA and Canada. This led to the enactment of the Traffic Damages Act in 1975. Under this Act, vehicle insurance is compulsory and the victim of an accident simply makes a claim to the vehicle insurer. The Act completely replaces the previous law. The Act contains some ideas familiar from tort law – especially the liability of the person causing the accident for fault.[57] But fault liability is now placed within a framework of insurance-based compensation, even if the level of appropriate compensation was fixed by reference to tort law.

In France the courts were able to play a more significant part in the move away from fault liability.[58] By the end of the nineteenth century the courts had confirmed that article 1384 of the *Code Civil* imposed liability without proof of fault for injuries caused by things.[59] This was not at first applied to road accidents, since the immediate cause of the accident was likely to be the negligence of the driver of the car rather than some defect in the car itself, but it was argued strongly by leading scholars that strict liability should apply here, and this line of argument was taken up by the Cour de cassation in the *Jand'heur* decision in 1930.[60] Thenceforth road accidents were taken outside the domain of fault liability. The problem in France was not the fixing of prima facie liability, but ensuring that the injured victim actually received compensation: there were still formal legal hurdles standing in the way of injured parties, and weaknesses in the system of insurance. A governmental commission to examine the system of compensation for road accidents was set up in 1964, though it was only in 1985, in the *Loi Badinter*, that major reforms were introduced. The dominant figure leading the demands for change in this period was the comparative lawyer André Tunc, who in 1964 had presented an *avant-projet* to remove traffic accidents totally from the law of delict. Tunc had spent time in the United States in the 1950s and was familiar with the work of scholars such as Keeton and O'Connell arguing for the replacement of the law of tort with a system of insurance. This was not in itself sufficient to trigger the reforms; the tipping point was achieved only by a

[57] Friberg and Dufwa, *Traffic*, pp. 215–216.

[58] Viney and Luégan-Lécuyer, *Traffic*, pp. 53–69.

[59] Cass. civ. 16 June 1896, *Oriolle, Guissez et Cousin c Teffaine*, S. 1897.1.17, note Esmein; DP 1897.1.433, concl. Sarrut, note Saleilles. This followed the lead of French administrative law: CE 21 July 1895, *Cames*, S. 1897.3.33, note Hauriou. See Y. Salmon, 'Technological Change and the Development of Liability for Fault in France' in *Technology*, p. 108, at 110–113.

[60] S.1930.1.121, note P. Esmein.

radical decision of the Cour de cassation in 1982,[61] based on the pro-victim opinion of Advocate-General Charbonnier that the cost of accidents should be borne by drivers and their insurers. This decision led to a good deal of uncertainty, with some judges following it and others refusing to do so, so that the legislature was effectively forced to act.

German law at the start of the twentieth century was very strongly focused on fault under § 823 BGB, reflecting the practice of the courts in the nineteenth century. It did not have anything equivalent to article 1384 of the French *Code Civil*, though it did have a model of strict liability in the 1871 Imperial Liability Law for railways.[62] The problems faced by the victims of road accidents were soon recognised: Millauer, writing in 1909, for example, pointed to the difficulty faced by the person trying to establish fault when machines were complex and the speed of events was such as to surprise driver, victim and witnesses.[63] After some years of debate, proposals first mooted by the legal profession in 1902 were enacted in the Motor Vehicle Act of 1909. This introduced a regime analogous to that already existing for railways, imposing strict liability on the keeper of the car unless it could be shown that there had been an inevitable accident which was not due to a defect or technical malfunction of the vehicle; similar liability applied to the driver, though only for injuries caused by his driving. In practice, the courts interpreted the test of inevitable accident very narrowly, thereby mirroring the English development towards a strongly victim-orientated interpretation. As a result of this, proposals for legislative changes were received half-heartedly (again as in England), and it was only in 2002 that any major amendment of the 1909 Act was introduced, replacing inevitable incident with a narrower *vis maior* in order to ensure compensation for children who had run into the road from behind parked cars. Under § 8(1), the 1909 Act only provided for compensation to those outside the vehicle, so that an injured passenger who wished to sue the custodian or driver had to rely on the fault liability of BGB § 823. In addition, § 12 established a statutory ceiling on compensation and no allowance was made for damages for pain and suffering. To get compensation in excess of the statutory ceiling or for pain and suffering, the victim had to rely on fault liability within the Code. Again,

[61] Cass. 2 civ. 21 July 1982, *Desmares*, D.1982.449, concl. Charbonnier, note Larroumet.

[62] Lohsse, *Traffic*, pp. 91–103.

[63] R. Millauer, *Die Haftung des Automobilhalters nach geltendem Recht und das zukünftige Rechs-Automobilgesetz unter besonderer Berücksichtigung des bisher ergangenen Rechtsprechung* (Stuttgart: Hess, 1909), 90–91.

as in England, the courts moved towards a form of strict liability here by interpreting fault in the interests of the victim.

In the first half of the twentieth century the development of the law in the Netherlands[64] tracked the German law very closely, and it is likely that there was some direct influence. Strict liability to other road users was introduced by legislation in 1924, leaving claims by passengers and the like to be dealt with under the general fault provision of article 1401 of the BW. The wording of the Dutch statute, however, was significantly different from the German, allowing the defendant to escape liability only if he could show *vis maior* rather than the broader inevitable accident: the problems thrown up in German law by child victims did not arise in the Netherlands. The case-law applying this provision reflected the development elsewhere in Europe, as the Hoge Raad adopted an increasingly narrow interpretation of what constituted *vis maior* and hence an increasingly strict view of liability. Intellectually, too, there was a change in the perceived justification for this stricter liability, away from an analysis expressed in terms of a presumption of fault to one based on the fact that the driver had, by the simple act of driving a car, increased the risk of injury to other road users. The same pro-victim tendency was visible in those cases where fault liability applied, culminating in the *Crossing Deer* case of 1983,[65] where the Hoge Raad held that a driver would be treated as legally blameworthy whenever a perfect driver might have chosen a safer course of action, even where it was recognised that he was not morally blameworthy for having acted as he did. From the 1960s there was a clear movement towards no-fault liability on the model of the French *Loi Badinter* of 1985. This was advocated by leading academic lawyers familiar with the current ideas both in Europe and North America, and formed the basis of a number of reform proposals. However, as in England, all of these proposals failed as the political will to enact them evaporated away. Instead, it was left to the Hoge Raad to take the lead in strengthening the liability regime. While it is impossible to identify individual contributions to the jurisprudence of the Hoge Raad, it is likely that a dominant role was played by Wouter Snijders, the driving force behind the attempts to amend the law by legislative means, and perhaps also Auke Bloembergen, the Leiden professor who was one of the first academic lawyers to press for reforms in the system of compensation and later a member of the civil chamber of the Hoge Raad.

[64] Van Dam and van Maanen, *Traffic*, pp. 132–149.
[65] HR 11 November 1983, NJ 1984, 331.

Spanish law looks more conservative.[66] The tort provisions of the *Código Civil* were very similar to those of the French *Code Civil*, with the notable exception that there was nothing paralleling the French article 1384 potentially imposing a general strict liability for injuries caused by things.[67] Nor did nineteenth-century Spanish law have any strict liability for railway injuries on the model of the 1838 Prussian law.[68] A reverse burden of proof was imposed where injuries were caused by animals, [69] but in the early years of the twentieth century the Tribunal Supremo refused to apply this by analogy to car accidents.[70] It followed that liability depended on proof of negligence under the general rule of article 1902. Spanish writers, however, were familiar with the developments in France and Germany and open to influence from them, and from 1943 there was a shift in the approach of the Tribunal Supremo, reversing the burden of proof in favour of the victim of the accident.[71] This was probably not a great step in the seminal case – the defendant driver was in breach of the Traffic Code and his conduct was the only plausible cause of the injury to a cyclist – but over the next twenty years it was built on the basis that the driver had brought about an increase in risk.[72] While there had to be clear proof of care to rebut this presumption of negligence, and hence a relatively strong pro-victim standpoint towards negligence liability, the Spanish courts did not go quite as far as Germany or the Netherlands in their very narrow view of what constituted *vis maior*. Legislation of 1962, with a strong focus on providing compensation for the fault-free victim of the road accident, aimed to consolidate this and link it to a system of compulsory insurance; but the resulting rise

[66] González Pacanowska, *Traffic*, pp. 173–185.

[67] The provision on liability for things was copied from the French Civil Code in earlier drafts of the Spanish Civil Code, but it did not find its way into the final draft: see D. Florencio Garcia Goyena, *Concordancias, motivos y comentarios del codigo civil español* (Madrid: Imprenta de la Sociedad Tipgráfico-Editorial, 1852), vol. 4, pp. 253–254. That commentary suggests that the liability for things and for persons was understood as a presumption of fault.

[68] See M. Martín-Casals and J. Ribot, 'Technological change and the development of fault liability in Spain' in M. Martín-Casals (ed.), *Technology*, 227, 231–233; González Pacanowska, *Traffic*, pp. 167–169.

[69] Código Civil, art. 1905.

[70] STS 27 October 1909, *Colección Legislativa. Jurisprudencia Civil*, 1909 no. 35; González Pacanowska, *Traffic*, pp. 174–176.

[71] STS 31 October 1943, RJ 1943\856. It is probably significant that the majority of the pre-1943 cases were dealt with in the criminal division of the Tribunal, as was common in Spain for claims to compensation for personal injury. The use of the civil division made it easier to break with the earlier tradition.

[72] *Colección Legislativa. Jurisprudencia Civil*, 1963 no. 354, discussing the decision of 1943 and the subsequent cases.

in insurance premiums was unpalatable, and the impact of the Act was reduced by imposing a relatively low level of compulsory insurance. This was alleviated somewhat by the raising of the level in line with European directives in 1986, and by the tendency of the Tribunal Supremo to apply the statute by analogy to cases where optional insurance had been taken out above the level of compulsory cover. That said, the operation of the statute has been described as 'frequently confusing',[73] involving a mixture of ideas of strict liability and negligence.

A further way of moderating the impact of fault occurred in most systems, altering the rules on contributory fault. At the beginning of the period in England, the 'last chance' approach had the effect that fault of the victim could remove his or her entitlement to recovery altogether. The approach was based essentially on strict notions of causation. The move to comparative fault made a considerable contribution to recovery for victims, but this did not happen in England until 1945.[74] In France and under the German law of 1909, fault of the victim was judged by the same criteria as primary fault of the driver. The Netherlands started with a similar position, but then narrowed the scope for this defence to situations in which the driver could not reasonably have foreseen the act of the victim.[75] In the 1990s, this was further restricted in relation to pedestrians and cyclists, road users who would not normally have insurance, a trend that had also been seen in France in the 1980s.[76] In the same period, Spain also restricted the scope of this defence on the part of the car driver, since it was shifting loss onto a person who was not insured.[77] Finally, German law restricted the impact of fault of the victim to cases of *force majeure* in 2002, thereby removing the problem of child victims who had been unable to recover under the earlier 'inevitable accident' test.[78] Thus we have a situation in which contributory fault of another driver remains an accepted defence, but that of the pedestrian or cyclist (who is probably not insured) becomes a defence only where it is unforeseeable.

Comparing the developments in these different systems, it is possible to see four distinct factors at work, each interacting with the others. First is the importance of the pre-existing rules in shaping later developments. These affected the ease with which changes could be implemented by the judiciary, most clearly visible in the way in which French law was able to introduce strict liability by the use of article 1384 of the *Code Civil*.

[73] Gonzalez Pacanowska, *Traffic*, p. 180. [74] See Bagshaw, *Traffic*, pp. 42–43.
[75] Van Dam and van Maanen, *Traffic*, p. 138. [76] *Traffic*, pp.139 and 66.
[77] Gonzalez Pacanowska, *Traffic*, p. 184. [78] Lohsse, *Traffic*, pp. 101–102.

They also affected the way in which statutes were framed and the receptivity of the legislature to proposals for their enactment, as seen in the developments of German and Dutch law by analogy with the antecedent rules relating to railway accidents. Secondly, the extent to which initiatives were taken by the courts was related to the perceived need to do so: the greater the intervention of the legislature, the less the pressure on the courts. As well, though, the way in which they were able to develop the law depended on the institutional framework of their system. In England, with a commitment to a strong doctrine of precedent, there were effective constraints on judicial creativity, whereas in countries such as France and Spain, where the commitment to following previous cases was weaker, judicial creativity was so much the greater.

Thirdly, perhaps most importantly, there was the unpredictability of the legislative process. In particular the economic crises of the 1930s and 1970s made it difficult for states to contemplate additional public expenditure on no-fault compensation schemes. Outside the law, but impacting on it, were social and economic factors such as the ease of credit determining whether those who were not wealthy could afford to buy cars, the number of car accidents and the ability of motorists' organisations and insurers to lobby politicians: factors such as these were important in, for example, the relatively slow development of strict liability in Spain. Most importantly of all, the rate and nature of change were related to the availability and forms of insurance. England's retention of fault liability, for example, can only be understood against a background of a very effective insurance system: already by the mid-1920s some 90 per cent of drivers were insured, and a rule of compulsory insurance was introduced in 1930. The creation of the Motor Insurers' Bureau in 1946, by agreement between insurers, made legislation unnecessary to compensate victims of identified but uninsured drivers, and this was further expanded voluntarily to cases where the driver was not identified. Alongside this, state insurance in the shape of social security benefits and free healthcare provided protection for injured parties, again minimising the need for a no-fault insurance scheme. Knock-for-knock arrangements between insurers provided swift resolution of cases without going to court (it is estimated that only 1 per cent of claims arising out of road traffic accidents went as far as a court judgment). Similar insurance practices and requirements existed elsewhere in Europe, always feeding in to the development of the formal liability rules.

In addition, and right across the countries surveyed, the development of road traffic liability benefited from considerable input from doctrinal legal writers. Particularly after the Second World War, when academic travel became more practicable, these writers constituted an informal international network, the members of which influenced each other. Most importantly, scholars such as André Tunc in France, Arthur Goodhart in England and Ivar Strahl in Sweden were channels through which both theory and practice from the USA and Canada were disseminated across Europe.[79] As well, though, going back as far as the latter years of the nineteenth century and the beginning of the twentieth, ideas of liability for risk-creation rather than the causation of harm were being discussed within Europe. This was most visible in France, where scholars such as Saleilles and Josserand promoted consideration of ideas which were then thoroughly unorthodox; Josserand was especially important since he later became a member of the Cour de cassation. These ideas were included in commentaries, and through these they encouraged the imposition of strict liability in the *Jand'heur* decision in 1930.[80] The baton was picked up by Picard in the 1930s, and then by Tunc from the 1950s after a stay in the United States, culminating in the *Loi Badinter* of 1985.[81] As Viney and Géguan-Lécuyer point out, the debate had advanced so far as to be really between the supporters of social insurance (the solution found for workmen's compensation in 1898 and for medical accidents in 2002) and a direct insurance-based system. It was the latter that prevailed, for various reasons connected with the place of legal and insurance lobbies in France.[82] The contrast with England, where these ideas made little headway, is very marked. From the 1960s scholarly writing explored the ideas which had advanced so far in France, but even where they were formulated by Goodhart or Parker – men of enormous influence within the legal establishment – practically nothing came of them. We cannot attribute this simply to the fact that scholarly opinion was by no means unanimous about them, which would have been the case elsewhere in Europe too. Far more significantly, in France *la doctrine* occupied a dominant place in legal reasoning whereas in England it was far more marginalised.[83] Everywhere else in Europe doctrinal writing had greater importance than in England, though its weight tended to be more visible through its influence on legislation rather than on the courts.

[79] See *Institutions*, pp. 7, 8, 25, 99.

[80] See the reference in the (successful) conclusions of Advocate General Matter, DP 1930.1 at 66; cf. the note from the lower court by G. Ripert, DP 1927.1.97, and the divergent views of others cited there.

[81] Viney and Géguan-Lécuyer, *Traffic*, pp. 61–65.

[82] *Ibid.* [83] Above, pp. 70–71.

C *Explaining change*

1 Regulatory law

If the development of tort law has to be understood against the background of insurance, so too it has to be set against the background of road safety. It is clear that the reduction in accidents resulted from very different legal interventions: three areas in particular might be noted. In the first place, drivers were screened by requiring driving licences and driving tests, and they were also subject to criminal law rules on driving, such as speed limits. A major reason for the reduction in deaths on the roads has been the control of drinking alcohol before driving. Secondly, from the very early years, the state prescribed minimum conditions for the design of vehicles to go on the road and manufacturers incorporated additional safety features as a selling-point for their products. These have become increasingly extensive. For example, airbags and seatbelts have become compulsory and reduced the impact of accidents. Thirdly, there have been considerable improvements in the quality of the roads on which vehicles travel. Improved surfaces, lighting, road signs and traffic management systems have been responsible for structuring the flow of traffic and reducing accidents. Tort law does not play a role in any of the three, but breach of the rules set out in each of the three areas can lead to tort liability.

In relation to road accidents, we see a new social problem which was quite similar across the legal systems both in time and in character and consequences. The function of tort law was also similar – to provide compensation and to make the user of the vehicle internalise the costs of the harm that it caused. Whilst, in practice, social and private insurance and voluntary payments typically provided most victims with compensation, tort law provided a framework both within which insurance operated and which allowed the cost of compensating victims to be shifted between the various types of insurer. This did not lead to the formulation of new tort rules in many countries, perhaps the reverse. England, France and Spain remained with existing texts until very late in our period. On the other hand, Sweden, Germany and Italy enacted new texts before 1914 and the Netherlands soon after. It is clear that the overriding concern everywhere was to enable victims outside the vehicle to obtain compensation, against the background of the difficulty of proving fault which was everywhere recognised. That meant that there was an issue about what the plaintiff had to prove. Knowledge was with the owner or driver, and so much effort was expended in arranging ways of making the person with knowledge bear the burden of disproving fault, rather than leaving the victim with the entire burden. Whereas English courts were keen to ensure that the particular action of a motor vehicle was evidence of fault,[84] other systems created a more structured presumption of fault arising from the very act of the thing (the vehicle). These were clearly differences in technique, but not significant differences in policy up until after the First World War.

There continued to be a debate, even in Germany and the Netherlands, in the 1920s and 1930s about whether the basis of liability was fault or risk. By the 1940s, risk had become the accepted basis in Germany, France, Italy, Sweden and the Netherlands, at least for motor vehicles. This was reflected in judicial interpretations and in academic writings. England and Spain were outliers, but for very different reasons. Spain was different because the pace of its growth in car ownership made the move from fault less urgent. In England, there was a resistance as a matter of policy to any departure from the ideas that were current and well known coupled with the strong constraint on judicial creativity flowing from the operation of the doctrine of precedent.

If we ask when were the tipping points in the development of liability for road accidents, the answer appears to be typically three key periods. The first is around 1910. It is clear from the dates of significant changes in the law that the initial pressure for reform was typically caused by the number of accidents in the early years of road traffic. Accidents were increasing at what was perceived to be an alarming rate. For example, in 1907 there were three accidents for every 22 vehicles on the roads in Germany. By 1910, the number of cars had grown by 50 per cent, but the accident toll had doubled.[85] With very rapid increases in car ownership, the number of accidents, particularly involving uninsured pedestrians and cyclists, became very significant. It was a novel and highly visible problem. Sweden, Germany, Austria and Italy all legislated in this first period. In a second period after the First World War, the number of cars grew very quickly, helped in part by the number of soldiers trained to drive during the War, by the cheaper costs of production, and by the growth in available credit. These created pressure on legislators to provide solutions. For the most part, legislators responded by traffic control measures and by compulsory insurance, the former designed to reduce accidents and the latter to increase the probability of the victim receiving compensation. Through legislation, the Netherlands did catch up on its neighbours in the 1924 law on motor vehicle accidents involving pedestrians and cyclists.

[84] *Wing v. London General Omnibus Co.* [1909] 2 KB 652; above, p. 122.

[85] Lohsse, *Traffic*, p. 93 note 66; von Gadow, *Die Zähmung des Automobils*, p. 46.

Meanwhile the French courts extended tort liability by extending strict liability to road accidents in 1930. But calls for more sweeping legislation were resisted in France, Germany and England. The third tipping point is the 1960s when vehicle numbers increased as did accidents. This period led to renewed academic interest in no-fault schemes, and to legislation in Sweden and Spain. Judicial interpretations in France, England, the Netherlands and Spain all become more pro-victim in this period.

If those are common problems, then the question arises why in England and France legislators were slower in reacting. In France, there were political problems related to the stability of governments, which made parliamentary legislation difficult, and led to other forms of legislation, e.g. in introducing driving licences by way of presidential decree.[86] The British Parliament was active in passing road traffic legislation, on the regulation of roads and on insurance requirements, but the compensation for road accidents never became a major topic of government concern or of significant debate among Members of Parliament. In both France and England, fault was preferred by the courts initially, since the accident was seen as the act of the driver and this was the framework within which liability for acts was traditionally conceptualised.[87] By contrast, members of the Dutch Parliament (though not the Government) were able to generate sufficient interest for legislation in the Netherlands.[88] Thus the actors involved in law reform and the intensity of their activity varied from country to country. But it would be wrong to attribute this to a 'culture', a typical approach to solving problems. Rather, there are political dynamics found in each country at particular times, such as the strength of motorist and insurance lobby groups, as well as the standing of particular individuals who proposed reforms. The pattern of the enactment of compulsory motor insurance reinforces this analysis. There was a measure of capriciousness in all of this; certainly the dynamics of legal change did not follow patterns of legal families.

2 Path dependence

The developments in the techniques and the policies used to deal with road accidents in each legal system can mainly be explained by two vectors. The most important was the analogy with liability for the accidents on railways. It is typical for lawyers to reason by analogy, and so the

[86] This procedure for enacting the rule was challenged in CE 8 August 1919, *Labonne*, Lebon 737.

[87] France: Req. 22 March 1911, S. 1914.1.213; on England, see Spencer, 'Motor Cars'.

[88] Van Dam and van Maanen, *Traffic*, pp. 132–133.

alternative to using the personal fault of the driver was either liability for animals or liability for railway engines and steam traction engines. The problem with liability for animals was that it depended on the dangerousness of the animal and, in any case, it was not applied to normal accidents caused by the horse and cart or horse and carriage, which were still in use for many years alongside the new motor car, initially the preserve of the rich. Accidents caused by a horse-drawn vehicle gave rise to liability on the basis of the fault of the driver or the vicarious liability of the owner in all systems, so it was difficult to use the liability for dangerous animals in relation to motorised vehicles. That left the analogy of railway accidents. The problems of the difficulties of proof in relation to complex and fast machines had arisen in relation to railway engines and in relation to steam-powered traction engines. In the countries studied here, different solutions had been adopted for railway accidents and that tended to dictate the way in which road accidents were handled.

The account of the development of the 1909 law on road traffic accidents in Germany makes it very clear that the 1871 Imperial Law on liability for railways was the reference point for discussion on liability for car accidents. While it was not copied exactly, there were specific reasons peculiar to road traffic situations why it was modified.[89] The Dutch road traffic liability law of 1924 was inspired by the railway law of 1875[90] and the Swedish preoccupation in 1906 with making the owner liable for the driver reflected a similar preoccupation in relation to railways in 1886. In England, liability for driving horse-drawn carriages was based on fault and this was applied to railway engines, steam traction engines and to cars, when they eventually came along. As has been noted,[91] attempts to use other bases of liability for traction engines and cars failed. Spain had used fault liability for railway accidents and so it was natural that it did the same with regard to motor vehicle accidents. Only the substantial increase of accidents in the 1960s led to a strict liability system, which followed foreign models.[92] In France, judicial decisions basing civil liability on article 1384, paragraph 1 started in respect of steam-powered boats and this was extended to railway engines by 1919 and eventually to cars by 1924. Contractual liability to passengers became strict in relation to boats in 1911, trains in 1913 and to cars in the 1920s.[93] French law aligned the solutions in the different forms

[89] Lohsse, *Traffic*, pp. 94–97. [90] Van Dam and van Maanen, *Traffic*, p. 129.
[91] Spencer, 'Motor Cars'. [92] Gonzalez Pacanowska, *Traffic*, pp. 163–168, 174–176.
[93] Viney and Géguan-Lécuyer, *Traffic*, pp. 54–56.

of transport around duties of security in contract and strict liability for things in delict, both of which were risk based.[94]

There are thus analogies with railways in terms of the legal techniques used to deal with road accidents, but also in terms of policy. The paradigm shift from attention on the driver (typical in relation to animal-drawn vehicle accidents) to attention on the vehicle (typical in railways) made it easier to establish rules of strict liability. The further move towards the socialisation of the consequences of injuries had not occurred on the railways, except in relation to the major victims, the employees with workmen's compensation in the period 1884–1910, the very period in which motor vehicles were emerging. With so many individuals driving their own car after 1920, the analogy with workmen's compensation was not appropriate and was not argued. It required a social welfare state in Sweden to provide the context for such a reform in the 1970s and a particular social welfare approach in France for their reforms of 1985.

There was a strong interconnectedness of legal systems in dealing with railways and this carried over into dealing with road traffic. The Prussian law of 1838 was based on English experience and, in turn, provided a model for the Netherlands and Italy. It is clear that the German law of 1884 on workmen's compensation (which included railway workers) provided a trigger and model for most other legal systems in the ensuing twenty-five years. Obviously cars could not be confined to a single country and so references to other countries became a staple of any system's approach to this new problem. Outside the area of compensation for accidents, the International Road Congress that met in Paris in 1908 was a significant point of exchange of ideas. So the problems associated with road transport were international matters from a very early date. But for the most part international agreements focused on the regulation of road vehicles and, later, on the documentation that drivers had to carry when moving from one country to the next.

Foreign models were cited in leading French cases in relation to contractual liability in rail transport[95] and in relation to delictual liability, e.g. in the arguments of the reporter Judge Le Marc'hadour in *Jand'heur*[96] and in the legislative proposals in France in 1985. But these models were encouragements to adopt a French solution, rather than to import a foreign model. Germany provided an explicit point of reference for the Netherlands in respect of both railways and roads, and this was a stronger comparative

[94] *Ibid.*, pp. 57 and 70–74.

[95] Viney and Géguan-Lécuyer, *Traffic*, pp. 55–56.

[96] DP 1930.1 at p. 64.

reference, based on a country with more experience in the area.[97] As in many areas, Spain was influenced by France, Germany and Italy in its debates in the 1930s and these ideas influenced the courts and eventually the legislator in 1962.[98] Sweden had modelled itself on foreign systems in relation to railway liability in 1886,[99] but in relation to cars it developed its own solutions, pushed in the first place by its own specific rules on vicarious liability and then by the inspiration of its own social welfare system. If anything, the points of reference were fellow Nordic countries, rather than other European countries.[100] Even the English refusal to adopt no-fault schemes was justified by the absence of sufficiently persuasive foreign precedents.[101] It is clear that Sweden and France were influenced in their no-fault schemes by ideas in the United States.[102] Indeed, ideas in the United States in the 1920s were discussed in many of the academic works in France and Germany. The Netherlands has considered Germany and the 1995 reforms in Belgium as a reference point for more recent debates on no-fault liability. As Gelter and Siems argue,[103] there are typical patterns of citation from other jurisdictions. But there are at least two features involved in the choice of the country to which reference is made. On the one hand, there is the country within the cognate legal family. Thus the Netherlands cited Germany, and the Nordic countries develop their own collective solution, whilst Spain cites Italy and France. But there is also the element of prestige. Some countries were considered advanced: in particular Germany (for the Netherlands, Italy and Spain) and the United States. Ideas could be used from countries that had confronted the problems before the rest of Europe. But, since most of the solutions influenced by foreign laws were to be adopted by the legislator, then local acceptability was also important.

Comparison also came through European and international agreements on motor car insurance and through insurance companies. These companies were not limited to one country but crossed borders.[104] As a result, they were able to influence opinion in a variety of countries.

[97] Van Dam and van Maanen, *Traffic*, pp. 129 and 133.

[98] Gonzalez Pacanowska, *Traffic*, p. 177.

[99] Friberg and Dufwa, *Traffic*, p. 191.

[100] *Ibid.*, pp. 206–207, 211.

[101] Bartrip, 'No-Fault Compensation'.

[102] Friberg and Dufwa, *Traffic*, p. 205 note 59, Viney and Géguan-Lécuyer, *Traffic*, p. 65; cf. also debates in England such as T. Ison, *The Forensic Lottery* (London: Staples, 1967), ch. 6 and see Bartrip, 'No-Fault Compensation' at pp. 272–273.

[103] M. Gelter and M. Siems, 'Networks, Dialogue or One-Way Traffic?' (2012) 8 *Utrecht Law Review* 88.

[104] M. Leimgruber, 'Accidental Crossings', paper for the European Social Science History Conference 2006.

Again, these cross-national experiences were of more significance in relation to road traffic regulation than in relation to accident compensation. The licensing of drivers and vehicles at a national level made it relatively straightforward to have national-specific approaches to insurance premiums, depending on the peculiarities of national law.

III Relations between neighbours and responses to industrialisation

A Social context

In many ways the problems of relations between neighbours were not so very different in the nineteenth and twentieth centuries from what they had been in earlier centuries. Gordley summarises the situation: 'The problems are the same everywhere. If the solutions are different – and often they are not – the reason is not a difference in culture or policy but that the problems are difficult and there is an understandable confusion as to how they might best be solved.'[105] His explanation suggests that a pragmatic search for solutions leads to different results because the problems are intractable. There is no obvious right answer and so individual legal systems experiment with what seems to be the most fruitful line of development for their own system. These solutions become part of the law of the individual systems, leading to a model of inevitable diversity due to constant experimentation.[106]

This analysis has undoubted explanatory force, particularly if the problem is stated at a high level of abstraction in terms of a person interfering with the enjoyment of land intending to harm a neighbour and situations where he did not.[107] At that abstract level, the problems have been with us for a long time and are practically universal. But if we ask the question about the extent to which neighbours should have to tolerate smells or pollution from industrial premises, then we have a problem which is not the same as in an agricultural economy which is supported by artisanal labour. Similar issues did arise from artisanal activity, from potters and their kilns or tallow chandlers and the smells associated with their work, but such problems were quite localised. The scale, intensity and potential persistence of noxious industries of an industrial era were altogether different. A copper smelting works might poison trees over a wide area. So, whereas the formulation of the rules might remain the same and even, at the highest level, the statement of the problem might remain the same,

[105] *Neighbours*, pp. 1–2. [106] Below, p. 179. [107] *Neighbours*, p. 3.

the real impact was different in the industrial era where nuisances might have effects over a far greater distance, exacerbated by the phenomenon of rapid urbanisation, which brought more people within the range of the nuisance. In England, for example, in the middle of the nineteenth century the common law had to address problems caused by pollution and industrial development using the tool of the old tort of nuisance, as the system of local regulation, which had for centuries operated well, began to fail. So too in Spain, where much of the background to the 1889 Civil Code was of an agricultural economy with craft workshops on the fringes of cities like Madrid, for which local regulation sufficed.[108] By 1889, more national solutions were needed to give greater consistency. That said, there was a marked contrast between England, where industrialisation was early and intense, and Spain, where the relative lack of industrial development relieved the pressure on the legislature and generated fewer debates in the courts.[109]

The essential background to the development of the law across Europe lies in the pace of change of urbanisation and industrialisation in different countries through the nineteenth and twentieth centuries.

Table 2 on the growth of cities shows the varied rates of growth in urbanisation between countries and between cities within the same country. France, England and Scotland had much earlier rates of urbanisation than Spain, Italy and the Netherlands. But it is clear that the middle of the nineteenth century was crucial for the fast industrialising countries.

Whilst France and the United Kingdom had an early start to their industrialisation, Germany and Italy were much later. If we look at the problems with which tort law is concerned, then there is a substantial increase in urbanisation already at the beginning of the period of our study in 1850, but industrialisation and the problems associated with it are more concentrated in France and England. It is unsurprising therefore that English and Scots law and French law were adapting to urbanisation and industrialisation in the period leading up to 1850, with a number of leading decisions dating from this period.[110] The German problems and

[108] A. Masferrer, 'Relations between Neighbours in Spanish Law 1850–2000' in *Neighbours*, 173 at pp. 177–178.

[109] *Ibid.*, p. 181 notes that there was little legislation and fewer cases before the courts than in more developed industrial countries.

[110] J. Morgan, 'Technological Change and the Development of Liability for Fault in England and Wales' in *Technology*, 40 at pp. 41–43; Salmon, *Technology*, pp. 93–97; G.D.L. Cameron, 'Neighbourhood Liability in Scotland 1850–2000' in *Neighbours*, 132 at pp. 135–138, 156–160.

Table 2: *European urbanisation*

City	Population (thousands)							
	1800/1	1850/1	1880/1	1900/1	1920/1	1930/1	1950/1	1970/1
France								
Lyon	110	177	377	459	460	460	471	523
Marseille	111	194	360	491	586	610	661	889
Paris	547	1053	2269	2714	2907	2891	2850	2489
Toulouse	50	94	140	150	175	195	269	370
percentage rate of increase*		186	207	121	108	101	102	100
Germany								
Berlin	172	419	1122	1889	3801	4243	3337	3208
Dresden	60	97	221	396	529	642	522	566
Frankfurt/Main	48	65	137	289	433	556	532	670
Munich	40	110	230	500	631	735	832	1294
percentage rate of increase		216	247	180	175	114	85	110
England								
Birmingham	74	233	437	523	922	1003	1113	1015
London	1117	2685	4770	6586	7488	8216	8348	7452
Manchester	90	303	462	645	736	766	743	543
percentage rate of increase		251	176	137	118	109	102	88

Scotland								
Edinburgh	83	202	295	394	420	439	467	454
Glasgow	77	357	587	776	2052	1093	1090	897
percentage rate of increase		349	158	133	211	62	102	87
Italy								
Milan	135	242	322	493	836	992	1260	1724
Rome	163	175	300	463	692	1008	1652	2800
percentage rate of increase		140	149	154	160	131	146	155
Netherlands								
Amsterdam	201	224	326	511	642	752	804	820
Rotterdam	53	90	153	319	511	582	646	671
percentage rate of increase		124	153	173	139	116	109	103
Spain								
Barcelona	118	175	346	533	710	783	1280	1745
Madrid	160	281	398	540	751	834	1618	3146
percentage rate of increase		164	163	144	136	111	179	169

* This relates to the average percentage increase of the selected cities from the country in question compared with the previous period.

Source: B.R. Mitchell, *European Historical Statistics 1750–1975*, 2nd revised edition (London: Macmillan, 1981), Table B4.

Table 3: *Industrial production (1913 = 100)*

	1850	1865	1880	1900	1913
France	33.5	39.9	49.4	67.9	100
Germany	9.5	16	26	61	100
Italy		33	42	61	100
UK	28	37.3	50.3	80.1	100

change came mainly after 1850.[111] Social change created problems which the law had to deal with, whether by re-interpreting existing civil law rules or by creating new regulatory rules.

B *Threads in the development of legal rules*

The legal issues thrown up by these phenomena were substantially the same from place to place, though with time lags reflecting the different rates of urbanisation and industrialisation. The variations in the mode of response were largely the result of how the problems were categorised and how they could be incorporated into the existing legal frameworks. On the one hand they could be seen as questions of property rights, especially the extent to which one person's activity on his or her land should be allowed to impact on others' enjoyment of their land. On the other hand, they could be seen as questions of tort, giving compensation for injuries flowing from the noxious activity; and within the law of tort there was room not only for arguments rooted in the mainstream of fault liability but also for arguments based on the Roman delict of *iniuria*, deliberate acts hurting another. Here there was a tension within the Roman law: on the one hand there were texts such as D.50.17.151, according to which a person who exercised his own right did no wrong to another, and on the other D.47.10.44 saying that the exercise of a right for the purpose of injuring another was an actionable *iniuria*.[112] The different categories interacted with each other, producing a patchwork of legal structures to reach very much the same results.

[111] A. Thier, 'Disturbances between Neighbours in Germany 1850–2000' in *Neighbours*, 87 at pp. 91–93, 95.

[112] For the tension in Roman law see S. Riccobono, 'La Teoria dell'Abuso del Diritto nella Dottrina Romana' (1939) 5 *Bullettino dell'Istituto di Diritto Romano* (NS) 1; A. Valiño, *La Aemulatio en el Derecho Romano: Su Examen en Sede de Relaciones de Vecindad y de Calumnia Procesal* (Santiago de Chile: Instituto de Historia del Derecho, 2002).

The problem of balancing the property rights of neighbours was not a new one. In the pre-industrial age the focus was on the property itself: rights of support, rights of way, rights to light and other servitudes. Legal issues were largely dealt with by asking whether the act of the alleged wrongdoer had interfered with the alleged victim's rights. The same mode of analysis could be used when dealing with problems of incommensurable uses – one person's peace is shattered by another's factory – but there was no clear approach to say where the balance should be struck. A famous text from the Digest had dealt with the question whether any action could be brought where smoke from one person's cheese shop interfered with a neighbour,[113] and a seventeenth-century English case had dealt with the stench emanating from a neighbour's pig-sty;[114] but it was in the eighteenth century that these questions became centrally important. This was noted by Lord Kames in relation to *Kinloch v. Robertson* in 1756:[115]

> The connection of close neighbourhood in a burgh introduces new duties among the inhabitants. Neighbours in town must submit to ordinary inconveniences from each other; but they must be protected against extraordinary disturbances, such as may render their property useless to them, or at least uncomfortable. Close neighbourhood introduces this temperament in equity, but not in such a manner as to deprive his neighbour of the use of his property. The only difficulty in matters of this kind is to bring this temperament under a general rule. If this cannot be done, the matter must be left to the discretion of Judges; *for when a man exceeds just bounds in the use of his property, justice demands a remedy.*[116]

The difficulty was to know what were the just bounds in the use of the property.

It is in Germany that we see these problems channelled most clearly into the law of property. Building on the Roman law, especially as interpreted by Bartolus and Caepolla,[117] by the beginning of the nineteenth century an action was allowed to a landowner whose property rights were interfered with by emissions from his neighbour's land. His primary remedy would be the *actio negatoria*, the denial of the defendant's right, but where the injury was done deliberately, as an act of *aemulatio*, damages might also be claimed through the *actio iniuriarum*.[118] The balancing of neighbours' rights took place primarily within the *actio negatoria*, and was encapsulated in §§ 903, 906 and 1004 of the BGB. The approach was

[113] D.8.5.8.5. [114] *Aldred's Case* (1610) 9 Co. Rep. 57 77 Eng. Rep. 816.
[115] (1756) Morison's Dictionary of Decisions 13164.
[116] Italics added by Cameron, *Neighbours*, pp. 134–135.
[117] Gordley, *Neighbours*, pp. 4–5. [118] Thier, *Neighbours*, pp. 89–90.

similar in the Netherlands in the nineteenth century, using the prohibition on interfering with the property rights of others in article 625 of the 1838 BW. In the twentieth century the conceptual focus shifted to the tortious remedy of article 1401 NBW, but the substance of analysis did not change at all since all depended on the unlawfulness of the defendant's behaviour. [119]

English law was completely the reverse, and in the nineteenth century began to influence Scots law in this respect too. Here the predominant legal mechanism was the tort of nuisance, which had probably originated as a proprietary remedy in the twelfth century but which had largely been absorbed into the law of torts in the sixteenth.[120] As elsewhere in the law of property, from the sixteenth century the common law had tended to use tortious actions to test proprietary rights, so when issues relating to balancing incommensurable land use grew with the onset of industrialisation it was the law of torts, in the form of nuisance, that was primarily called upon.

French law used a property analysis, but its focus was more on the rights of the active owner to exploit his or her lands to the maximum extent rather than on the rights of the passive owner to be maximally free from interference.[121] Moreover, since its list of servitudes had been established by law in articles 640–682 of the *Code Civil*, French lawyers in the nineteenth century did not have the flexibility of their German counterparts to expand on this. Other routes had to be found. One was to bring the relations between neighbours within the conception of *faute* of article 1382, such that any activity by one landowner which improperly interfered with a neighbour's enjoyment of his or her land was in itself a *faute* triggering liability. Liability of this sort for *troubles de voisinage* was created before 1850,[122] and by 1865 it was treated as a well-established head under which to claim for smoke or noise caused by industrial activities.[123] The difficulty, inevitably, was to work out what interferences were improper. Attempts by scholars to give shape to this area of law were not notably successful, and in practice appellate courts treated it as a question

[119] A. Verheij, 'Fault Liability between Neighbours in the Netherlands 1850–2000' in *Neighbours*, 107 at pp. 110–112.

[120] D. Ibbetson, *Historical Introduction to the Law of Obligations* (Oxford University Press, 1999), 98–106.

[121] French *Code Civil*, art. 544. The same approach to property is found in some German writers too: Gordley, 'Immissionschutz, Nuisance and Troubles de Voisinage in Comparative and Historical Perspective' (1998) 6 *Zeitschrift des Europäischen Privatrechts* 13, 17.

[122] DP 1845.1.13 (citing decisions since 1843).

[123] DP 1850.2.56; DP 1860.2.116; DP 1865.2.144.

of fact to be decided by the court of first instance.[124] It was not until 1907 that the Cour de cassation took on itself the mantle of making decisions, in the wake of an article by Henri Capitant and the doctoral thesis of Georges Ripert.[125] Parallel to this, by the middle of the nineteenth century the absolute nature of property rights under article 544 was qualified by a general requirement that rights must not be abused, such that article 544 could not be relied upon where the defendant had acted specifically to disturb the neighbour. The roots of the abuse of rights doctrine lay in pre-Napoleonic law, and were traceable back to Justinian, and even though there was no specific reference to it in the *Code Civil* it was immediately treated as still being part of the law.[126] By the second half of the century it was being used routinely in a property context, exemplified most clearly in a decision of the Court of Appeal of Colmar in 1855, allowing an action against a landowner who had erected a dummy chimney on his roof for no purpose other than to injure his neighbour.[127]

A similar mid-position combining both proprietary and tortious reasoning is represented by Spain.[128] Articles 552–593 of the *Código Civil* of 1889, located in the property section of the Code, delineated the property rights of neighbours by listing natural servitudes, thereby prohibiting certain sorts of activities in the vicinity of others' land and striking a balance between the interests of the parties. Elsewhere in the Code, in the delict section, article 1908 imposed liability on owners in four cases: (a) explosions of machines not kept with due care, or of explosives not stored in safe places; (b) excessive smoke injurious to the person or property; (c) the falling of trees onto roads where this had not been caused by *force majeure*; (d) emanations from sewers and the like which had been constructed without precautions appropriate to the place in which they were situated. Although this parallels the strict liability for

[124] DP 1907.1.385, note Ripert, referring to Demolombe, Proudhon, Baudry-Lacantinerie, Laurent, and Aubry and Rau.

[125] H. Capitant, 'Des Obligations de Voisinage' (1900) *Revue Critique* 156, 278; G. Ripert, *L'Exercice du Droit de Propriété dans les Rapports avec les Propriétés Voisines* (thesis Aix-Marseille, 1902).

[126] J.-M. Pardessus, *Traité des Servitudes ou Services Fonciers* (Paris: Garnery, 1838), 1.209–1.210, § 86, based most immediately on Fromental, *Decisions de Droit Civil* (1740), 656 (with further references there to the *ius commune* literature); Metz 10 November 1808, *Lingard*, S-VC 1808.2.438 ('Qu'il est permis a chacun de disposer de sa propriété comme il lui plaît, mais sans cependant nuire à autrui': 'Everyone is permitted to dispose of his property as he wishes, but not however to harm another.'); Metz 16 August 1820, *Mercy*, S-VC 1821.2.309.

[127] D.1856.2.9. [128] Masferrer, *Neighbours*, pp. 181–183.

damage caused by things in article 1384 of the French Code, it is a very different type of provision: the second and fourth provisions are those we would associate with the regulation of rights between neighbours in the face of industrial nuisances. Its source, too, is different. Although by no means a wholesale borrowing, it is likely that a principal influence on it was article 1133 of the Argentine Code of 1869 (the fourth provision of the Spanish Code is almost identically worded to the Argentine, and the second and third are closely parallel), which was in its turn influenced by article 3690 of the draft code prepared for Brazil by Teixeira de Freitas[129] and articles 2323 and 2329 of the Chilean Code of 1856, behind all of which there was a link to the casuistic treatment of Roman law traceable through the Spanish *Siete Partidas*.[130] The shifts of legal rules from Chile to Argentina to Spain are noteworthy: in Chile there is a list of examples of when liability will lie for fault, which added little or nothing to the general principle; in Argentina there is a list of specific cases in which there will be fault liability with a reverse burden of proof, i.e. fault liability still applies but there is a rebuttable presumption that the requirement has been satisfied; in Spain, the necessary link with fault is broken, with clearly strict liability applicable to the escape of smoke.

It can be seen, therefore, that the pattern of development varied from system to system, depending on the relationship between property and tort. Building on this, there was a clear tendency for tortious remedies to fall into line with the orthodox undercurrent of fault liability, while proprietary remedies would be granted independently of any fault criteria. In Spain, therefore, despite the strict liability formulation in parts of article 1908 of the *Código Civil*, by the early years of the twentieth century the provision was being interpreted as if it was based on fault.[131] Similarly in England; although the tort of nuisance as it had developed up to the nineteenth century was free from the fault criterion of the tort of negligence, from the middle of the twentieth century it moved in the direction of negligence: where the defendant had not personally created the nuisance, negligence in the strict sense was required, and where he had created it

[129] B. Llerena, *Concordancias y Comentarios del Código Civil Argentino*, 2nd edn (Buenos Aires: Peuser, 1900), §§ 4.208–4.209. For the influence of Teixeira de Freitas on the law of Argentina, see E. Martinez Paz, *Freitas y su Influencia sobre el Código Civil Argentino* (Córdoba: Imprenta de la Universidad, 1927).

[130] The relevant texts of the *Partidas*, P.7.15.6–7, are cited by Andres Bello, the draftsman of the Chilean Code, in his notes to article 2329.

[131] Masferrer, *Neighbours*, p. 190 note 36.

was said that there would nearly always be fault 'in some form'.[132] As was already seen in France in the nineteenth century and the Netherlands from the start of the twentieth, the fault criterion had a high degree of plasticity, which enabled it to be adjusted to situations where it could be said that there was blameworthiness in any way. Alongside this, there was a parallel tendency for fault to be irrelevant in proprietary remedies, but for the remedy to be simply the vindication of the property right, clearly visible in systems such as those of France and Spain where tortious and proprietary remedies existed side by side.

That said, there was scope for one type of remedy to cover the ground of the other. In Germany, therefore, from the middle of the nineteenth century 'denial damages' could be awarded in an apparently proprietary action, on the grounds that any decision that allowed the defendant to continue with an activity that interfered with the plaintiff's property rights constituted an expropriation which had to be compensated.[133] Equally in England, it was recognised that in the tortious action of nuisance the court could award an injunction to forbid the continuation of the nuisance (technically, a positive order to abate the nuisance); and where this was the remedy awarded fault had little or no part to play. It followed, therefore, that in every system, whatever the formal configuration of its rules, the courts were able to grant both proprietary relief and compensation, and use a mixture of fault-based and non-fault-based criteria of liability. Although in formal terms this is a clear example of divergent development, as a matter of substance this was by no means necessarily the case.

Adding to the complexities of comparison was the doctrine of abuse of rights. As has been seen, this was a principle known to the *ius commune* and embraced by the French as a qualification, or antidote, to their absolutist conception of property rights contained in article 544 of the *Code Civil*.[134] The same idea was found in Germany in the Prussian *Allgemeines*

[132] P. Giliker, 'Relationships between Neighbours: England and Wales 1850–2000', in *Neighbours*, 29 at pp. 38–46. See *Sedleigh-Denfield v. O'Callaghan* [1940] AC 880, *The Wagon Mound (no. 2)* [1967] 1 AC 617.

[133] Thier, *Neighbours*, pp. 90, 100–103. Similar considerations could apply to give compensation in French public law for the activities of public authorities (J. Gordley, 'Disturbances among Neighbours in French law' in *Neighbours*, 65 at pp. 77–78), while in England statutory compensation schemes were sometimes established to deal with damage caused by socially useful activities (e.g. in relation to fires caused by the running of railway engines: Morgan, *Technology*, pp. 48–51).

[134] Above, p. 144.

Landrecht of 1794,[135] and adopted from a theoretical perspective by Rudolf von Jhering.[136] In their turn, Jhering's ideas influenced the early twentieth-century French theorisation of Josserand, stressing the social functions of legal rights.[137] Meanwhile, after considerable debate, the doctrine was incorporated into the German BGB as § 226, prohibiting the exercise of any right with the sole purpose of harming another.[138] It was recognised in Dutch doctrine before the end of the nineteenth century, with the leading decisions in the Hoge Raad coming in 1937.[139] In Spain, it was introduced into doctrinal writing by José Calvo Sotelo in 1917 and adopted by the Tribunal Supremo in 1944;[140] and there are hints of the idea in Scots law in the nineteenth century.[141] In contrast to this, English law, and in its wake Scots law, emphatically and decisively rejected this in *Mayor of Bradford v. Pickles* in 1895.[142] We may identify, perhaps, three reasons for this difference: first, English case-law in the nineteenth century had developed a set of precise rules deciding who was entitled to take water (the context of *Bradford v. Pickles*), and any abuse of rights doctrine would have rendered this unstable; secondly, the principal area in which the question of the malicious exercise of rights was being discussed in the 1890s was that of labour relations, and the courts in *Bradford v. Pickles* would have been reluctant to introduce a general rule which would inevitably have applied to this area too; and thirdly, there was nothing at all in the history of the common law to parallel the doctrine of the *ius commune* that rights could not be exercised for an improper purpose. Once established by the House of Lords in *Bradford v. Pickles*, the rule was fixed. Instead of a general rule against the abuse of rights, English law adopted a principle within the tort of nuisance, that malicious conduct would be treated as unreasonable and hence of no weight when balancing the interests of neighbours.[143] The result, in this context, was the same as that reached elsewhere, but the legal mechanism was very different.

135 *Allgemeines Landrecht für die Preussischen Staaten*, § 1.8.27.

136 'Zur Lehre von den Beschränkungen des Grundeigentumers im Interesse der Nachbarn' (1863) 6 *Jherings Jahrbücher* 81.

137 L. Josserand, *L'Abus de Droits* (Paris: Rousseau, 1905).

138 H.C. Gutteridge, 'Abuse of Rights' (1933) 5 *Cambridge Law Journal* 22, 36–37.

139 Verheij, *Neighbours*, pp. 110, 112–114.

140 Masferrer, *Neighbours*, p. 185. Sotelo subsequently became a right-wing politician, whose assassination in 1936 precipitated the Spanish Civil War.

141 Cameron, *Neighbours*, p. 157.

142 [1895] AC 587.

143 *Hollywood Silver Fox Farm v. Emmett* [1936] 2 KB 468, building on *Christie v. Davey* [1893] 1 Ch 316.

Behind all of this variation we may see four themes in common across the countries studied. First, there was a shift in focus from direct or indirect interferences with the neighbour's land itself to interferences with the enjoyment of the land, marked most visibly by Jhering's re-theorisation of German law in this way in 1863.[144] Secondly, in balancing the interests of neighbours the law adopted a test of what was reasonable in the place where the alleged nuisance occurred, a test which gave a great discretion to courts in its application. Thirdly, it is observable that as a country industrialised there was a shift in the direction of favouring industrial activities rather than treating them as alien invasions into traditional communities: in England, France and Germany, for example, the tipping point was reached in the 1860s, in the Netherlands in the 1870s.[145] Fourthly, and most importantly, everywhere the rules of tort and property law were supplemented, and largely superseded, by administrative regulations and planning law. It may be that the long-term picture of the development of legal control over nuisances starts with local controls over land use. These break down with the onset of industrialisation, and very general principles of tort law and property law were used *faute de mieux*. These general principles gave authority to judges to strike a balance between individuals' uses of land. Finally, nationally imposed systems were being created to regulate the operation of particular activities and the permissible uses of land.[146]

C *Analysis of legal development*

It is only when we look at tort law and property law in isolation from their context that the relative stasis pointed to by Gordley[147] is seen. All legal systems build on their existing remedial framework, whether derived from developed Roman law, the common law or a mix of both. Unlike in the field of road traffic, there was less of a tendency to create new rules

[144] 'Zur Lehre von den Beschränkungen'. The distinction between interference with land and interference with enjoyment was drawn at almost exactly the same time in England in *St Helen's Smelting Co v. Tipping* ((1865) 11 HLC 642), though there is no evidence that this was influenced by Jhering's work.

[145] Thier, *Neighbours*, pp. 100–101; Salmon, *Technology*, pp. 103–108; *St Helen's Smelting Co v. Tipping* (1865) 11 HLC 642; Verheij, *Neighbours*, pp. 124–125.

[146] J. F. Brenner, 'Nuisance Law and the Industrial Revolution' (1974) 3 *Journal of Legal Studies* 403; J.P.S. McClaren, 'Nuisance Law and the Industrial Revolution – Some Lessons from Social History' (1983) 3 *Oxford Journal of Legal Studies* 155. Compare Cameron, *Neighbours*, pp. 133–134; Masferrer, *Neighbours*, p. 177.

[147] *Neighbours*, pp. 1–2; above, p. 138.

and more of a broadly common move to recognise amenity rights by way of interpretation of existing rules. This involved the need to engage in a more explicit balancing, something which was made possible by the open-ended nature of concepts used, particularly that of reasonableness.

But the most important theme in the development of the law relating to neighbours, especially in the context of industrialisation, is the relative insignificance of tort law. The amount of litigation in the nineteenth century, so far as we can judge from reported decisions, was relatively slight. Tort law has to be seen in the context of other responses or vehicles for achieving protection for the victims of industrial interference. There was a range of these, including local courts and regulatory law, as well as private ordering between neighbours by the use of such devices as conventional servitudes and restrictive covenants.

The most important context for the operation of tort law was the existence of public regulatory law. Local control over activities was extensive and long-standing. Such local regulation was able to moderate rules proscribing activity in a way which was sensitive to the locality and the value of the social activity. Such local regulation existed well before the Industrial Revolution and was a first way in which the law could adapt to industrialisation and urbanisation. Whereas tort law would strike a balance between the rights of individual landowners (including entrepreneurs), statute law was able to identify particular industries for special treatment. So, for example, in England, the alkali production industry was regulated from 1862 with inspectors; other industries, such as smelting, were regulated only later, so the leading case of *St Helen's Smelting Co v. Tipping* can be seen as an example of a common law case trying to fill the gap in relation to an industry then not subject to statutory regulation and inspection. [148] Regulatory law provided systematic and proactive rules governing the conduct of particular industries. Property law and tort law could only provide individualised solutions, often only after problems had occurred.

Different countries had differing patterns of legislation. The French developed generic legislation on the authorisation of noxious industries in 1810; this provided a framework, typically a local one channelled through the prefect or mayor of the commune, for the prior authorisation of activities without specifying particular industries. The Spanish and Dutch inherited this legislation, though the Spanish did not have the

[148] (1865) 11 HLC 642. See A.W.B. Simpson, *Leading Cases in the Common Law* (Oxford University Press, 1995), ch. 7, especially pp. 176–179.

administrative structure to police the standards imposed.[149] The Dutch legislation of 1824 established three levels of permission: national for activities which had to be sited away from human habitation, regional for activities to be carried out without nuisance, and local for activities not to be carried out in residential areas. Within this structure, modified regularly over time and made subject to a presumption in favour of industrial development in 1875, it was possible to develop differing attitudes to industrial development. Independently of this, the Industrial Code for the North German Federation of 1869 adopted a similar system of administrative regulation and licensing.[150] English law did not have the same general system of national approvals and standards, except in so far as activities such as the running of railways were subject to authorisation by way of private Act of Parliament. Instead, from the 1840s onwards, specific laws were passed to deal with threats to public health and to regulate specific industries.[151] Although the shape of the legislation was different from that in continental Europe the result was the same, that changing attitudes could be reflected over time. The structures of the administrative regulation and the extent of inspection varied depending on the administrative structure of the country and the pace of industrialisation. Political considerations might affect this, as for example with the Italians' concern to protect nascent industries.[152] More generally the pace of change reflected the degree of industrialisation, with such countries as France, Germany and Great Britain more active in the nineteenth century than Spain or Italy. Moreover, since the nineteenth century also witnessed significant changes in structures of local and central government and their capacity to police industrial activities, the kinds of legislation introduced to deal with issues between neighbours also varied from place to place. Identical industrial activities, therefore, might be socially different from place to place, and hence require different legislative treatment.

A final feature that needs to be noted is the extent of mutual influences between different countries. This was not purely, or even primarily, legal, though a writer such as Jhering affected attitudes far outside his native Germany, and the French legislation of 1810 was imposed or adopted elsewhere. Industrialisation was not a purely local phenomenon,

[149] M. Martín-Casals and J. Ribot, 'Technological Change and the Development of Liability for Fault in Spain' in *Technology*, 227 at pp. 240–242.

[150] Thier, *Neighbours*, pp. 94–95.

[151] Giliker, *Neighbours*, pp. 54–55.

[152] C. Favilli, 'Technological Change and the Development of Liability for Fault in Italy' in *Technology*, 185 at p. 204.

and industrialists visited other countries and took ideas and technologies from them. In the early Industrial Revolution, many technologies were exported from Britain, whilst from the 1860s, the newer and more expensive technologies were imported from the United States and Germany.[153] Investment in other countries was also very significant. For example, half the capital invested in French railways up to 1847 came from Britain, and in 1914 over half French foreign investment went into other European countries.[154] In such a context, it would not be surprising if methods of dealing with the problems of industrialisation also crossed borders. There were associations of industrialists setting their own standards for inspection and the avoidance of injuries; ministries looked to other countries for ideas to deal with similar problems; and to the extent there were academic, as opposed to professional, writings on the subjects, there was also a willingness to look at foreign legislation.[155] All of this fed in to a degree of homogeneity in the ways in which real-life problems caused by urbanisation and industrialisation were dealt with, despite the differences in purely formal legal responses.

[153] N. Ferguson, 'The European Economy, 1815–1914' in T.C.W. Blanning, *The Nineteenth Century: Europe 1789–1914* (Oxford University Press, 2000), 78, 90–91.

[154] *Ibid.*, pp. 90–91 and 111.

[155] See, for example, *Technology*, pp. 141–142, 156, 193, 206, especially notes 49 and 113.

5

Convergence and divergence in the development of fault liability

It was suggested in the first chapter that the understanding of the changes in the law of tort that we are aiming to describe is best achieved by a model of law that is the union of the law in the books, legal rules and principles that are capable of being formulated in words, and legal outcomes, the results reached in actual cases.[1] These are related to each other: the law in the books provides a justification for the legal outcomes, both actual and hypothetical, and to some extent generates them; and the legal outcomes feed back into the law in the books by giving it more precise definition, by favouring one formulation of a rule over another, or by replacing one rule by another. The way in which this feedback loop operates depends on the legal institutions operating in a system at any given time: such factors as the ease with which existing rules and principles can be reformulated; whether judges are required to give reasons for their decisions, and if so what constraints exist on their reasoning; the extent to which questions can be shifted out of the legal domain by being defined as matters of 'fact' rather than 'law'; the openness of any system to foreign models, and the relative weight of academic opinion and judicial decisions. These exist against the background of the legal and extra-legal environment: the way in which the law of tort relates to other fields of law and the social, economic and ethical background against which law functions.

We link these elements together by means of a diagram (Figure 3).

I The big picture

The large-scale picture of the development of fault liability since 1850 can be characterised in terms of two interlocking themes: a move from fault towards strict liability, with an increasing focus on the victim rather than the wrongdoer; and the rejection of the near-axiomatic assumption that legal liability should go hand in hand with moral responsibility.[2] There has been a change in legal values, not just in legal techniques.

[1] Above, pp. 46–48. [2] Jansen, *Doctrine*, p. 9.

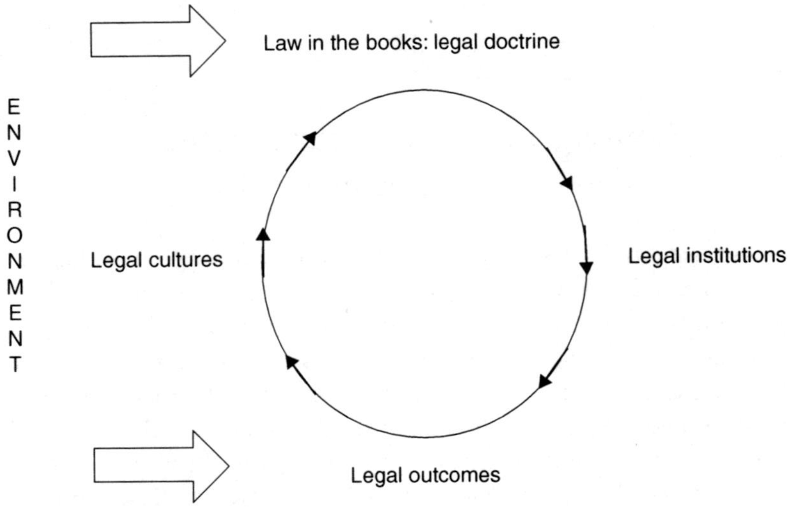

Figure 3. Legal development

The move towards a more victim-centred approach to liability is visible in different ways; the mechanisms used are exactly the same as those already found in the mid-nineteenth century. Within it there are two distinct elements, although they are often connected: fault liability itself has come to be seen more from the point of view of the victim than of the wrongdoer, and also there is a greater sense that, at least in some significant area, compensation should be awarded not only to those who are injured by others' wrongful acts but also to those who are injured by socially desirable ones. The techniques for achieving this change of emphasis are varied. Sometimes it has involved no more than a changing interpretation of fault, away from the defendant and towards the victim: we might point to the increasingly high standard of care imposed on car drivers and doctors when and where fault liability prevails.[3] In these situations the fault principle is not formally displaced, though the effect is in practice much as if it had been.

Sometimes there is a shift in the burden of proof, so that prima facie liability is imposed once the causation of injury is proved. This may occur because the defendant has superior knowledge, as occurred for example when liability came to be imposed on negligent manufacturers of goods. It may alternatively be based on considerations of fairness between

[3] Above, pp. 97, 103, 123, 128.

wrongdoer and victim, particularly where the wrongdoer has created a risk of injury but it cannot be shown by the victim that it was his or her acts that actually caused the harm. We see this technique being used, for example, in relation to injuries caused by cars in Spain in 1943 and in relation to manufacturers' liability in Germany in 1968. Alongside this, there has been a weakening of the requirement of proof of a causal connection between the defendant's act and the victim's injury, particularly in cases of diseases caused by the ingestion of asbestos fibres where there are a number of possible tortious causes but it is a medical impossibility to demonstrate which was the effective cause on the facts.[4] In these cases, and others like them, the defendants' liability can be justified in terms of the creation of a risk rather than the causation of harm. This may be done explicitly or, as has happened in French law, by treating the chance of not suffering an injury as a form of compensable damage in itself.

Sometimes there has been an express imposition of strict liability. This has normally taken place in a piecemeal way, as legislation has taken some well-defined situation outside the core of fault liability: road traffic accidents in Germany, Sweden and France; medical negligence in France and Austria; or generally across Western Europe liability for injuries caused by defective products. Occasionally, though, it has occurred across a wider front, as for example with the use of article 1384 of the French *Code Civil* to impose strict liability for things since the end of the nineteenth century, or with the Swedish reforms since the middle of the twentieth century linking legal liability with insurance mechanisms. In part this has involved a change in legal technique as strict liability has shifted the burden onto the defendant to show that the injury occurred in one of a defined set of ways in which the defendant should be exonerated. In part, though, it has involved a genuine change in the basis of liability, as when legal liability and moral responsibility have been separated in cases of car accidents or defective products, both situations in which damages are almost always covered by insurance or by some other means of loss-spreading.

This change towards a victim-orientated approach has two aspects. On the one hand, it has unsurprisingly had the result that those suffering injuries have a greater overall chance of recovering compensation at the start of the twenty-first century than they would have had in the middle of the nineteenth. Secondly, there is a rhetorical dimension in the supposition that those who have suffered injury at the hand of another (whether

[4] Martín-Casals, *Technology*, pp. 31–33.

or not they are obviously careless) should in principle be entitled to redress. This aspect is very clear, for example, with the imposition of strict liability for defective products in the wake of the EC Product Liability Directive, which may have made very little difference in practice to the fault-based liability which existed beforehand.

This shift in rhetoric can be seen in terms of the fortunes of two different natural law principles: a waning of Grotius's natural law principle that a person who acts in a blameworthy way should compensate a person suffering injury from this, and an increase in the weight given to the alternative natural law principle that a person injured by another should in principle receive compensation.[5] Equally, it might involve the separation of the legal liability of the actor from his or her moral responsibility. Already in the later nineteenth century it was being argued by the German Victor Mataja that economic rather than moral ideas might be used to determine legal liability,[6] and similar ideas were put forward in France by scholars such as Saleilles and Josserand.[7] These ideas gained in influence after the 1950s. In Italy, under American influence, the imposition of liability came to be seen as a mechanism for allocating risks in a socially desirable way;[8] in England there was a greater focus on legal policy in deciding new cases;[9] and in Sweden the introduction of no-fault insurance-based systems reflected a concern to give compensation to victims of certain types of accident as a matter of social rather than corrective justice.[10] That said, it has not completely displaced the use of traditional ideas of individual moral responsibility as the primary justification of tortious liability; these continue to be dominant in Germany, Spain and Holland (and perhaps also in France), though behind their façade it is likely that notions of public policy have been at work.[11]

This big picture, however, fails to capture the detail of the different legal systems. Even at the most abstract doctrinal level each system has developed in its own way, with a criss-cross patchwork of mutual influences together with influences from outside Europe, in particular from the United States.[12] Where functionally similar results have been reached, this has occurred by the use of different legal mechanisms and at different rates. Moreover, even within the same legal system changes have not occurred homogeneously; we need to be sensitive to the factual contexts of legal liability.

[5] Above, p. 55. [6] Jansen, *Doctrine*, p. 98.
[7] Halpérin, *Doctrine*, p. 88. [8] Graziadei, *Doctrine*, pp. 161–162.
[9] Ibbetson, *Doctrine*, pp. 65–66. [10] Modéer, *Doctrine*, pp. 216–221.
[11] Jansen, *Doctrine*, pp. 25–26. [12] Ibid., pp. 31–40.

II Internal changes

While much legal change is responsive to the external environment, we may see some changes as purely internal. These take three forms: the increasing precision of the law in the books as a result of legal decisions; the formulation of legal principles at a level of generality, particularly in the drafting or redrafting of codes; and more generally in lawyers' shaping of legal doctrine.

A Concretisation of legal rules

The first of these may seem relatively uninteresting from the point of view of the development of legal doctrine. Within most legal systems, the division between law and fact is such that decisions at a high level of detail are largely characterised as questions of fact and are typically made by first-instance judges whose reasoning is not reported, with the result that they generate no legal rule. The only important exception to this is English law in the nineteenth and early twentieth century, where duties of care were formulated with a very high degree of precision. Behind this there lies the institutional factor of the relationship between judge and jury: whether there was a duty of care in the first place was a matter of law to be decided by the judge, whether the duty had been breached was a matter of fact for the jury.[13] The principal device by which judges controlled jury discretion in the tort of negligence was by defining duties of care at a very concrete level, and hence generating rules of law. The law became increasingly sharply defined, 'a wilderness of single instances', so that the main text before the seminal decision in *Donoghue v. Stevenson* and before the effective disappearance of the jury, the fourth edition of *Beven on Negligence*, which appeared in 1928, was 1570 pages long with a table of cases running to 175 pages.[14]

Apart from this, though, the institutional frameworks within which the law operated were not conducive to this type of development; in general, most legal decisions could be treated as simple instantiations of the operation of general principles. This is not to say that the feedback loop between the legal outcome and the law in the books was irrelevant, but its

[13] D. Ibbetson, 'The Tort of Negligence in the Common Law in the Nineteenth and Twentieth Centuries', in E.J.H. Schrage (ed.), *Negligence* (Berlin: Duncker & Humblot, 2001), 229, 240–241.

[14] T. Beven, *Negligence in Law* (London: Sweet and Maxwell, 1928). Even the first edition, published in 1889, devoted more than 700 pages to the question.

importance lay in the way in which legal decisions responded to the external environment and brought about change in the law in the books rather than in the way in which they created precise legal rules.[15]

B Codification and legal principles

Changes brought about in the process of codification are more easily demonstrated. The rules with which we are concerned here are those of a very high level of abstraction; they are more a reflection of the perceptions of the lawyers responsible for the drafting (or redrafting) of the codes as to the proper shaping of the law rather than any concern about the outcome of legal disputes.

The relevant provisions of the Spanish *Código Civil* of 1889, articles 1902–1909, are very strongly influenced by the French *Code Civil*, with some slight differences to deal with specific types of case.[16] The major exception to this is that the provision of article 1384 of the *Code Civil* imposing liability for things, the source of the strict liability recognised after the *Teffaine* decision in 1896, was omitted from the equivalent article, article 1903. This can only have been a conscious decision, for not only was it present in the *Code Civil*, but it was also found in the Goyena draft code of 1851 (article 1901). The omission clearly reflects the perception of the dominance of fault-based liability at the time of the drafting of the Code. It is unlikely, though possible, that it was intended to avoid the imposition of strict liability for things in concrete cases, since even in French law this was recognised in practice only some years later.

The fault principle is similarly dominant in the drafting of the German BGB of 1900.[17] It is at the forefront of the relevant provisions, § 823 I, and underpins the rest of the tort principles. In this it reflects both the ideological commitment to fault liability of the late nineteenth century and its place within German pandectist thought. Although there had been a very general recognition in practice of liability for causing any loss by fault in the nineteenth century, scholarly opinion required a greater definition; this too is reflected in the BGB. Pandectist thought, picking up on some strands of natural-law thinking and behind them the Roman lex Aquilia,

15 We may, of course, see nineteenth- and early twentieth-century English decisions operating in this way too, but we need to distinguish this from change that was little more than increasing precision.

16 Martín-Casals and Ruda, *Doctrine*, pp. 184–190.

17 Jansen, *Doctrine*, pp. 100–103.

had stressed that liability stemmed from unlawful conduct;[18] unlawfulness was explained by Windscheid and others in terms of the interference with some right of the victim, and this also is reflected in the formulation of § 823 I. The fact of greater precision in drafting was undoubtedly ends-related, imposing a degree of discipline on trial courts in determining whether or not to impose liability. But the shape in which § 823 I was formulated, with its list of protected interests, was purely doctrinal, the product of the way in which legal scholars believed that the law ought to be structured.

C *The shaping of legal doctrine*

The sort of purely doctrinal change evidenced in the formulations of codes is also sometimes found more generally in the development of law. It is well illustrated by the relevance of a requirement of unlawfulness additional to, or independent of, fault. This brings out, too, the further idea of path dependence:[19] lawyers' perceptions of the way in which the law ought to be framed are to some extent conditioned by their own upbringings in the law, and their sense of the history of their own system.

Behind the requirement of unlawfulness we may identify two principal, if related, roots: Roman law and natural law. Within the Roman lex Aquilia, unlawfulness had an ambiguous role. Although the lex itself had spoken of loss having been caused (*iniuria*), this was explained by Gaius as being equivalent to deliberate or blameworthy conduct, *dolus* or *culpa*. Gaius's analysis was repeated in the Institutes of Justinian. Texts in the Digest reveal a more ambiguous relationship, with *culpa* playing the dominant part but *iniuria*-based ideas still visible in explaining why a person who had acted pursuant to a legal right should not be liable. This latter point was strengthened by a maxim found elsewhere in the Digest, that a person acting with a right does not act wrongfully. Since Roman law had formed the basis of the *ius commune* which had dominated all of continental Western Europe, these ideas of unlawfulness interlinked with fault were a major point of reference.[20] For some natural law theorists, such as Grotius and Pufendorf, simple fault was the basis of liability. However, in the eighteenth century, Christian Wolff[21] added the element of unlawfulness to this. So whilst we cannot say that unlawfulness was as relevant

[18] Above, p. 52; below, p. 160. [19] Above, pp. 24–32.

[20] Above, pp. 64–65; Jansen, *Doctrine*, pp. 5–15.

[21] Jansen, *Doctrine*, p. 102 and especially note 44.

to natural law thinking as it was to Roman law, it was very significant in some strands, less so in others.

Against this background, we can identify three rough groupings. In Germany, where Wolff's theory of natural law was dominant, unlawfulness was a central pillar. In the French tradition, where there was a Roman law base but where natural law thought was channelled through Domat rather than Wolff, unlawfulness occupied a far more subordinate position: there was no place for it in articles 1382–1386 of the *Code Civil*, but the background influence of the lex Aquilia meant that it could not be ignored. Finally, in England neither Roman law nor Wolff's version of natural law had had any substantial influence, and here it was fault alone that determined liability.

Wolff's influence in Germany was strong enough to create a climate within which unlawfulness was seen as a major plank in establishing liability, but this was locked in place by Johann Christian Hasse's work on *culpa* in Roman law, first published in 1815 and with a second edition in 1838.[22] Hasse distinguished between the objective unlawfulness, what it was that made the act wrongful, and the subjective element, which made the actor responsible. So far as the former was concerned, wrongfulness was analysed in terms of the breach of a statutory duty or the infringement of an individual right. His analysis was generally accepted by the Pandectists of the nineteenth century, and underpins the approach to liability taken in the BGB. Although the independent role of unlawfulness rather ebbed away in practice in the twentieth century, the structure of the BGB has had long-term effects on liability rules. Most obviously, it has ensured that the breach of statutory duties has remained within the scope of the general principles of fault liability and allowed for the retention of a strongly subjective approach to responsibility exonerating young children and the mentally ill. As well, the BGB's focus on the interest or right that has been infringed enabled German law to adopt a framework of analysis within which the scope of liability was controlled by looking at the victim's interests rather than at the actor's conduct.

England was completely the reverse. The lex Aquilia was not a reference point, and although the influence of natural law was crucial, it was Pufendorf's version rather than Wolff's that shaped English thinking. Fault, or negligence, was paramount therefore, with no place for any additional requirement of unlawfulness. English law was therefore able to treat breach of statutory duty as a tort independent of negligence, and

[22] *Ibid.*, pp. 102, 115–118.

subjective factors such as infancy or mental incapacity had no part to play in determining liability in tort. The principal control device was the duty of care (itself probably taken from Pufendorf), and even when there has been a question whether certain types of harm were recoverable, English law has tended to analyse these in terms of the scope of the actor's duty rather than in terms of the nature of the victim's interest.[23]

The French tradition, in which we include Holland, Italy and Spain, whose civil codes were very strongly shaped by the French model, is the most complex of the three. The *Code Civil* itself was concerned solely with the actor's fault, with no place for any consideration of unlawfulness.[24] Behind it, though, was a division between delict, deliberate or criminal wrongdoing, and quasi-delict, causing loss by fault, which meant that the unlawfulness of the actor's conduct was something which could simply be ignored. Added to this was article 5 of the Declaration of the Rights of Man and Citizen, that everything that was not prohibited by law was allowed. From as early as the 1820s this text, coupled with the traditional formulation of liability on the basis of Roman law, was used by some as a means to equate fault with unlawfulness, with a focus on the breach of a positive law. From the 1850s the analysis of fault in terms of unlawfulness was more or less axiomatic, though unlawfulness might have had little meaning beyond fault. Under German influence – Zachariae von Lingenthal's commentary on the *Code Civil* translated into French by Aubry and Rau – it was even argued that unlawfulness meant an interference with the rights of the victim (an idea that was already to be found in the debates leading up to the enactment of the *Code Civil*), and, although this was not generally accepted at the time, it was to be picked up by writers such as Josserand in the 1930s and used as a theoretical base for the imposition of strict liability. The debate over the proper role for unlawfulness, and its proper definition, continues today. So far as French law is concerned, the important feature is that unlawfulness had no part to play in the formal law as laid down in the *Code Civil*, but that it could be brought into play when needed to justify some particular conclusion. The acceptance of the strict liability for things, and hence the French rules relating to road traffic accidents, are a consequence of this.

The Spanish and Italian experiences were similar to each other.[25] In Spain, the Aquilian tradition was very strong, routed through the

[23] See *ibid.*, pp. 1, 9, 15, 49–53. [24] Halpérin, *Doctrine*, pp. 80–85, 88–90.

[25] Martín-Casals and Ruda, *Doctrine*, pp. 207–208; Graziadei, *Doctrine*, pp. 131–132, 138–142.

thirteenth-century *Siete Partidas* which remained an active source of formal law. Hence, although the *Código Civil* of 1889 followed French lines, with liability dependent on fault or negligence, almost immediately commentators analysed the law as containing a requirement of unlawfulness following the contours of the *Partidas*. The Italian Code of 1865 similarly had no reference to unlawfulness (its relevant provisions were a word-for-word translation of the French), but immediately after its enactment it began to be read as if it did, following the contemporary German-French interpretation of Zachariae von Lingenthal and Aubry and Rau. When a new Code was enacted in 1942, the requirement of unlawfulness was included. Consequently, while modern Spanish law is able to question whether there is in fact a role for an independent requirement of unlawfulness (as in France), this is not possible in Italy.

The Dutch development was rather different.[26] The equivalent provisions of the Code of 1838 were almost identical to the French, with the crucial difference that there was an additional explicit requirement of unlawfulness. There was disagreement whether this was something distinct from fault, but by the 1880s it was accepted that it might be found either in the breach of a statutory provision or of some right of the victim. Dutch law, therefore, in many ways resembled German law. Its focus on the infringement of rights, however, enabled this provision to be brought into play in the early twentieth century to deal with situations of unfair competition, ensuring that the tort had a broad scope. We may surmise, too, that it is this that lies behind the ease with which a marked pro-victim leaning was able to develop in the Netherlands in the latter part of the twentieth century.

D Internal changes and doctrinal divergence

These internal changes have a tendency to cause legal systems to diverge from each other. Legal actors favour different ideas at different times, and some of these ideas become embedded in their systems. Over time, this individualised selection and retention of ideas tends to push legal systems apart. There are, however, a number of countervailing factors which put some check on this process of divergence. First, tort law in Europe has a strong shared heritage in the natural law tradition, supplemented in continental Europe by Roman law as developed by the jurists of the Middle Ages and the early modern period. Although there were variations in this

[26] Hol, *Doctrine*, pp. 165–176.

background – English law was influenced by Pufendorf's treatment of the duty to take care, for example, while German law was more dependent on Wolff's analysis of protected interests – at their core all of these embodied a similar commitment to the ethical principle that legal liability should be based on fault. With this principle at the heart of the law, the range of options available for its formulation has been relatively limited and liability not based on fault has been largely fragmented and relegated to the periphery of the law. It is only in Scandinavia that this basic principle was subjected to fundamental criticism, first by Lunstedt in the 1920s and then by Strahl after the Second World War, culminating in the Tort Liability Act of 1972, which was focused on insurance-based compensation for those suffering harm rather than on the fault or wrong of the actor.[27] Secondly, national legal systems have not developed in total isolation from each other. Ideas shaped in one place have influenced lawyers in other places, providing ready-made models to be followed. The French *Code Civil* formed the background to all the codes of the later nineteenth century except the German, for example, and in the twentieth century the legal systems of Italy, Spain and the Netherlands have been notably porous to legal ideas from abroad.[28] Thirdly, flowing from the previous two factors, legal systems have been able to reach almost identical results despite having different institutional structures. The doctrine of abuse of rights, for example, was adopted in France from pre-1804 law, in Germany after substantial doctrinal discussion building on a journal article by Jhering, in Holland first by scholars and then in case-law, and in Spain by explicit borrowing from abroad later accepted by the Tribunal Supremo.[29]

III External changes

Although some legal change takes place in the way we have just described, by lawyers trying to achieve an intellectually satisfying body of rules and principles, most change takes the form of a response to the external environment. Technological changes produce new challenges, economic changes alter perceptions of desirable solutions and at the same time generate possible new ways to deal with problems, social changes bring about different expectations. The legal response to these may be legislative, or it

[27] Modéer, *Doctrine*, pp. 216–221.

[28] J. Bell, 'The Relevance of Foreign Examples to Legal Development' (2010) 21 *Duke Journal of Comparative and International Law*, 431, 434–449.

[29] Above, pp. 147–148.

may occur through courts; and behind both there has frequently lain the work of scholars.

These external influences do not necessarily bring about legal change. They do not operate automatically, but only when individuals act in response to them. Law, however, is inertial, in the sense that it requires positive effort to change it. Judges and other legal actors are expected to work within the law, applying it rather than changing it, and legislation is costly in terms of time and so comes up against competition from other potential statutes. Change only occurs when a tipping point is reached. To some extent this is a matter of chance; we can say that the greater the pressure for change the more likely it is to occur, but this does not get us very far. We may, however, identify some factors influencing the likelihood of a tipping point being reached. Legislative change is more likely to occur as a response to a particular event or moral panic, as for example where statutory changes followed in the wake of mass food poisoning or disastrous side effects of therapeutic drugs.[30] So far as court-based change is concerned, the tipping point is more easily reached where there is a greater range of legal formants available.[31] Where there are a number of different formulations of the law in the books a court can choose to follow one of these, simultaneously applying 'the law' and changing it by increasing the strength of one formant as opposed to others. By contrast, where there is a narrow range of formants available, courts have less choice open to them if they are not to be seen as exercising a quasi-legislative role.

It is here, perhaps, that we see the most significant institutional difference between English law and continental legal systems. Continental scholarship has greater freedom to restructure the law, and because of the greater respect afforded to academic opinion in the tradition of the *ius commune,* both as *communis opinio* and individual writings,[32] their arguments have weight as statements of what the law is. Continental systems are, of course, not identical in this respect; in France, for example, it is the writings of individuals that predominate, whereas in Germany since 1860 these have been complemented by the existence of an identifiable *communis opinio* produced by the regular Deutsche Juristentage. But the similarities among the continental systems are far greater than the differences. English scholarship, by contrast, is highly court centred: it is expected to reflect what courts are doing, not to remodel it. Inventive scholarship, therefore, commonly takes the form of saying how and why the law might

[30] Above, pp. 76, 82–83. [31] For legal formants, see above, p. 2.
[32] Above, pp. 68–71.

be different from what it is, rather than saying that it is in fact different from what it is generally thought to be. Because of this relative paucity of legal formants in English law and the strength of its doctrine of precedent, legal argument and the justification of legal decisions tend to be framed in terms of the law in the books as it is generally accepted unless there is a diversity in the decisions of lower courts without any authoritative resolution.[33] It is harder to reach a tipping point than in continental systems.

A *Tort and its competitors*

We might say that the tipping point has been reached when the pressure to do something about a problem becomes too strong to resist. If the response occurs in the setting of a court, it will almost by definition involve a change in the law of tort, since the dispute will have been framed within the law of tort.[34] Where it is legislative the position is very different. Here there is a range of possible responses, of which alteration of the tort system is only one. The present study provides several examples of this.

Legislatures across Europe have all had to face up to the problem of death or personal injury being caused in road traffic accidents.[35] One possible reaction to the perceived need to do something was to strengthen tort law by the enactment of some form of strict liability statute, as happened in Germany and Sweden in the early twentieth century. Another was to retain the fault-based system but to strengthen the position of victims by introducing a requirement of compulsory insurance, perhaps coupled with a state-funded guarantee where the wrongdoer could not be identified or was not in fact insured. A third response was to make the roads safer so as to reduce the risk of accidents: drivers are required to be licensed, regulations relating to the fitness of cars for use on the roads are introduced, together with speed limits, parking restrictions, traffic lights and the like. Informal solutions may be reached, as occurred in Great Britain with the Motor Insurers' Bureau's 'voluntary' agreements to compensate the victims of unidentified or uninsured drivers.

From the perspective of French law, the *Teffaine* decision of 1896, introducing or reintroducing strict liability for things, the problem of exploding steam boilers appears to be a major trigger for the reform of tort law

[33] C. Perelman and R. Vander Elst (eds.), *Les Notions à Contenu Variable* (Brussels: Bruylant, 1984).

[34] There may, however, have been an antecedent question of how the dispute should be framed. See below, p. 166.

[35] Above, pp. 120–129.

from within. But the *Teffaine* decision itself arose against the background of a regulatory system traceable back to 1810, consolidated in 1843, and partly reduced in stringency in 1865.[36] Elsewhere we find regulation of boilers envisaged in the Italian Civil Code of 1865, a limited strict liability in tort introduced in Germany in 1871 and a form of strict liability in article 1908 of the Spanish Civil Code of 1889 (albeit strict liability emasculated by an underpinning idea of fault), while in England statutory reform in 1881 was primarily focused on a regime of inspection together with the investigation of accidents which did occur with a view to their better prevention in the future.[37] These developments took place against the background of self-regulation by associations of steam boiler users, and in the context of moves to give better compensation to workers injured in industrial accidents.

In some systems, most notably those of the United Kingdom, asbestos-related industrial diseases have put very considerable stresses on tort law in the last few decades, with problems relating to the operation of orthodox ideas of fault, causation, damage and limitation periods.[38] In most countries, though, tort has played a subsidiary role, and in Germany and Spain it has played hardly any part at all. Commonly, the legislative response has been to impose regulations to improve workplace safety (as was the case in England from 1931), to rely on the social security system to provide support for victims and their families by classifying asbestosis and mesothelioma as occupational or professional diseases, or to set up a statutory compensation scheme as happened in France in 2002. It follows that in some systems the principles of tort law have had to be adjusted, either through case-law or through legislation, in order to deal with these problems, while in others tort law has remained fundamentally untouched by them.

Examples could be multiplied. Medical negligence can be dealt with through criminal processes rather than tort law; though in Italy, France and Spain, where the *partie civile* procedure applies,[39] tortious liability might be a by-product of such processes. Alternatively, disciplinary processes may be the dominant mechanisms for dealing with medical practitioners whose competence falls below an acceptable level. More generally, through the twentieth century systems of social insurance have played an increasingly important part in cases of personal injury and disease, either ousting tort law or relegating it to a subsidiary position. Similarly,

[36] Salmon, *Technology*, pp. 100–108. [37] Martín-Casals, *Technology*, pp. 12–18.
[38] *Ibid.*, pp. 29–39. [39] Above, pp. 72–73.

the ultimate response to problems of industrial nuisances has been the use of planning law or detailed regulatory frameworks, contrasting with the use of tort or property law in the middle of the nineteenth century.

The effect of the existence of this range of possible approaches has been that there has been a degree of divergence in the law in the books notwithstanding the similarities in the external environment. Even where social, technological or economic change has been reflected in functionally equivalent consequences in different systems, the legal mechanisms adopted may not have been the same, so that different legal structures have been produced.

B The non-use of tort

Except where it was formally ousted, tort law retained at least a residuary role. The fact that a different legislative solution to a perceived problem might have been adopted does not explain why there did not continue to be pressure to reform tort law from within. Individuals who had suffered injuries might still wish to bring actions in tort to obtain compensation. There might, however, be disincentives to bringing tort actions or barriers to doing so. Most importantly, financial support for victims or their families might be available by other means. Social insurance has already been mentioned. Private insurance might also be in general use: loss insurance of various forms (insurance of workers by their employers, for example, or private health insurance taken out by individuals, or insurance against property damage), or liability insurance. The latter of these may be especially important where it is heavily used in some particular sector so that it becomes a means in itself for spreading losses. It is easy to surmise that the stasis of the English tort of negligence as it applies to road traffic accidents has been possible only because of the practice of motor insurance companies not to waste time and money investigating the precise whereabouts of fault, nor to take advantage of their rights of subrogation in order to bring actions against other motorists who may have negligently injured the insured party. State-funded compensation systems might similarly reduce the pressure to use the tort system, as may provisions for compensation contained within regulations, such as those governing safety in the workplace.[40] In addition, tort litigation may be headed off by potential defendants making *ex gratia* payments to victims, as occurred notably in

[40] See below, p. 173, for the question whether regulatory compensation operates within the core of the tort system or outside it.

the English asbestos industry through much of the twentieth century;[41] and there are very strong pressures to limit the costs of litigation by settling actions before they come to court. These alternative forms of payment might be lower than those potentially obtainable by an action in tort, but the simple fact of their availability without the need for additional exhausting and costly litigation reduced the incentive to bring a claim in tort.

The barriers to tort litigation could be considerable. If individuals have to fund their own actions it might be simply too costly seriously to contemplate bringing a law-suit. Before the general availability of legal aid for the relatively poor after 1949 in England, and outside the context of the treatment of industrial injuries where the support of trade unions might be available, it is noticeable that many of what appear to be claims for medical negligence in fact arose by way of defence or counter-claim when a doctor brought an action against a patient for his fees.[42] There is similarly a hint that some of the cases that established the extra-contractual liability of negligent manufacturers were brought by insurance companies exercising their rights of subrogation rather than by the victims themselves, or that they were being managed by the defendant manufacturers in order to establish a clear legal rule of liability or non-liability rather than endure a situation of legal uncertainty.[43] The use of private-law claims for asbestos-related injuries in France over and above the statutory compensation scheme can be linked to the practice of insurance companies rather than the individual initiative of victims.[44]

A second set of barriers to tort litigation are those stemming from difficulties of obtaining evidence and proving liability. It is often the case that the person causing an injury is in a better position to discover how it occurred than the victim, though this may be partially alleviated by reversing the burden of proof or imposing strict liability, or by procedural mechanisms such as judicial investigation or rules requiring the discovery of evidence. Even beyond this, though, victims may be put in a weak position to demonstrate liability. Where the defendant was a member of a well-organised professional group, for example a doctor, it may be difficult to get other members of that group to give evidence against him.[45] It is said that one purpose of tall chimneys in nineteenth-century factories was to make it difficult to show that damage caused by pollution came

[41] Morgan, *Technology*, p. 77. [42] Above, p. 93. [43] Above, p. 77.

[44] Salmon, *Technology*, pp. 130–133; www.viva.presse.fr/spip.php?page=articlemutuelles&id_article=11898 (accessed 5 January 2012).

[45] Above, p. 93.

from any one factory in particular,[46] prefiguring the way in which the victims of mesothelioma were at a major disadvantage in proving the tortious responsibility of any one person who had exposed them to asbestos fibres before mechanisms were put in place to remove this hurdle.

Thirdly, there might be ideological barriers. Before the changes in medical care after the Second World War there appears to have been a reluctance on the part of patients to sue their doctors, and the further back we go the greater this reluctance seems to have been.[47] Workers in the English asbestos industry accepted the risks of that work as an unavoidable side effect, and even the Asbestos Regulations of 1931, which have been described as a 'licence to kill', were drafted with the full co-operation of the Trades Union Congress.[48] More generally, one reason for the failure of the private law tort of nuisance to provide a remedy for injuries caused by industrial pollution in the nineteenth century was that the people who suffered the injuries were typically the workers in the polluting factories, who were wholly dependent on the factories for their livelihood.[49]

Whatever the causes of victims not bringing actions or pursuing them to completion, the effect was always to reduce or remove the pressure for judicial change to the law, since this can only occur through litigation which is actually brought before the court. The pressure is further reduced when the disincentives and barriers to litigation are combined with legislation which has alleviated some of the social consequences of an activity, so that a tipping point for change is yet less likely to be reached. Formal law, the law in the books, has been able to remain stubbornly resistant to change notwithstanding the massive changes in the external environment over the last century and a half. This is visible in all systems, but it is particularly noteworthy in England where, as has been seen, the institutional structures militate against judicial change.[50]

C Mechanisms for change

Pressure for change may be felt both by the courts and by the legislature. Court-based change is largely incremental, working within the existing

[46] J.F. Brenner, 'Nuisance Law and the Industrial Revolution' (1974) 3 *Journal of Legal Studies* 403.

[47] Above, p. 95.

[48] Morgan, *Technology*, p. 67, citing N.J. Wikeley, 'The Asbestos Regulations 1931: A Licence to Kill?' (1992) 19 *Journal of Law and Society* 365.

[49] Brenner, 'Nuisance Law and the Industrial Revolution', pp. 419–20.

[50] Above, pp. 70–71.

law. Major changes are more appropriate to the legislature, which has the capacity to investigate the implications of any alteration, with its potential benefits and disadvantages, and to mould it in different ways; and it is only the legislature that can engineer a change which involves the payment of money by the state or the imposition of regulations which may have criminal sanctions attached to them.

The pressure on courts is outcome-related, in the sense that it is precipitated by the law in the books seeming to require what is perceived (or at least argued) to be the wrong answer. Where the wrong answer is not actually necessitated, but the courts can reach what they see to be the right answer within the existing rules, this will be the easiest course to follow. The idea of fault is highly plastic, so that changes in the incidence of legal liability can occur purely by interpretation. The shifts in the liability of medical practitioners in both England and France happened in this way. In England the negligence principle remained intact despite major changes in the approach to liability between the 1950s and the 1980s; the only formal variation in the standard of care required of the doctor, through the so-called *Bolam* test, was an offshoot of the rules relating to the interpretation of expert evidence.[51] So too in France, where the changes in liability occurred behind the language of *faute*, as the liability rule moved from *faute lourde* to the less stringent *faute simple*.[52] Similarly, the liability of car drivers in England remained formally fault based while the interpretation of what constituted fault seemingly became stricter,[53] as did the liability for defective products across Europe until statutes intervened.[54]

Courts, if they choose not to act simply by interpreting the existing rules, are nonetheless constrained by them. But where there is a greater range of legal formants available, it becomes easier to justify a change without appearing to do so.[55] Hence in France the Cour de cassation in *Jand'heur* in 1930 was able to admit a substantially strict liability on drivers who had caused injuries. The *Teffaine* decision of 1896, as interpreted, had recognised a measure of strict liability for things under article 1384 of the *Code Civil*, and leading scholars (Ripert, Josserand, Capitant, Esmein) had argued that this might equally be applied to road traffic accidents.[56] The same step might have been taken in England in 1909 in *Wing v. London*

[51] Above, p. 99. [52] Above, p. 92.
[53] Above, pp. 122–129. [54] Above, pp. 77–82.
[55] Above, pp. 2–3. We might prefer to describe this as a change in the dominant formant rather than a change in the law.
[56] Above, p. 131.

General Omnibus Co., but it was rejected by the Court of Appeal.[57] Once compulsory insurance had been introduced in 1930 the climate might have been more favourable to strict liability, but the decision in *Wing* was by this time too well established to be displaced.

Legislative change is not so constrained. In theory, it is not constrained at all. It is commonly, however, very slow and often proceeds incrementally.[58] The radical restructuring of compensation for personal injuries in the Swedish Tort Liability Act of 1972 and the Traffic Damages Act of 1975 can be traced back to the arguments of Vilhelm Lunstedt in 1923 and proposals of Ivar Strahl made in 1947 and discussed at the Nordic Convention for Lawyers from the beginning of the 1950s.[59] Andre Tunc's proposals for the removal of road traffic accidents from the law of tort were made in 1964, finally becoming (in muted form) the basis of the statutory reforms of 1985.[60] Gino Gorla in Italy and Werner Lorenz in Germany had introduced American ideas of strict product liability into Europe in the years after the Second World War, but it was only in 1985 that the European Product Liability Directive was enacted.[61]

There is a measure of competitive synergy between legislative and court-based change. Where the legislature has failed to act, the courts may do so within the limits available to them in any system. French case-law developed strict liability for motor accidents in 1930, half a century before there was a statutory regime; proposals for similar statutory reform in the Netherlands came to nought, but the Hoge Raad was able to move the law towards the position which had been proposed by scholars such as Wouter Snijders and Auke Bloembergen, both of whom sat on the Hoge Raad; German courts gave a very narrow reading to the defence of inevitable accident for decades before this was given a statutory recognition in 2002 by replacing it with a requirement of *vis maior*.[62] The same can largely be said of the approach of the courts to manufacturers' liability between the 1930s and the enactment of the Product Liability Directive in 1985;[63] and a similar phenomenon can be seen with medical liability in an environment in which there are arguments for no-fault schemes for some types of injury (found already in Sweden in 1971, and subsequently introduced in

[57] Above, p. 122.

[58] N. Ghei, 'The Optimal Timing of Lawmaking', in F. Parisi (ed.), *Production of Legal Rules* (Cheltenham: Edward Elgar, 2011), 54.

[59] Modéer, *Doctrine*, pp. 217–218.

[60] Viney and Guégan-Lécuyer, *Traffic*, pp. 64–69.

[61] Above, pp. 74, 83.

[62] Above, p. 126.

[63] Above, pp. 82–83.

France) as well as embryonic legislation at a European level.[64] Equally, the courts can trigger statutory changes. The French reform of traffic law of 1985 was, probably deliberately, provoked by the decision of the Cour de cassation in *Desmares* in 1982,[65] just as the British Parliament acted with untypical rapidity immediately to reverse the effect of the House of Lords' decision in *Barker v. Corus plc*.[66]

As well as operating to affect legal outcomes, legislative change may also have a rhetorical function. It is likely that this is the primary consequence of the Product Liability Directive and the statutes made in accordance with it. In so far as the courts had already in practice made liability more strict by their interpretation of what constituted fault and by the use of procedural devices such as the reversal of the burden of proof, the formal enactment of statutes imposing strict liability made very little change, while the Directive itself (and therefore the national legislation) created a simulacrum of fault liability by defining defects in products in terms of the level of safety that users were entitled to expect. In the same way, in England, section 1 of the Compensation Act of 2006 provided that in determining whether a duty of care should be held to have existed, courts should take into account whether the imposition of liability would have knock-on effects of discouraging desirable activities. Explicitly, the purpose of this section was not to change the law at all, but to 'improve awareness' of this aspect of the law and to 'provide reassurance' for those concerned about possible litigation.[67]

IV Convergence and divergence

Within the development of fault liability in the law of tort in the last 150 years, therefore, it is possible to see a competing dynamic, partly towards convergence of the law and partly towards divergence. In this final section we try to reconcile this tension.

Where change has been brought about by purely internal mechanisms, the tendency has been for this to lead to divergence between systems, counterbalanced by a degree of convergence resulting from a common heritage and from the adoption of foreign models.[68] Such changes take

[64] Taylor, *Medical*, pp. 93–98; Hondius in *Medical*, pp. 19–23.

[65] Viney and Guégan-Lécuyer, *Traffic*, pp. 66–67.

[66] Morgan, *Technology*, pp. 87–88.

[67] Compensation Act 2006, Explanatory note 10, quoted by Morgan, *Technology*, p. 88 note 232.

[68] Above, p. 163.

effect within the law in the books, so that the formulations of the rules and principles in systems have come to differ without this having any necessary effect on the legal outcomes. It does not matter, for example, whether actions for the breach of regulatory duties are treated as falling within the main core of tortious liability, as has occurred generally in continental Europe where unlawfulness is a component of ordinary liability, or as a specific tort of breach of statutory duty, which has been the position in England since the 1940s.

Changes which have occurred as a response to the external environment are rather different. They typically affect the legal outcomes, but may do so in different ways. In very general terms it can be said that there is convergence at a functional level, in terms of the outcomes which are reached, but that there is divergence as a result of these outcomes being reached in different ways except – as with internal changes – where there have been common or mutual influences on the ways in which the changes are made.

A *Functional convergence*

Functional convergence can be illustrated in several ways from the European Legal Development project: it is present in all of the fields examined in the earlier volumes in this series. In the nineteenth and early twentieth centuries there are similar responses to industrialisation, visible most clearly in the pro-industrial responses to pollution. Negligent manufacturers were similarly protected in this early period, with a reversal of this trend in the middle of the twentieth century and an increasing move towards strict liability thereafter. Medical liability has moved in the direction of the protection of patients, and the liability of car drivers has similarly become stricter.

As legal systems responded to industrialisation we see a shift first from the protection of traditional activities to the protection of emergent industries. This is visible in England, France and Germany in the 1860s, with each system adopting within its law of nuisance (however this is structured in the individual system) a presumption in favour of industrial developments;[69] in Italy and Spain, where industrialisation occurred rather later, the explicit protection of industry also occurred rather later.[70] This did not necessarily involve an economic subsidy to industry, but might paradoxically involve the imposition of strict liability on industrial

[69] Above, pp. 150–151. [70] Above, p. 151.

enterprises. In Germany, for example, damages were awarded under the *actio negatoria* without any proof of fault, just as it was unnecessary to prove fault in order to succeed under the English tort of nuisance or under article 1908 of the Spanish *Código Civil*[71] and strict liability for the escape of water from reservoirs and the like was introduced at more or less the same time in England, Scotland, France, Germany and Italy.[72] What was important was that the new rules bent the law in the direction of allowing the industrial activity to take place notwithstanding the risk of damage, refusing to grant injunctions against them. This pro-industrial approach was not formally reversed but rather neutralised by the imposition of regulatory codes, planning rules and the like; state control at a level of detail largely replaced open-textured private law.

Manufacturers of defective goods were to some extent immunised from liability in the nineteenth century for a number of reasons.[73] Perhaps the most important was the way in which remedies for injuries caused by goods were primarily seen in contractual terms, so that direct recourse against a manufacturer who had not himself supplied the goods to the victim was unavailable because of the rules of privity of contract. Yet the use of tort was not unimaginable, and here manufacturers were largely protected against claims except in so far as liability could be passed through a chain of contracts. We may surmise that behind this there lay a desire not to burden emergent industries with liabilities; as well, since much production was still on a relatively small scale, there may have been a feeling that it was problematic to impose a potentially very high level of liability which might have a very low probability of occurring, something which could not be factored in to the manufacturer's pricing.[74] By the 1930s there was a clear move towards the imposition of liability for personal injury on negligent manufacturers in those jurisdictions where there was a strong manufacturing sector, with the changes occurring almost simultaneously in France, the United Kingdom and Holland. By now the structure of manufacturing industry was moving towards larger concerns which had a greater capacity to absorb losses and pass them on to their customers,

[71] Above, p. 146.

[72] *Rylands v. Fletcher* (1868) LR 3 HL 330; *Kerr v. Earl of Orkney* (1857) 20 SC 298; D.66.1.271; von Jhering, 'Zur Lehre von den Beschränkungen des Grundeigenthümers' (based on decisions of the previous three decades); Torino 18 May 1869, Giurisprudenza Italiana 1869.2.342.

[73] Above, p. 76.

[74] See for example the remarks in *Winterbottom v. Wright* (1842) 10 M & W 109, 111; 152 ER 402, 403.

and liability insurance was generally available to spread losses (as it had not been in the nineteenth century), though it is impossible to find data demonstrating whether this was in fact the cause of the changes in the law. There was no real sense in which the liability of the negligent manufacturers could or should be linked to an idea of moral responsibility, and courts invented mechanisms to shift the balance towards the injured consumer, reflecting the more general societal moves towards consumer protection. Finally the functional convergence was consolidated by the achievement of a formal near-uniformity as a result of the enactment of the European Product Liability Directive in 1985.

A similar shift in the liability of medical practitioners occurred over the period we have examined. Here there was a mixture of forces at work.[75] The late nineteenth and early twentieth centuries saw a change in medical practice as a result of technological developments, most importantly X-rays, as well as antiseptic procedures and new drugs. These scientific innovations were, inevitably, pan-European and not limited to any particular place. Alongside them, particularly after the First World War, there were changes in the nature of hospitals, as they became places where sick people went to be cured rather than simply to be looked after. This brought about a change in expectations of doctors and other medical professionals. This change was not uniformly reflected in the formal legal rules. It has been seen that in England the rules remained the same and their interpretation was strongly weighted in favour of the doctors, whereas in France there was a change in the formulation of the rules of both private and public law, lowering the level of negligence which would trigger liability on the part of the doctor. Even here, though, the application of the rules might not have been significantly different from what it had been before.[76] There were substantial changes in public health provision after the Second World War, and also changes in the availability and costs of legal services. These did bring about a change in the rules and their application in France, both in private law and in public law, but in England it was not until around 1980 that this became visible. The comparative slowness of the changes in English law can be explained by the activity of the Medical Defence Union in the early part of the twentieth century and then by the dominant part played by the conservative (in this respect) Lord Denning in the 1950s, 1960s and 1970s. England was similarly lagging behind at the start of the twenty-first century, as France

[75] Above, pp. 84–85. [76] Above, p. 96.

began to introduce strict-liability schemes for certain types of medical injury. That said, the trajectory of development is identical.

Finally, we have seen a similar functional convergence in the imposition of liability on drivers for motor accidents.[77] Underpinning this has been the relation between legal liability and insurance, whether explicitly (as in Sweden, for example) or implicitly (as in England). While the question to which the law initially responded was when car owners or drivers should be held legally liable, as a result of the growth of the insurance market by the second half of the twentieth century the question was recharacterised as one of creating efficient mechanisms for compensating the victims of accidents (the fact that we speak of them as 'accidents' perhaps reveals the extent to which genuine fault has become largely irrelevant). Compulsory insurance, accompanied by schemes to deal with uninsured or unidentified drivers, has been the preferred solution; the recalibration of liability in favour of the victims of accidents, by whatever means this has been achieved, has been the common response of all the legal systems examined.

These responses were not automatic or mechanistic responses by 'the law'. They were the responses of individuals – of judges, of legislators and of scholars – whose attitudes had been moulded by the economic changes that were taking place. They may or may not have been reflecting popular opinion, which would probably in any event have been fragmented, though without a substantial measure of support from the principal legal actors it is perhaps doubtful whether they would have become established in the law. Sometimes changes occurred almost simultaneously. This might be the result of deliberate reforms, as with the introduction of workmen's compensation rules in the 1890s as a result of concerted action by the international trades union movement, though frequently there is no such clear link: we are left guessing whether the change in approach to industrial polluters in the 1860s or to negligent manufacturers in the 1930s was the result of influences from one system on another or simply of chance. Commonly, though, there have been time lags in the changes brought about in different systems, either because of the different rates of external changes between countries (industrialisation occurring earlier in some places than in others, for example, or private car use growing faster in some places than in others), or because of the sheer capriciousness flowing from political circumstances or the decisions of particular individuals.

[77] Above, pp. 111–114.

Common to all these situations was that the external changes brought about changes in the way in which the world was viewed, and these were in their turn reflected in the legal rules. Parallel development of the law was possible without this, though. We have seen that in both England and France there was a greater concentration on questions of patient consent to medical procedures in the second quarter of the twentieth century,[78] but do not have to attribute this to any widely held belief in patient autonomy, nor even to influence from one system on the other. A more attractive explanation is that English law and French law independently shifted their focus onto this in order to counteract the problems faced by patients in demonstrating fault on the part of a doctor who had been using technologically sophisticated equipment whose working was understood neither by the patient nor by the judges trying the case. By focusing on consent there was a question which was susceptible of examination, which provided a proxy for the requirement of proving fault.

A further examination of the same phenomenon is provided by the nineteenth-century question of legal liability when sparks escaped from a railway engine and set fire to property lying next to the track. Here there was no agreement about the correct answer, even within the same system; Lord Hoffmann, commenting on the nineteenth-century English decisions, speaks of the way in which they displayed no coherent development but rather showed the shifting ascendancies of one view or the other.[79] Notwithstanding this, between the middle of the nineteenth century and the middle of the twentieth, all the systems examined moved in practice towards the imposition of strict liability on the railway operator. In Germany this was achieved early by legislation, the Prussian Railways Act of 1838, which was adopted in other German-speaking territories.[80] In France, the clear nineteenth-century view was that liability depended on fault under article 1382, though by the 1850s it was held that the necessary degree of fault was present even where the railway was being run 'according to all the rules of ordinary care'.[81] In effect, a form of strict liability was being smuggled in behind the façade of fault. The façade was rapidly dropped in the early twentieth century, once it had been recognised that article 1384 could be used to impose strict liability for things.[82] Italian law[83] followed the French in the nineteenth century, imposing liability for

[78] Above, pp. 104–110.

[79] *Wildtree Hotels Ltd v. Harrow London Borough Council* [2001] 2 AC 1, at para. [3], quoted by Morgan, *Technology*, p. 44.

[80] Scherpe, *Technology*, pp. 140–144.

[81] S.1867.1.77; Salmon, *Technology*, p. 95.

[82] S.1905.2.105; Salmon, *Technology*, p. 98.

[83] Favilli, *Technology*, pp. 185–203.

fault without requiring proof of fault. At the end of the century, however, just as the French were discovering the potential of article 1384, Italian law began to require a strict proof of fault. In effect, it was moving in the opposite direction from French law. In practice, though, the courts shifted the responsibility for determining what constituted fault onto the public administration, which was empowered to make regulations: failing to act in conformity with the regulations was fault, acting in accordance with them was prima facie sufficient to relieve the railway from liability. Finally, as steam trains began to be phased out in the middle of the twentieth century, liability became stricter as the courts imposed a high standard of care over and above what was required by the regulations. Spanish law was rather similar.[84] Fault liability was applied in the nineteenth century, though there was considerable ambiguity in the way in which fault was interpreted. From the early twentieth century attention shifted to whether the regulations had been observed, and from the 1950s this was supplanted by a high standard of care beyond what the regulations laid down. English law, too, displayed a marked leaning towards strict liability in the nineteenth century,[85] but in 1869 – against the advice of the judges – the House of Lords held that where the railway was being run with a statutory authorisation liability should lie only for negligence.[86] In practice, most railways did have statutory authorisation, so negligence liability became the general rule. This was substantially reversed by statute, the Railway Fires Act of 1905, imposing strict liability for loss up to the value of £200. The reasons offered in justification of the Act during its passage through Parliament were not so much theoretical or moral as practical. Even where the railway company had in truth been negligent, it was commonly very difficult for the landowner to prove this and always very expensive to do so; moreover, it was very difficult for landowners to insure against this form of loss.[87] The real benefits of the strict liability regime were that it enabled compensation to be obtained without these difficulties of proof and that it would operate as an incentive on railway companies to develop and adopt more effective means to avoid the escape of sparks from their engines. Although the routes followed by each system were different, each reached the same stable position.

[84] Martín-Casals and Ribot, *Technology*, pp. 227–238.
[85] Morgan, *Technology*, pp. 40–51.
[86] *Hammersmith and City Railway v. Brand* (1869) LR 4 HL 171.
[87] Parl. Deb. (4th series), vol. 142, cols. 348–374.

B Path dependence and doctrinal divergence

Functional convergence may go hand in hand with divergence at the level of the law in the books. In the absence of influence from one system on another, we would expect such divergence to be the norm because of the way in which each system develops by the accretion of changes. Judges decide cases in terms of their own systems, and each of these will have its own characteristics. Legislators have a menu of options open to them, but even where the menu is the same in each system the choice made from it may be different.

A degree of doctrinal divergence is inevitable, but our study has suggested that this divergence is not uniform. Liability for medical injuries and defective products is relatively homogeneous in different systems (even before the imposition of common rules by the European Commission in the latter case), while nineteenth-century responses to industrial pollution and early twentieth-century responses to road accidents reveal systems seeming to move apart. This can be attributed to the fact that the former two situations were generally dealt with in terms of the ordinary rules of fault liability in 1850, whereas in the latter two situations different legal structures were already in place at that time.

The divergences observable in industrial pollution and road traffic cases were brought about in different ways, the former through case-law and the latter through a mixture of case-law and legislation. They reveal two different forms of path dependence.[88]

That there should be path dependence in developments achieved through case-law is unsurprising. Judges operate within the existing law, and even where different formants are available the way in which things have been done in the past provides an easy guide to the way in which they should be done now. The natural way for the pollution cases to be dealt with in continental Europe was through the law of property – specifically the law of servitudes – together with a doctrine of abuse of rights based on the earlier law of malicious wrongdoing, *aemulatio*. In England, by contrast, the traditional way to deal with them was through the tort of nuisance rather than the law of property. In the absence of any pre-existing ideas of abuse of rights within the common law, the House of Lords in *Bradford v. Pickles* in 1898 was not persuaded to adopt one, all the more so because of the potential consequences which this might have for legal liability arising out of industrial disputes. Once this was locked in place

[88] Above, pp. 24–32.

it was impossible for courts to displace it, given the absolutely binding quality of House of Lords' decisions at the time. Instead, English courts developed their own rules of malice within the tort of nuisance, treating malicious acts as unreasonable and hence potentially actionable.[89]

More needs to be said about motor accidents, where both legislation and judicial decisions had their parts to play. In the early years of the twentieth century those countries with the largest rates of motor vehicle ownership – the United Kingdom, France and Germany – were faced with the same problem: pedestrians and cyclists were increasingly being injured by motor cars driven by or on behalf of wealthy individuals or companies. The burden of proof imposed on the victim made recovery in tort difficult because the speed of events and the novelty of technology made it difficult to provide reliable evidence from witnesses. With good communication and international discussion, such as at the International Road Congress of 1908 in Paris, there was a real possibility of finding international solutions. Each country, though, had its own pre-existing law, which offered solutions that could be applied by analogy. All had rules relating to liability for animals. In Germany there was also the Prussian Railways Act of 1838, imposing strict liability for trains, the scope of which had been expanded in the Imperial Law on Liability of 1871. In France, article 1382 of the *Code Civil* had based liability on fault but the *Teffaine* decision had opened the possibility of strict liability for things under article 1384. England had its main core of negligence liability, which had been applied to railway accidents, but other analogies were possible: strict liability for dangerous things under the rule in *Rylands v. Fletcher*, public nuisance for blockages on the highway, animals.

In Germany, the Motor Vehicle Act of 1909 imposed liability on the operator of the car, not the driver, thereby enabling the victim to recover compensation from the person with the deep pocket who would otherwise have been immune from liability because of the fault-based vicarious liability of the BGB.[90] The reform was necessary if compensation was to be practically recoverable, though the precise details of the legislation were influenced by the effective lobbying of the motoring organisations. This was closely modelled on the liability rules that were already applied to railways: the fact that these rules existed already operated as a focus for the legal practitioners' discussions in the Deutsche Juristentag and made the acceptance of the proposal more palatable to the legislature. Statutory schemes for the imposition of strict liability were proposed at about the

[89] Above, p. 148. [90] Above, pp. 119–120, 124; for details, Lohsse, *Traffic*, pp. 93–96.

same time in both England and France but succeeded in neither: the tipping point for legislative change was not reached, in part because the vicarious liability rules were more generous to victims and in part because the lack of existing rules, such as those applied to German railways, meant that there was greater reluctance to accept strict liability.

In both England and France, change was achieved through case-law. When the question of liability arose in England in *Wing v. London General Omnibus*,[91] where a passenger had been injured escaping from a bus which had skidded into a lamp post in wet conditions, the choice open to the Court of Appeal was between the adoption of a rule of fault liability by applying the tort of negligence or one of strict liability through the tort of nuisance. The latter would entail holding that it had been wrongful for the defendant company to put the vehicle on the road in wet conditions, with the implication that they should not have done so and hence that they should not do so in the future. As Pollock noted at the time, common sense suggested that the public would prefer to be able to use vehicles in the rain and run the risks of non-negligent injury.[92] English law simply followed its near-axiomatic adherence to fault liability.

In France the question was rather different, whether the potentially strict liability for things of article 1384 could be applied to motor car accidents. *Teffaine* had applied this to steam boilers, and hence to one typical case of injury or damage caused by railway trains,[93] an approach confirmed in decisions of the Cour de cassation around 1920.[94] At first the courts would not apply this to car accidents, since the injury was caused by the driver's driving rather than by the vehicle itself,[95] but these later decisions of the Cour de cassation encouraged a different approach to motor vehicles, and in 1924 the Cour de cassation simply took the form of words which it had used in relation to railway engines in 1919 and applied it to cars.[96] The *Jand'heur* decisions of the Cour de cassation in 1927 and 1930, faced with criticism from leading doctrinal writers such as Ripert and Capitant and with reluctance on the part of the lower courts to apply no-fault liability to motor cars, took this further.[97] In the *rapport*

91 [1909] 2 KB 652. 92 (1909) 26 LQR 3, 4.

93 Cass. civ. 16 June 1896, S. 1897.1.17; Halpérin, *Doctrine*, p. 88.

94 Cass. civ. 21 January 1919, DP 1922.1.25; Cass. civ. 16 November 1920, DP 1920.1.169; Cass. civ. 15 March 1921, DP 1922.1.25.

95 Req. 22 March 1911, D.P. 1911.1.354.

96 Cass. civ. 29 July 1924, DP 1925.1.5, note Ripert.

97 GP 1927.1.407; Cass. ch. réunies 13 February 1930, DP 1930.1.57, *rapport* Le Marc'hadour, concl. Matter, note Ripert.

of Judge Le Marc'hadour and the conclusions of avocat général Matter, we are presented with very long and careful illustrations of legal reasoning on both sides from within the judiciary. Le Marc'hadour opposed the extension to cars on the grounds that this would constitute an illegitimate form of judicial law-making. By contrast, avocat général Matter argued that the extension was not contrary to the 'tradition' of the *Code Civil*: the case-law on article 1384 only dated from 1896, and, adopting a risk-based theory propounded by Saleilles in 1897, he preferred to apply a 'liberal and humane' interpretation of the text to provide greater protection to victims. What is significant is that the two sides argued within the same framework. Neither called in question the line of case-law since 1896, and both recounted fundamentally the same history going back at least to 1804. The same corpus of legal experience and knowledge formed the subject-matter of their legal interpretation, even if their interpretations led to different results. Fidelity to the tradition was an ambition which imposed a way of working, such that analogy and re-interpretation went hand in hand. The debates in English law about the appropriate level of judicial legislation were far less sophisticated than those in France, but what is more significant is that the options open to the court in *Wing* were very different from those available in *Jand'heur.*

French law's acceptance of liability without fault for motor accidents made its adoption of a fully-fledged no-fault system backed by insurance, introduced by legislation (the *loi Badinter*) in 1985, easier than in Germany or in England. Although in all three systems American models of such systems were being discussed as early as the 1920s, none of these discussions resulted in legislation at the time. There was renewed interest in such schemes in the 1960s; but in Germany the suggestion did not fall on fertile ground, while in England the recommendation of the Pearson Commission in 1978 that a no-fault scheme should be introduced was not adopted by Parliament. France was less unreceptive, though it required the decision of the Cour de cassation in *Desmares* finally to stimulate the legislature into action.[98] Perhaps more significant, though, was that Badinter, the Minister of Justice, was a colleague at the University of Paris I of André Tunc, the principal proponent of change since the publication of his *La Sécurité Routière* in 1964.

Path dependence, with its ideas of normative consistency and incremental decision-making, provides some explanation for these examples of legal divergence. But we must not lose sight of the fact that there has

[98] Above, p. 126.

been no simple, invisible hand guiding the process, but rather conscious choice and debate throughout. If certain individuals had occupied key positions, the law could have gone in different directions. All that can be said is that certain analogies and arguments are more legally plausible in one environment than another. Path dependence thus provides a useful pointer to reasons why, sometimes, the law of different countries may formally diverge, but it cannot offer a complete explanation; and no explanation can ever be deterministic.

APPENDIX: MAIN CODE AND LEGISLATIVE PROVISIONS CITED

The texts provided in this Appendix provide the main texts of national codes dealing with delict or tort that applied in the period 1850 to 2000, together with the major legislation on road traffic.

France

Civil Code (1804)[1]

Property

544 Property is the right to enjoy and to dispose of things in the most absolute manner possible, provided that one does not use it in a way prohibited by laws or regulations.

649 Servitudes established by law have as their purpose communal utility, or the utility of private individuals.

650 Those established for public or communal utility have as their purpose the towpath alongside navigable or floatable rivers, the construction or repair of paths and other public or communal works.

Everything concerning this kind of servitude is determined by special laws and regulations.

651 Legislation subjects owners to various obligations with regard to each other independently of any contract.

652 These obligations are governed in part by laws on rural policing. The others relate to party walls and ditches, to rights of support, to views over the property of a neighbour, to drainage from roofs, and to rights of passage. [These rights are then regulated in detail in articles 653–685.]

686 Owners may establish servitudes on their properties and in favour of their properties, as seems best to them, provided nevertheless that the designated services neither are imposed nor are in favour of a person, but merely on or for

[1] Later amendments in italics.

a property, and provided that the services contain nothing contrary to public policy.

The use and extent of the servitudes thus established are governed by the title document which creates them; in the absence of such a document, by the following rules [set out in articles 687 to 710].

Delict

1382 Any human act whatever which causes damage to another obliges him by whose fault it occurred to make reparation.

1383 Every person is liable for the damage which he causes not only by his own act but also by his negligence or imprudence.

1384 [para.1] He is liable not only for the damage which he caused by his own act, but also for that which is caused by the act of persons for whom he is responsible, or by things which he has in his keeping.

[para. 2][2] *However, he who possesses by whatever right all or part of a building or of personal property in which a fire occurs is liable vis-à-vis third persons for damage caused by such fire only if it is proved that it should be attributed to his fault or to the fault of persons for whom he is responsible.*

[para. 3][3] *This provision does not apply to relations between owners and tenants which remain regulated by articles 1733 and 1734 of the Civil Code.*

[para. 4][4] The father, and the mother after the death of the father, are liable for damage caused by their minor children living with them.

[para. 5] Masters and principals (are liable) for damage caused by their domestics and employees in the functions for which they have been employed.

[para. 6] Teachers and artisans (are liable) for damage caused by their pupils and apprentices during the time when they are under their surveillance.

[para. 7] The above liability arises unless the father and mother, [*teachers*][5] and the artisans prove that they could not prevent the act which gave rise to such liability.

[para. 8] *As to teachers, the faults, imprudence or negligence alleged against them as having caused the damaging act must be proven according to ordinary law by the plaintiff in the suit.*

1385 The owner of an animal or he who avails himself of it while it is being put to his use is liable for the damage which the animal causes, whether the animal was in his keeping or whether it had strayed or escaped.

[2] Text resulting from the law of 7 November 1922. [3] *Ibid.*

[4] Text resulting from law n° 70–459 of 4 January 1970: the father and mother, to the extent that they exercise the right of custody, are jointly liable for damage caused by their minor children living with them.

[5] The law of 5 April 1937 removed this word and added paragraph 8.

1386 The owner of a building is liable for damage caused by its ruin, when this occurred through want of maintenance or by a construction defect.

Sale (extracts)

1641 The vendor is held to guarantee against defects in the thing sold which render it improper for the use for which it was intended, or which so diminish this use that the purchaser would not have bought it, or would only have given a lower price, if he had known.

1644 The purchaser has the choice of returning the thing and being reimbursed for the price, or of keeping the thing and having part of the price reimbursed, which sum is fixed by experts.

1645 If the vendor knew of the defect in the thing, he is liable not only to reimburse the price he has received but also for any damages to the purchaser.

1646 If the vendor did not know of the defect in the thing, he is liable only to reimburse the price he has received and to repay to the purchaser the expenses incurred in the sale.

1648 The action for defects has to be commenced by the purchaser within a short time, according to the nature of the defects, the usage of the place where the sale took place.

Road Traffic Law 5 July 1985

1 The provisions of the present chapter apply to the victims of traffic accidents in which a motor vehicle or its trailer is involved, even if the victims are being carried pursuant to a contract; they do not apply to trains or trams which run on their own tracks.

2 Neither force majeure nor the act of a third party provides the driver or custodian of a motor vehicle with any defence against victims, including drivers.

3 (1) Victims other than drivers of motor vehicles are indemnified for the harm resulting from personal injury regardless of their own fault, unless it was inexcusable and constituted the sole cause of the damage.

(2) If such victims are less than sixteen or more than seventy years old or, whatever their age, have been held to be permanently disabled or incapacitated to at least eighty per cent, they are entitled in all cases to full damages for their personal injuries.

(3) However, no damages are due in such cases if the victim deliberately incurred the harm suffered.

4 The fault of the driver of a motor vehicle can limit or exclude his claim for damages.

5 Fault on the part of the victim can limit or exclude the damages he may claim for damages to property, save that the rules relating to personal injury apply if the items damaged are medically prescribed.

6 Claims by third parties are subject to the limitations and exclusions which affect the claim of the primary victim of a traffic accident.

Germany

Civil Code (1900)

226 The exercise of a right is unlawful if it can only have the purpose of harming another.

459 (1) The seller of a thing warrants to the purchaser that, at the time when the risk passes to him, it is free from defects that diminish or destroy its value or its suitability for normal use or for the use provided for in the contract. A trivial reduction in the value or suitability is not taken into consideration.

(2) The seller also warrants that, at the time the risk passes, the thing has the qualities promised.

460 A seller is not responsible for the defect in anything sold if the purchaser knew of the defect at the moment of entering into the contract. If a defect of the kind specified in § 459(1) has remained unknown to the purchaser because of his gross negligence, the seller is liable only where he has fraudulently concealed it, unless he warranted that the thing was free from defect.

462 By reason of a defect for which the seller is liable under §§ 459, 460, the purchaser may claim that the sale be annulled (cancellation) or a reduction in the purchase price.

463 If a promised quality in the thing sold was absent at the time of the purchase, the purchaser may claim compensation for non-performance, instead of cancellation or reduction. The same applies where the seller has concealed a defect.

Delict

823 (1) A person who wilfully or negligently injures the life, body, health, freedom, property, or other right of another contrary to law is bound to compensate him for any damage arising therefrom.

(2) The same obligation attaches to a person who infringes a statutory provision intended for the protection of others. If according to the purview of the statute infringement is possible even without fault, the duty to make compensation arises only if some fault can be imputed to the wrongdoer.

826 A person who wilfully causes damage to another in a manner *contra bonos mores* is bound to compensate the other for the damage.

828 (1) A person who has not completed his seventh year of age is not responsible for any damage which he does to another.

(2) A person who has completed his seventh but not his tenth year is not responsible for the harm which he inflicts on another in an accident with a motor vehicle, a railway or a hover rail. This does not apply if he has caused the injury deliberately.
(3) A person who has not yet completed his 18th year is, in so far as his responsibility is not excluded under paragraphs 1 or 2, not responsible for the harm which he inflicts on another if, on the commission of the action causing the harm, he does not have the necessary intelligence to realise his responsibility.

831 (1) A person who employs another to do any work is bound to compensate for damage which the other unlawfully causes to a third party in the performance of his work. The duty to compensate does not arise if the employer has exercised ordinary care in the choice of the employee, and, where he has to supply appliances or implements or to superintend the work, has also exercised ordinary care as regards such supply or superintendence, or if the damage would have arisen, notwithstanding the exercise of such care.

(2) The same responsibility attaches to a person who takes over the charge of any of the affairs specified in para. 1, sentence 2, by contract with the employer.

839 (1) If an official wilfully or negligently commits a breach of official duty incumbent upon him towards a third party, he shall compensate the third party for any damage arising therefrom. If only negligence is imputable to the official, he may be held liable only if the injured party is unable to obtain compensation elsewhere.

(2) If an official violates his official duty by a decision on a legal matter, he is only responsible for the harm arising from this if the violation of duty consists of a criminal act. This provision has no application to a refusal or delay which is contrary to duty in exercise of the office.
(3) The duty to compensate does not arise if the victim has intentionally or negligently refrained from averting the harm by the use of a legal remedy.

847 [REPEALED IN 2002, see now § 253 (2)] In the case of injury to body or health, or in the case of deprivation of liberty, the injured party may also demand an equitable compensation in money for damage which is not a pecuniary loss.

Property

903 (1) Insofar as the law or the rights of third parties do not conflict with this, the owner of a thing can deal with the thing at his discretion and can exclude others from any interference with it …

906 (1) The owner of land cannot forbid the introduction of gases, steam, smells, smoke, soot, heat, noise, vibrations and similar things coming from the land of others insofar as these do not interfere with his use of his land or interfere only to a negligible extent. A negligible interference typically occurs where the limits or targets established by statute or regulation are not exceeded by the interferences laid down and assessed by these provisions. The same applies to standards in general administrative provisions that have been promulgated under art. 48 of the Federal Environmental Impact Protection Act and represent the state of art.

(2) The same applies to the extent that a material interference is caused by a use of another plot of land that is usual in that location and cannot be prevented by measures that are economically reasonable for users of this kind. Where an owner is obliged under these provisions to tolerate an interference, he may require the user of the other land to pay compensation, if the interference impairs a use or revenue of the former's land that is usual in that location beyond a degree that the owner can be expected to tolerate …

907 (1) The owner of a plot of land may require that no facilities are created or maintained on a neighbour's plot of land where it can be predicted with certainty that their existence or use will have an impermissible effect on the owner's land. Where an installation satisfies the provisions of the law of the *Land* concerning the distance from the boundary or other protective measures, then the removal of an installation may only be required if the impermissible interference actually occurs.

(2) Trees and bushes are not facilities within the meaning of these provisions.

1004 (1) Where ownership is interfered with through the removal or deprivation of property, the owner can request that the interfering person remove the interference. Where further interferences are anticipated, then the owner can demand a prohibitory injunction.

(2) Such claims are excluded where the owner is bound to tolerate the interference.

Road Traffic Law (KFG) of 3 May 1909[6]

7 (1) If in the course of the operation of a motor vehicle a person is killed; the body or the health of a person is injured or an object is damaged, the keeper of the motor vehicle is obliged to compensate the injured party for the damage resulting therefrom.

(2) The duty to compensate is excluded, if the accident was caused by an unavoidable event which is not due to a defect in the construction of vehicle

[6] This law (the Kraftfahrzeug Gesetz) was re-enacted in a slightly modified form by the Straβenverkehrsgesetz (StVG) of 19 December 1952, see below.

or to the failure of its mechanism. An event is deemed to be unavoidable in particular if it is due to the conduct of the injured party or of a third party who is not involved in driving or an animal, and if both the keeper and the driver of the vehicle have applied that care which is required in the light of the circumstances.

(3) If someone uses the vehicle without the knowledge or wishes of its keeper, that person is liable to compensate for the damage in the place of the keeper. *However, the keeper remains liable for the damage, if the use of the vehicle has been made possible through his fault.*[7] *The first sentence has no application if the user is appointed by the keeper to drive the vehicle or if the vehicle is handed over to him by the keeper.*[8]

8 The provisions of § 7 do not apply

1. where the person harmed or the property damaged was being transported in the vehicle at the time of the accident,
2. where the person harmed was active in driving the vehicle,
3. to [goods] vehicles which cannot travel at faster than 20 kilometres an hour on the level.[9]

9 If the injured party contributed to the damage by his negligence, § 254 BGB applies with the proviso that if an object was damaged, negligence on the part of the person exercising factual control over the object is treated as equivalent to negligence on the part of the injured party.

12 [Sets out the maximum amounts of compensation]

16 Legal provisions remain unaltered whereby the keeper of the vehicle is liable for the damage caused by the vehicle with wider scope than under this law or whereby another person is liable for the damage.

17 (1) If damage is caused by several motor vehicles and if the keepers of the vehicles involved are bound by law to pay compensation to a third party, the liability to pay compensation of the keepers of the vehicles and the extent of the compensation to be paid as between themselves depends upon the circumstances, especially according to whether the damage has been caused predominantly by one or the other of the parties. The same applies to the liability of one of the keepers of the vehicles if the damage was caused to another keeper of a vehicle involved in the accident.

[7] Sentence added by the Law of 21 July 1923.
[8] Sentence added by the Law of 7 November 1939.
[9] Extended by the Law of 21 July 1923 to all vehicles not capable of travelling above 20 kilometres an hour.

18 (1) In the circumstances covered by § 7(1), the driver of the motor vehicle is also liable to pay compensation in accordance with the provisions of §§ 8 to 15. No liability exists if the damage was not caused by the blameworthy conduct of the driver.

Road Traffic Law of 19 December 1952

7 (1) If in the course of the operation of a motor vehicle a person is killed, the body or the health of a person is injured or an object is damaged, the keeper of the motor vehicle is obliged to compensate the injured party for the damage resulting therefrom.

(2) The duty to compensate is excluded, if the accident was caused by an Act of God which is not due to a defect in the construction of vehicle or to the failure of its mechanism. An event is deemed to be unavoidable in particular if it is due to the conduct of the injured party or of a third party who is not an employee or an animal and if both the keeper and the driver of the vehicle have applied that care which is required in the light of the circumstances.

Italy

Italian Civil Code (1865)

1151 Any human act whatever which causes damage to another obliges him by whose fault it occurred to make reparation.

1152 Every person is liable for the damage which he causes not only by his own act but also by his negligence or imprudence.

1153 Everyone is liable also not only for the damage which he caused by his own act, but also for that which is caused by the act of persons for whom he is responsible, or by things which he has in his keeping.

The father, and, if there is no father, the mother are responsible for harm caused by their minor children living with them.

Guardians (*tutori*) are liable for the harm caused by the wards living with them.

Masters and principals (are liable) for damage caused by their domestics and employees in the functions for which they have been employed.

Teachers and artisans (are liable) for damage caused by their pupils and apprentices during the time when they are under their surveillance.

The liability outlined above does not occur where parents, tutors, teachers or artisans prove that they could not have prevented the act for which they would have been liable.

1154 The owner of an animal or he who avails himself of it while it is being put to his use is liable for the damage which the animal causes, whether the animal was in his keeping or whether it had strayed or escaped.

1155 The owner of a building is liable for damage caused by its ruin, when this occurred through want of maintenance or by a construction defect.

Italian Civil Code (1943)

Delict

2043 Any intentional or negligent act which causes unlawful harm to another obliges the person who committed the act to provide compensation.

2046 A person is not liable for the consequences of a harmful act where he did not have the capacity to intend or will it at the moment when he committed it, unless the state of incapacity arose by his fault.

2047 In the case of harm caused by a person who lacks capacity to intend or will, compensation is due from the person obliged to supervise the incapable person, except in the case where he shows that he could not have prevented the act.

2048 The father and mother, or the guardian, are liable for the harm caused by the unlawful act of the minor, unemancipated children, or of persons within their custody, who reside with them. The same applies to a parent by affiliation.

Teachers and others who teach an art, trade or profession are liable for the harm caused by the unlawful act of the pupils or apprentices under their supervision.

The persons mentioned in the preceding paragraphs are only relieved of liability if they prove that they were unable to prevent the act.

2049 Masters and employers are liable for the harm caused by an unlawful act of their servants or employees in the exercise of the functions to which they are assigned.

2050 Whoever causes harm to another in the performance of activities hazardous by their nature, or by reason of the means employed, is liable in damages, unless he proves that he has taken all appropriate measures to avoid the harm.

2051 Everyone is liable for harm caused by things in his keeping, unless he proves that the harm resulted from a fortuitous event.

2052 The owner of an animal, or a person using it for the period of his use, is liable for harm caused by the animal, regardless of whether the animal was in his custody or had strayed or escaped, unless he proves that the damage resulted from a fortuitous event.

2053 The owner of a building or structure is liable for the harm caused by its collapse, unless he proves that such harm was not caused by defective maintenance or defect in construction.

2054 The custodian of a vehicle that is not guided by rails is liable for the harm caused to person or property by the operation of the vehicle, unless he proves that he did all that was possible to avoid the harm.

In the case of the collision of vehicles, it is presumed, in the absence of proof to the contrary, that each operator contributed equally to the cause of the harm suffered by each vehicle.

The owner of the vehicle, or in his stead the usufructuary or purchaser with reservation of ownership is liable *in solidum* with the custodian of the vehicle, unless he proves that the vehicle was being operated against his will.

In any case, the persons mentioned in the preceding paragraphs are liable for the harm resulting from defects in the manufacture or maintenance of the vehicle.

2056 The damages owed shall be determined in accordance with the provisions of articles 1223, 1226 and 1227.

The damages arising from loss of earnings shall be assessed by the judge according to the circumstances of the case.

2059 Non-patrimonial damages may be awarded only in cases provided by law.

The Netherlands

Civil Code (1838) (ordinary delict provisions)

1401 Every unlawful act by which harm is caused gives rise to an obligation on the part of the person by whose fault it has occurred to make reparation for it.

1402 Every person is liable for the damage which he causes not only by his own act but also by his negligence or imprudence [lack of foresight].

1403 One is liable not only for the damage which one caused by one's own act, but also for that which is caused by the act of persons for whom one is responsible, or by things which one has in one's keeping.

The father, and, if there is no father, the mother are responsible for harm caused by their minor children living with them.

Masters and those who appoint others to look after their things are liable for damage caused by their domestic servants and subordinates in the activities in which they make use of them.

Teachers and employers are liable for damage caused by their pupils and servants during the time when they are under their surveillance.

The liability outlined above ceases where the father or mother, teacher or employer proves that the act for which they would have been liable could not have been prevented by them.

1404 The owner of an animal or he who avails himself of it while it is being put to his use is liable for the damage which the animal causes, whether the animal was in his keeping or whether it had strayed or escaped.

1405 The owner of a building is liable for damage caused by its ruin, when this occurred through want of maintenance or by a defect in its construction or in its fitting out.

Civil Code (1992) (ordinary delict provisions)

6:74 Any failure to perform an undertaking obliges the debtor to compensate the damage suffered by the creditor, unless the failure cannot be attributed to the debtor.

6:99 Where the damage may have resulted from two or more events for each of which a different person is liable, and where it has been determined that the damage has arisen from at least one of these events, the obligation to repair the damage rests upon each of these persons, unless he proves that the damage is not the result of the event for which he himself is liable.

6:101 When the damage is partly caused by an occurrence that can be imputed to the injured party, the obligation to pay compensation is reduced by apportioning the damage between the injured party and the liable party in proportion to the degree in which the occurrences that can be imputed to the parties have contributed to the damage, provided that account is taken of the disparity in the seriousness of the respective faults, or other circumstances of the case, to decide whether fairness demands that an alternative apportionment or full recovery takes place or that the obligation to pay lapses.

6:106 (1) For damage which is not property damage, the victim has the right to compensation fixed according to fairness:

a. where the person responsible had the objective of bringing about such damage;
b. where the victim has suffered physical injury, his honour or good name is harmed or he is affected in any other way in his person; or
c. where the damage relates to the memory of a deceased person and the claim is brought by a spouse who is not separated, a registered partner, or a blood relative to the second degree, that person may take the place of the deceased if, were he still alive, the deceased would have had a right to compensation for injury to his honour or good name.

(2) The right to compensation set out in the previous paragraph is not capable of being transmitted by way of seizure unless an agreement is established or a claim is made in law. The transfer is complete under the general title when the person has informed the other party responsible for making compensation.

6:162 A person who commits an unlawful act towards another, which can be imputed to him, must repair the damage which the other person suffers as a consequence thereof.

Except where there is a ground of justification, the following acts are deemed to be unlawful: the violation of a right, an act or omission violating a statutory duty or a rule of unwritten law pertaining to proper social conduct.

An unlawful act can be imputed to its author if it results from his fault or from a cause for which he is answerable according to law or common opinion.

6:163 No duty to compensate arises whenever the violated norm does not protect against the damage that the victim has suffered.

6:168 (1) The judge may reject a claim to forbid unlawful conduct on the ground that it should be tolerated by reason of pressing social interests. The victim retains his right to compensation under the relevant title [of this Code] ...

(3) Where an order for compensation or for conserving a situation is not complied with, then the judge may, if necessary, forbid the conduct.

6:169 A person who exercises parental authority or guardianship over a child of under fourteen years of age is liable for damage done to another by such conduct of that child *which must be considered as an act*, where this act, but for the child's age, could be imputed to him as an unlawful act.

Road Traffic Law (Wegenverkeerswet)[10]

185 (1) If a motor vehicle which is being driven on a road is involved in a traffic accident which causes damage to persons or goods not carried by that motor vehicle, except for the limitation following paragraph 3 below, the owner of the motor vehicle, or – if there is a keeper of the motor vehicle – the keeper is obliged to compensate that loss, unless it is plausible that the accident is due to force majeure, even where it is caused by someone for whom the owner or keeper is not liable.

(2) The owner or keeper, who does not drive the motor vehicle himself, is liable for the conduct of the person whom he causes or allows to drive the motor vehicle.

(3) [This provision was abolished in 2005. It contained a limitation of the compensation for property loss to the value of the motor vehicle at the moment of the accident, with a minimum of € 250.]

(4) Paragraphs 1–3 do not apply to damage caused by a motor vehicle to unleashed animals, to another moving motor vehicle or to persons or goods which are being transported by the motor vehicle.

[10] Translation W.H. van Boom, in: Ulrich Magnus and Miquel Martín-Casals (eds.), *Unification of Tort Law: Contributory Negligence* (The Hague-London-New York: Kluwer, 2004), p. 129.

(5) [This article leaves unimpaired the liability following from other statutory provisions.]

Spain

Civil Code (1889)

Property

7.2[11] The law does not protect the abuse of rights or the antisocial use of them. All action or omission that, by the intention of its author, by its object or by the circumstances in which it is done, would exceed the normal limits of a right, with nuisance to another individual, will give rise to compensation or to the necessary administrative or judicial measures to prevent the abuse from continuing.

590 No one may build sewers, aqueducts, ovens, forges, chimneys, stables, stores for corrosive materials, steam-powered machinery or installations which, of themselves or by their outputs, are dangerous or noxious, near to a communal well or a neighbour's well without following the distances prescribed by regulations and local custom and without taking any protective measures necessary for the work, as also laid down by regulations. Where there is no regulation, the builder shall take all precautions which are deemed necessary, according to the established opinion of experts, to avoid harm to neighbouring tenements or buildings.

Delict

1902 The person who by action or omission causes damage to another by fault or negligence is obliged to repair the damage caused.

1903 The obligation imposed in the preceding article applies not only for a person's own acts or omissions, but also for those persons for whom a person is responsible.

The father and the mother are responsible for the harm caused by their minor children who are living with them.

Tutors are liable for the harm caused by minors or incapacitated persons under their authority and living with them.

Employers or directors of an establishment or firm are liable for the harm caused by their employees in the performance of tasks that are entrusted to them or of their functions.

The State is liable under this head for the acts of its special agents, but not when the harm has been caused by a civil servant entrusted with practical administration, for which case the preceding paragraph applies.

[11] As inserted by Decree of 31 May 1974.

Masters and directors of arts and trades are liable in respect of the harm caused by their pupils or apprentices, as long as they remain under their control.

The liability under this article ceases when the persons mentioned prove that they have shown the diligence of the good father of the family to avoid the harm.

1905 The possessor of an animal or a person who makes use of one is liable for the harm that it causes, even where it had strayed or escaped. This liability only ceases when he proves that the harm resulted from a fortuitous event or from the fault of the person who suffered the harm.

1906 The owner of a building is liable for the harm caused to neighbouring property when he has not taken the necessary steps to prevent them increasing ….

1907 The owner of a building is liable for the damage resulting from its total or partial ruin, if this was caused by the failure to make necessary repairs.

1908 The owner of objects is also liable for harm caused:

1. By the explosion of machines that had not been kept with due care and by the burning of explosive substances that were not stored in safe and suitable place.
2. By excessive smoke, that is injurious to persons or property.
3. By the falling of trees located on thoroughfares, when this is not caused by force majeure.
4. By emanations from sewers or deposits of toxic matter, built without the precautions appropriate to the place in which they were.

INDEX

Lightning Source UK Ltd.
Milton Keynes UK
UKOW05f0804101014

239856UK00014B/568/P

9 781107 475625